Events Project Management

This book provides events management students with an accessible and essential introduction to project management.

Written by both academics and industry experts, *Events Project Management* offers a unique blend of theory and practice to encourage and contextualise project management requirements within events settings. Key questions include: What is project management? How does it connect to events management? What is effective project management within the events sector? How does academic theory connect to practice? The book is coherently structured into 12 chapters covering crucial event management topics such as stakeholders, supply chain management, project management tools and techniques, and financial and legal issues. Guides, templates, case study examples, industry tips and activity tasks are integrated in the text and online to show practice and aid knowledge.

Written in an engaging style, this offers the reader a thorough understanding of how to successfully project manage an event from the creative idea to the concrete product. It is essential reading for all events management students.

Hanya Pielichaty is a Senior Lecturer at Lincoln International Business School, University of Lincoln and coordinates the BSc (hons) Events Management programme. Before joining the University of Lincoln Hanya worked as a practitioner for the Youth Sport Trust and Lincolnshire Sport in connectivity to sports events and developing community provision.

Georgiana Els (Dr) is a Lecturer in Tourism and Events Management at Lincoln International Business School, University of Lincoln. Prior to joining the University of Lincoln, she taught in European universities and accumulated work experience within international tourism and events companies. Georgiana has more than nine years' experience in events, mainly in the business/trade and educational events segment.

Ian Reed is the Emergency Planning & Business Continuity Manager for Lincolnshire County Council. He specialises in event planning and event safety management and has a wide range of event planning experience. He has chaired many event SAGs and has also facilitated both exercises and structured debriefs for event organisers. He regularly presents on Lincolnshire's multi-agency approach to event safety at a strategic level, and at a variety of forums around the country. He also guest lectures at the University of Lincoln as part of its Events Management degree course.

Vanessa Mawer works as a course trainer in event safety and with event organisers in managing safety at their events. Prior to this, as a police officer, she was responsible for putting together the policing of many planned and spontaneous events. In this role she was also one of the founders of Lincolnshire Event Safety Partnership, a multi-agency group who work with event organisers to ensure safe and successful events.

Events Project Management

Hanya Pielichaty, Georgiana Els,
Ian Reed and Vanessa Mawer

Routledge
Taylor & Francis Group

LONDON AND NEW YORK

First published 2017
by Routledge
2 Park Square, Milton Park, Abingdon, Oxon OX14 4RN

and by Routledge
711 Third Avenue, New York, NY 10017

Routledge is an imprint of the Taylor & Francis Group, an informa business

British Library Cataloguing in Publication Data
A catalogue record for this book is available from the British Library

Library of Congress Cataloging in Publication Data
Names: Pielichaty, Hanya, author.
Title: Events project management / Hanya Pielichaty, Georgiana Els,
Ian Reed and Vanessa Mawer.
Description: Abingdon, Oxon ; New York : Routledge, 2017. |
Includes bibliographical references and index.
Identifiers: LCCN 2016020668| ISBN 9781138832688 (hbk) |
ISBN 9781138832664 (pbk) | ISBN 9781315735900 (ebk)
Subjects: LCSH: Special events--Management. | Project management.
Classification: LCC GT3405 .P54 2017 | DDC 394.2--dc23
LC record available at https://lccn.loc.gov/2016020668

ISBN: 978-1-138-83268-8 (hbk)
ISBN: 978-1-138-83266-4 (pbk)
ISBN: 978-1-315-73590-0 (ebk)

Typeset in Frutiger
by RefineCatch Limited, Bungay, Suffolk

Visit the Companion Website: www.routledge.com/cw/pielichaty

Printed and bound by CPI Group (UK) Ltd, Croydon, CR0 4YY

I would like to dedicate this book to my wonderful family: Gavin, Smidge, Helena, Peter and Joe. Thank you for your continued support, guidance and inspiration.

Hanya Pielichaty

To my husband, Johan, for his constant support, encouragement, advice and unconditional love. You are my everything.

Georgiana Els

To Laura, Hannah and Ellen for their patience xxx

Ian Reed

To Fred, Phil and Darren for their support always

Vanessa Mawer

Table of contents

Figures

Tables

Case studies

Acknowledgements

There are many people we would like to thank for the time, effort and involvement that has empowered us to make this textbook a reality. Our sincerest thanks go to Paul Gibbons (Head of Visitor Experience at the Design Museum, London), City of Lincoln Council, Lincolnshire Event Safety Partnership, Kristina Skvrce (Wedding Planner and Coordinator), Verity Parmley (Front of House Supervisor, Lincolnshire Showground), Dr Jeremy Pearce (Senior Lecturer, Lincoln International Business School, University of Lincoln), Judy Jackson (Managing Director, MRL Safety Limited), José Martinez Tormo (Secretary General, Junta Central Fallera), Roberto Daniele (Senior Lecturer, Oxford Brookes University), Lethea Louw (Owner and Manager at First Choice Conferences & Events), Martin Knight (Senior Lecturer, Lincoln International Business School, University of Lincoln), Nick Sentance (Divisional Resilience Manager, East Midland Ambulance Service).

Contains public sector information published by the Health and Safety Executive and licensed under the Open Government Licence.

Crown copyright information is reproduced with the permission of the Controller of HMSO and the Queen's Printer for Scotland.

Abbreviations

This textbook will refer to many different abbreviations throughout the chapters and this section will assist in understanding what the abbreviations represent.

AAC	Arctic Ambassador Centres
A-on-N	Activity-on-Node
AR	Augmented Reality
BVEP	Business Visits and Events Partnership
CAN	Community Ancillary Notice
C-PEST	Competitive, Political, Economical, Sociocultural and Technological
COSHH	Control of Substances Hazardous to Health
CSAS	Community Safety Accredited Stewards
CSF	Critical Success Factors
DCMS	Department for Culture, Media and Sport
DEFRA	Department for Environment Food and Rural Affairs.
EIA	Economic Impact Analysis
EIF	Events Industry Forum
EMBOK	Event Management Body of Knowledge
e-WOM	Electronic Word of Mouth
FIFA	Fédération Internationale de Football Association
FNA	Frontiers North Adventures
GHG	Green House Gases
GIS	Geographical Information Systems
GPS	Global Positioning System
HM Government	Her Majesty's Government
HRM	Human Resource Management
HSE	Health and Safety Executive
IMC	Integrated Marking Communications
IOC	International Olympic Committee
IOSH	Institute of Occupational Safety and Health
IPC	International Paralympic Committee
ISO 20121	International Standard for Sustainable Events

Abbreviations

LBS	Location Based Services
LESP	Lincolnshire Event Safety Partnership
MEV	Manchester Event Volunteers
OECD	Organisation for Economic Co-operation and Development
PBI	Polar Bears International
PR	Personal Relations
PRINCE	PRojects IN Controlled Environments
RBS	Risk Breakdown Structure
RFL	Rugby Football League
ROI	Return On Investment
SAG(s)	Safety Advisory Group(s)
SDGs	Sustainable Development Goals
SMART	Specific, Measurable, Attainable, Realistic and Time-limited
SMP	Sustainable Management Practices
SOC	Sense of Community
SWOT	Strengths, Weaknesses, Opportunities, Threats
TBL	Triple Bottom Line
TEN	Temporary Event Notice
UIA	Union of International Associations
UTAUT	Unified Theory of Acceptance and Use of Technology
VOC	Volatile Organic Compounds
VQ	Virtual Queuing
WBO	World Boxing Organisation
WBS	Work Breakdown Structure
WCED	World Commission on Environment and Development
WOM	Word of Mouth
WWF	World Wildlife Fund

Chapter 1

Project management for events

1.1 Introduction

There has been a rapid growth in the number of events and festivals delivered since the 1980s (Brown, 2014) and in relation to this an increase in the number of institutions offering events management programmes to both undergraduate and postgraduate students. The academic research connecting to events, however, has not developed at the same pace and there are gaps in some areas of academic event theory. This book seeks to address the paucity of literature available to students studying events-management-based degrees specifically in connectivity to project management. The aim of this book is to provide students with an understanding of project management theory and practice within a global events setting. The authors of this book offer expertise from both an academic and events industry perspective.

Key questions that this book seeks to address include:

- What is project management?
- How does project management connect to events management?
- What does an effective project management set-up look like within the events sector?
- How does academic theory around project management connect to practice?

This book is divided into 12 chapters and is presented in a specific order which mirrors the way a practitioner may structure the organisation of an event in industry. The book begins with an exploration of the relationship between events and projects and then develops to look at key stakeholders, structures and teams, and supply chain management. The middle third of the book provides the practical project management tools and techniques necessary to strategically manage client, community and organisational event objectives within a legal setting. Finally the book addresses the financial, legal and contemporary issues regarding event projects and project close. Students will be able to follow the textbook from start to finish in a logical sequence or read the chapter linked to their module content as a standalone resource. Each chapter ends with a case-study example in order to help students connect theory with practice and provide inspiration for assignment ideas.

1.2 Events, projects and characteristics

From ancient through to contemporary times events have been part of society, defining different beliefs, preferences, and fashions across a variety of cultures. Events can range from small family gatherings such as birthday celebrations to mega-events like the Olympic and Paralympic Games. It must be noted that not all events have an appointed event organiser; instead traditions and local rituals may pave the way for unorganised or spontaneous events. Examples of these include gatherings in public spaces at New Year's Eve and end-of-war celebrations. This makes events a very interesting and innovative subject area to both study and work in and it also means it is difficult to provide one single definition of events. According to Smith (2012, 1) public events are 'themed occasions that take place at a stipulated time'; arguably, they are designed in a unique way, as each one offers a synergy between location, the range of people involved and the culture/rituals in place. It is thought that one must experience an event in order to fully understand it. Typically, 'an event is generally a complex social endeavour characterized by sophisticated planning with a fixed deadline, often involving numerous stakeholders' (Van Der Wagen and White, 2015, 5). This is a useful definition as it strongly connects to project management influences linking events to planning, timelines and stakeholders. For the purposes of this book, events can be understood as social occasions that are limited in time, involve an audience and fulfil complex and varied objectives dependent on the stakeholders involved. Event management pulls together the practical tools, resources and expertise needed to bring an event to fruition.

Similarly to the definition of events, the relationship between projects and events can be multiple and changing. This chapter will help to define and pinpoint the meaning of a project and, in turn, how this relates to events and event management. Bladen, Kennell, Abson and Wilde, (2012, 23) state that 'projects are distinct from the day-to-day processes of an organisation'. They argue that events are projects because they share many similar characteristics. These similar characteristics and traits include life cycle, budget, leadership, teams, one-time tasks and cross-functionality. The listed descriptors are all appropriate and logical but perhaps do not fully encapsulate the entire relationship between events and projects.

Bowdin, Allen, O'Toole, Harris and McDonnell, (2011, 257) simply state that 'the production of a festival or event is a project', and they endorse the use of project management tools to ensure the successful completion of the event. This definition emphasises the production and implementation side of event management as being project-led rather than the entire process. The initiation, planning, implementation, monitoring and shut-down stages are described by Bowdin et al. (2011) as key elements of project management linked to events. Cserháti and Szabó (2014), however, do not separate the two fields and refer to them instead as event projects in their study exploring World and European Championships from a project management perspective. They acknowledge that 'organisational event projects have well-confined parameters, such as fixed deadlines, strict competition rules, numerous stakeholders and environmental aspects' (Cserháti and Szabó, 2014, 613). This view can be encapsulated by understanding events as the setting in which project management processes and values are being utilised. This connects to the core aim of this book, which involves exploring and mastering the use of project management theory and skills against an events management backdrop. The phrases 'event projects' and 'events project manager', therefore, will be used frequently in this book to refer to the amalgamation of events with project management techniques and processes.

Rowe (2007) defines project management as being both an art and a science. The art of project management implies the coordination of technical and business resources, the team and the client and all the stakeholders involved. The science of project management is based on processes and techniques. To be an artist in project management means to be proficient in the science of project management. This notion of project management adheres very well to the events industry, which is a fusion of art and technical application. The use of project management skills and theory is necessary in the events sector because it provides useful processes and project tools and the framework for defining the event scope and associated objectives. Furthermore, as for events, the project manager directs the team to focus on tasks and helps with the management of time scales and resources.

In essence, a project is an idea that is implemented into action until completed. Project management involves the careful monitoring and management of each project stage to ensure that it is completed efficiently, professionally and to brief. The simple stages of the project management cycle can be viewed in Figure 1.1. The event concept or idea is the initial stage of the process which in order to be agreed upon by key stakeholders must also have the appropriate financial backing. An event organiser presenting their particular event project to a panel of Safety Advisory Group (SAG) members is unlikely to reassure the SAG of their event safety if the correct finances and legalities are not in place.

An initial feasibility study of the event project along with an internal and external analysis of the strengths, weaknesses, opportunities and threats (SWOT) connected to the event idea is needed. Only then is it encouraged to progress to the project planning and implementation (doing) stages. These stages of project management align directly with event planning, and the final stage of this involves completion, shut-down and review, which will be discussed in greater detail in the final chapter of this book.

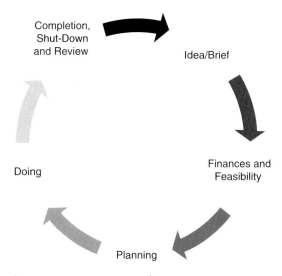

Figure 1.1 The project management cycle

1.2.1 The connection between events and projects

As already introduced, the relationship and connection between events and projects can be difficult to understand and apply. The characteristics of projects are listed below and the processes by which they are developed and implemented are of interest to event managers:

- They are time based: every aspect of a project has a time constraint.
- They are unique and involve either using new resources or using standard resources in a new combination.
- They have start and finish dates.
- They involve considerable unfamiliarity and the possibility of unforeseen risks.
- The level of activity varies over the duration of the project.
- They constitute a dynamic system subject to change from internal and external sources.

Source: O'Toole and Mikolaitis (2002, 21)

The constrained element of time within events and projects is undeniable, both of which have deadlines at the micro and macro level. Due to the fast-paced nature of the events industry it is always necessary to search for new resources and methods of planning and managing an event. Inevitably, there may be unforeseen risks and unexpected occurrences may take place. It is the role of the project manager, however, to eliminate all reasonable and predictable risks and challenges by creating detailed, thorough and organised plans.

Maylor (2010, 5–6) provides several key characteristics of project management which are sited below and have been adapted for this book to encapsulate event management practices:

- *Social construction*: an event is organised and led by people so it is complex and dynamic.
  - ○ Live Aid (1984, 2008 and 2014).
- *Uncertainty*: a characteristic also linked to events management as it is a dynamic industry and vulnerable to internal and external threats and changes. For example, at an outdoor event organisers are dependent on the weather conditions. In addition, there can be uncertainty regarding the costs and resources involved in organising the event. Event organisers need to know how to cope and deal with uncertainty.
- *Uniqueness*: each event will have an individual output as the time, space and resources involved (human and material) will vary from event to event.
- *Emergence*: events have a definite set of activities that need to meet the event objectives within limited resources; however, in some emerging/changing situations all objectives and the measures to achieve it must adapt.
  - ○ In 2011 the Lincoln Christmas Market planned for 250,000 to attend throughout the event, in fact 330,000 visitors arrived.
- *Change*: can intervene at any stage in the organisation of an event as with its progression the initial idea/scope/mission evolves.
- *Focused*: each event has a particular aim and needs to achieve its result/ mission (some events can have multiple purposes that need to be achieved).
- *Temporary*: events have a definite time: a start date when objectives are set and a finish date when all objectives have been achieved.

- *Integrated*: the project manager has the role of interlinking all the activities and make sure that each member of the team understands their role. Resources (material and human) need to be put together in a complex structure to make the event successful.

As demonstrated previously and as highlighted by Bladen et al. (2012, 23), 'events are projects because they are of limited duration, require a degree of coordination of tasks towards goals, usually have a fixed budget, and are unique occurrences'. Some major events may have several project officers working on them who are dedicated to work across specific sections of the event. The crossover between events management and project management is endless; however there are some key differences which exist and are illustrated in Figure 1.2 in relation to event and project descriptors.

As shown in Figure 1.2, there are many more similarities between events and projects than there are differences. The use of a Venn diagram helps to illustrate the crossover between event and project descriptors. Some of the differences, however, are essential to both this book and in understanding the relationship between events and projects and the management of each in general. The concept of 'overlay' (Bowdin et al., 2011, 258) is a valuable one and describes the way in which project management utilises all of the tasks involved in general management. When this overlay is placed on top of event management, however, there are some aspects that are not covered. An event is not a project in its entirety, but rather an event utilises many key characteristics of project management but is distinctive because an event involves an *audience* and a rigid performance date (the event itself). It is the elements connected to the notion of audience, such as promotion, ticket sales, event date and leisure, that summarise the departing characteristics of events away from the project management overlay. The attendance of an

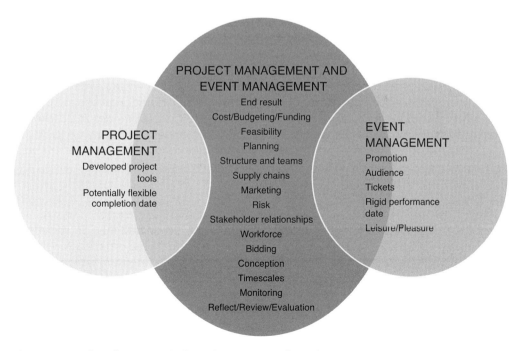

Figure 1.2 The characteristics of events and projects

audience at an event is arguably the ultimate aim for an event organiser; it is not one discrete aspect of a project task but rather a holistic vision of event success.

As documented by previous scholars there is still a great deal of crossover between events and projects: 'By virtue of the fact that major sports events have pre-defined start and end dates, they are similar to projects' (Parent and Smith-Swan, 2013, 49). Parent and Smith-Swan acknowledge that event managers do use project management tools to organise and host events. As referred to in Figure 1.2, the similarities between projects and events are more prevalent than their differences, but event management is not the same as project management. Event management concerns the organising and hosting of an event using project management resources and knowhow, and this incorporates the wants and needs of an audience. In their discussion of event projects, Cserháti and Szabó (2014, 623) comment that: 'Project management methods and techniques are essential in the definition and planning phases of an event. However, during the implementation, soft skills, relationships and appropriate communication can ensure the fulfilment of success criteria.'

This links back to the audience (soft skills, relationships) as being a separating factor when analysing the difference between project and event management. Project management is used throughout event management stages to effectively plan, realise and develop the right processes, structures and techniques required for event success. But once the implementation stage is enforced – namely marketing, publicity, event delivery – different skills are required and a movement is made away from a pure concentration on project management. This book, therefore, seeks to critically apply project management tools and techniques to specific event management contexts, namely *event projects*.

1.3 Event initiation

The event planning process as outlined by Masterman (2009) and illustrated in Figure 1.3, provides the order and flow in which to plan for and implement events. This chapter focuses on the preliminary stages of event planning: the initiation stage, which incorporates objectives, concept and feasibility from Masterman's (2009) model. Event objectives, concept and feasibility are all crucial initial phases to ensure event success at the later implementation milestone. This is in line with the initiation phase as outlined in the Event Management Body of Knowledge (EMBOK, 2016) model. It is acknowledged that 'events are about people. They concern change and creativity' (O'Toole, 2011, 108) and therefore comprehensive but flexible planning and research at the start of the process will assist in the handling of the dynamic and creative industry.

1.3.1 Objectives and concept

Event objectives are interlinked with the event concept, vision and mission statement of the organisation. The objectives state the goals and aims of the organisation and/or event. According to Lock (2014, 5) initial objectives are used to measure later success in relation to the following three aspects:

1 Project completion within approved cost budget;
2 The project finished on time;
3 Good performance, which requires that the project satisfies its specifications and delivers the intended benefits.

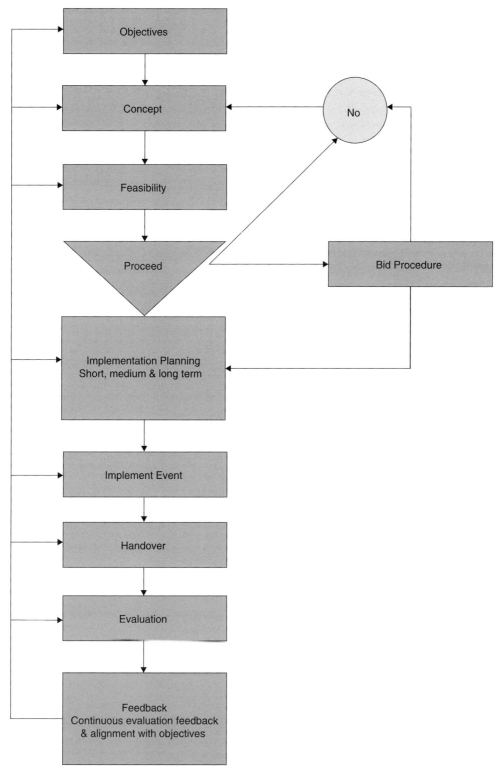

Figure 1.3 The event planning process

Source: Masterman, 2009, 58

It is very important to set realistic and measureable targets from the outset in order to gauge success levels in a reliable and reasonable manner at a later stage. In order to make clear and coherent event objectives it is useful to take time to complete them, and to utilise the research and expertise of colleagues and stakeholders to assist with the decision making. A long-standing method of guiding objective setting is the SMART technique, which stands for **S**pecific, **M**easurable, **A**ttainable, **R**ealistic and **T**ime limited (Heagney, 2012). Some considerations for using the SMART technique are discussed in Table 1.1.

Study activity

Create three event objectives which align to the SMART method for an event you are planning on hosting or volunteering at in the near future. Think about how well you will be able to answer the questions in Table 1.1.

Event concept is concerned with the idea of the event which may connect to a target market or set theme (e.g. school sports day, community charity bike ride or student vintage clothes show). The objectives and concept must be substantiated with a vision of the overall event and an organisation mission statement. Event visions can often be hopeful, ideological and utopian. See Table 1.2 for two examples of event visions.

Table 1.1 SMART objective considerations

Specific	• Who is the objective aimed at? • Is the concept and vision clear?
Measurable	• Is the objective tangible or intangible? • What methods are available to measure achievement? • Is this a new concept or one that can be benchmarked against previous ones?
Attainable	• Is funding in place to meet the objectives? • Does the events team have the right expertise and staff numbers in place to bring the objectives to fruition? • Is the external and internal climate right for this event to take place?
Realistic	• Does the budget align to the event aspirations? • Is the time-frame appropriate and does it account for potential delays? • Is the infrastructure already in place?
Time Limited	• Is the time frame appropriate to ensure the event can take place? • Has research been undertaken to understand lead times on certain project areas? • Are any stakeholders involved going to cause time issues?

Table 1.2 Event visions

Event	Vision
Rio 2016 Olympic and Paralympic Games	'All Brazilians uniting to deliver the greatest event on earth and proudly advancing through sport our national promise of progress.'[1]
San Sebastian European Capital of Culture 2016	'The San Sebastian European Capital of Culture 2016 project aspires to the hope that, by 2026, ours will be a society where people have the know-how and tools to overcome conflicts and live together, sharing in peace and collaborating in a supportive community.'[2]

1 *Source*: Rio 2016 (2011) *Rio 2016 presents strategic pillars to IOC members in Durban*. Available from: http://www.rio2016.com/en/news/rio-2016-presents-strategic-pillars-to-ioc-members-in-durban

2 *Source*: San Sebastian European Capital of Culture (2016) *Mission, vision and values*. Available from: http://dss2016.eu/en/transparency-portal/mission-vision-and-values

In both the Rio 2016 vision and that of the Capital of Culture in Table 1.2, the words used are emotive and aspirational: 'uniting', 'proudly', 'progress', 'aspires', 'hope', 'sharing' and 'collaborating'. A mission statement often outlines how the organisation in charge of the event will ensure the event vision is realised. It details the purpose of the event organisation and can be understood by answering two questions: 'what are we going to do?' and 'for whom are we going to do it?' (Heagney, 2012, 49). The vision and mission of the Design Museum, London is discussed in the case study at the end of this chapter. The way in which objectives and event concepts are implemented and decided upon is based on feasibility planning, which is discussed next.

1.3.2 Event feasibility

Conducting a feasibility study is of great importance within the events world. Having effective, well-researched and informed content to wrap around the event will assist in applying for funding, gaining stakeholder support and, in turn, hosting a successful event. It is important to understand the scope (Lock, 2014) of the event project, meaning the reach and extent to which the event tends to impact. Event organisers all operate differently and may collate one or more feasibility studies depending on their preference; financial feasibility (as discussed in Chapter 9), venue feasibility, workforce feasibility may all feature within the overall study. It is important to have in place a strategic plan from the event stakeholders initially to assist in the feasibility and progression of the event(s) (O'Toole, 2011). A strategic plan will highlight the business objectives and organisational vision for the event stakeholders; these may be more generic to their business sector rather than specific to events as such. Parent and Smith-Swan (2013, 13) provide a list of potential feasibility considerations for a sporting event: 'a facility review and assessment; the event fit-out requirements; hosting capability; internal and external transportation capability; community support; sport expertise; and economic impact projections'.

The repeated word 'capability' is important to note because this is how feasibility can be simply summarised: the extent to which the organisation and local infrastructure is capable of hosting an event. The definition provided by Parent and Smith-Swan (2013) covers the general areas of facility/venue appropriateness, workforce and expertise, infrastructure, community and legacy. These five areas will help event organisers to compile a feasibility study for their planned event, and it is clear from these themes that financial support is ingrained within each area as the backbone of feasibility. It must be noted that staff competency levels can affect how thorough and effectively the feasibility study will be conducted (O'Toole, 2011, 39) and therefore it is important to provide support and guidance to the team member or team conducting the study.

Masterman (2009) argues that the design and set-up of the event can be tried and tested at the feasibility stage of the planning process. The following considerations are taken into account when testing the event design:

- who is responsible
- resources required
- coordination of bidding process
- long-term plans
- timing implications
- identifying new partners
- cost vs. benefits analysis
- determining critical path
- aligning to objectives.

Adapted from Masterman (2009, 59–60)

To extend the five themes as manifested from Parent and Smith-Swan's (2013) definition, here the concept of pragmatics can also be added to facility/venue appropriateness, workforce and expertise, infrastructure, community and legacy. Pragmatics covers the coordination, timing and critical path analysis, which is all crucial to feasibility planning, as referenced by Masterman (2009). As stated in this section, there are varying views and definitions of what exactly a feasibility study should cover. It is argued here that using the following broad themes will assist in developing a useful feasibility study:

- pragmatics
- facility/venue appropriateness
- workforce and expertise
- infrastructure
- community
- legacy.

It is important to consider cost and financial planning as threaded through the entirety of this list and embedded within each theme, as discussed in relation to budget and feasibility at the Design Museum in this chapter's case study. Conducting a thorough event project feasibility study will ensure event managers are equipped with the information and detail they require to bid for work, satisfy stakeholder needs and raise any capital investment. In addition to this, event managers who conduct valuable feasibility studies from the outset will arguably lead to gaining a positive reputation linked to professionalism and trust.

1.4 Events management environment

An important aspect of event planning is that of situational analysis and a common method to analyse this is to look at strengths, weaknesses, opportunities and threats (SWOT) (Bowdin et al., 2011) linked to the current events environment. The strengths and weaknesses of this situational analysis connect with aspects that affect the internal running of the organisations such as staff team, organisational policies and workplace. In contrast, opportunities and threats connect with the wider world and what is happening externally to the event organisation that may affect event procedures. This section will focus primarily on the external environment in relation to the current events management sector. Much of the current literature and media focus on events has been on public spending and legacy. Li and McCabe (2013, 390) define mega-event legacy as 'Tangible and intangible elements of large-scale events left to future generations of a host country where these elements influence the economic, physical and psychological well-being at both community and individual levels in the long-term.'

As stated, the economy, physical environment and psychological satisfaction have considerable impact on those who are connected in some way to mega-event hosting. When analysing potential opportunities and threats from the external context, it is important to consider the following environments: political/legal, economic, social/cultural, technological, demographic, physical/environmental and competitive (Bowdin et al., 2011, 206–207). The sections to follow will therefore cover these areas in more detail in relation to the current events sector climate.

1.4.1 Political/legal environment

Like the events world, the political and legal environment surrounding events management is continually shifting and changing in line with societal demands and pressures. The UK government is made up of several ministerial departments and the Department for Culture, Media and Sport (DCMS), in particular, is very closely linked to the events sector. This specific government department is tasked with helping 'make Britain the world's most creative and exciting place to live, visit and do business' (DCMS, 2016, online). Event hosting is inextricably linked to living, visiting and doing business within a location and plays a very significant role within both a national and global economy. It is noted that the way in which the events industry has evolved over recent time does lean towards a more professionalised approach:

> By its nature the event industry tends to be highly entrepreneurial, which encourages innovation. However, the last decade has seen it also becoming increasingly professional in its approach with a great deal of time being devoted by event organisers and suppliers to developing professional standards across the market, from specialist guidelines for the erection of temporary structures and stages to information for those organising events such as the 'Purple Guide'.
>
> (Business Visits and Events Partnership, 2014, 10)

The changes in the professionalisation of the industry have consequentially impacted on the legal and political environment in terms of guidelines, reports and policy; refer to Chapter 8 for more information about this. All event managers must be aware of new and revised legal guidelines and policies made in relation to the events industry; these may cover hospitality, construction, community, road closures, licensing and selling of goods.

1.4.2 Economic environment

The Organisation for Economic Co-operation and Development (OECD) is made up of 14 member countries and promotes policies around the world to instil and encourage economic growth and improved social wellbeing (OECD, 2016). 'Economically, it has been estimated that sporting events contribute 3% of the gross domestic product of OECD countries' (Gezici and Er, 2014, 44).

Much research has indicated that the reason nations choose to host events is due to the potential economic benefits for their country (Chan, 2015; Lee et al., 2015), although there is still some debate as to the extent of which economic benefits do manifest from event hosting (Mitchell and Stewart, 2015). This aside, the perceived positive impact of event hosting on the national economy has been prioritised and embedded with mega-event culture. The recession that occurred in 2008 meant 'the bubble economy of the Western economies burst' (Sloan, Legrand and Chen, 2013, 9) and businesses and organisations globally sought new, more sustainable ways to manage and progress business event objectives. There are many opportunities and threats connected to events management in relation to this, including cost implications, responsible project management and, of course, innovation for future sustainable economic drivers. It is important that the events industry is proactive in dealing with sustainable issues going forward in order to protect and develop the sector; this is discussed in section 1.4.6.

The Business Visits and Events Partnership (BVEP) is an organisation that works with different businesses and government agencies connected to the events sector. Their role is to:

> Garner the cohesive opinion of these stakeholders and to collectively influence and develop policies, practices and strategies that support and generate growth in the sector and, raise sector awareness through clear communications of the social and economic benefits of the business visits and events sector.
>
> (BVEP, 2012, online)

In 2014 the BVEP produced a report entitled *Events Are Great Britain*, claiming that the British events industry is worth £39.1 billion and is broken down into the parts shown in Table 1.3.

Table 1.3 demonstrates the value of the events sector to the UK and this will continue to be a feature of UK culture in the future. It is important for event projects to contribute to local economies as well as to operate on a social and equitable level to ensure that events are wide-reaching and fully inclusive. More about event legacy and evaluation can be found in Chapter 12 of this book.

1.4.3 Social/cultural environment

Events have been heavily woven into the global tapestries that form the cultural and social web of our lives. Events have recently been used to develop 'social capital and/ or community cohesion' (Bladen et al., 2012, 352) in their bid for inclusivity and promo-

Table 1.3 Value of Britain's events sector

Event Type	Worth (£billion)
Conferences and Meetings	£19.9
Exhibitions and Trade Fairs	£11.0
Incentive Travel and Performance Improvement	£1.2
Corporate Hospitality and Corporate Events	£1.2
Outdoor Events	£1.1
Festivals and Cultural Events	£1.1
Music Events	£1.3
Sporting Events	£2.3

Source: BVEP (2014, 5)

tion of equality and diversity of cultures, religions, faiths, customs and rituals. Events are not only utilised by governments and local authorities to make profit and physical investments but to also provide the softer, psycho-social benefits to communities involved with the event. There is increasing pressure on event managers to provide events that are 'multi-purpose' to meet many stakeholder requirements that may span across economic objectives as well as social, environmental and community objectives. Social and cultural opportunities developed from event hosting may cover:

- attendee/volunteer sense of wellbeing and satisfaction
- confidence development of volunteers
- apprenticeship schemes
- civic pride
- teamwork provision for workers/volunteers
- overall sense of achievement, community sense of belonging.

In their book *Events and the Social Sciences*, Andrews and Leopold (2013) draw attention to the social and cultural aspects of events where previous research has focused on the practical side of events management. It is crucial to think not only about profit, strategic management and planning when organising events but also about audience participation, identity formation and community 'voice'. Events will always 'say something' about the event organisation, host community, entertainment and/or audience members. This may link to event image, organisation image, organisation effectiveness and professionalism of the business, and community acceptance. It is crucial to include cultural and social environmental factors in the initial event planning states in terms of situational analysis and acknowledgement of future prospects.

1.4.4 Technological environment

It has been noted that the 'diversity of events, together with the unique demands of some venues particularly for outdoor events, has required the development of specialist skills' (BVEP, 2014, 10). This need for new specialist skills and the proliferation of technology and digital technology usage within contemporary society has inevitably impacted upon the way audiences engage with events. 'The postmodern society is seen as being dominated by transnational companies, advanced capitalism, trading blocs and common policies, the introduction of the web and rapid development of new technologies' Andrews and Leopold (2013, 26). The term 'rapid' here illustrates the speed at which technological advancements are being made, and using technology in a smart and appropriate way in the events sector can increase competitive advantage and audience engagement. The events sector is now immersed in a world of e-ticketing, website bookings, online reviews, social media engagement and b/vlogging. The influx of technological usage can manifest in large opportunities and also significant drawbacks. Opportunities come in the form of increased ease of operating systems, efficiency in planning models, speedy promotion and greater customer satisfaction. Drawbacks, however, may surface in relation to high initial costs, staff training, management of public audience engagement and competitive pressures. The emphasis is on multi-communication pathways and a need to successfully manage and monitor these: 'Citizens, living digitised and social mediated lifestyles, are now important co-creators, shaping the design, delivery and dissemination of events to a wider audience' (McGillivray 2014, 96).

Arguably, there has been a power shift away from the event organiser towards the consumer in which they now help to 'co-create' the event to suit their own needs. Technology extends the reach for events and helps to engage with potentially disaffected audience types. The contemporary event organiser must be confident to embrace technological advances at an appropriate rate for their own organisation.

1.4.5 Demographic environment

There are many different ways for an events organisation to investigate their current and/or target audience demographic. These can include segmenting markets by the following categories:

- gender
- age
- location
- marital status
- personality and motivations
- income.

Situational analysis concerns understanding what 'type' of people currently attend the event in question and how this compares to business objectives, and future goals as well as to business competitors. With a good understanding of the event market, it will be easier to plan a successful event in relation to consumer needs and demands. Demographic information may have a considerable effect on the design and implementation of an event. For example, the way in which audience members showcase their gender identities in event/festival environments can have repercussions for event managers in terms of managing excessive consumption, costume and enjoyment (Pielichaty, 2015). In addition, in their research on attendees at an international culinary event, Smith and Costello (2009) discovered two dominant market segments: the 'food focusers' and 'event seekers'. By understanding the personality types of event goers and their linked motivations, event organisers are better able to accommodate for their needs.

> # Tip box
>
> You can use audience observation to get a very general view of your event attendees' attributes and demographics. During your own event make a note of the type of people you see. Are they families, groups of friends, dominated by one gender, younger, older? You can find out a lot simply from noticing what is around you.

1.4.6 Physical/environmental context

Events, for the most part, are physical occasions which occupy a space on the Earth. They take up physical room and inevitably impact on the environment they are part of. 'Humankind consumes what nature has to offer and in return we create waste and deplete the Earth's natural reserves. All our actions have an impact on the Earth's ecosystems that are only able to renew themselves at low levels of consumption' (Sloan et al. (2013, 1). There is a need for event managers to be aware of and implement sustainable practices in their business where possible. As cited by Bladen et al. (2012, 374), after the Rio Earth Summit in 1992, there was a growth in interest and popularity surrounding issues of sustainability, use of resources, responsibility and environmental concern. Events organisations may continue to seek to customise their event offering by developing events that prioritise ethical products, sustainable practices and/or responsible resourcing.

It is the urban environment, as well as the rural one which may be impacted upon by events. As researched by Gezici and Er (2014, 46) during the hosting of the Formula 1 Grand Prix in Istanbul, 'the real long-terms effects are the positive and negative legacies generated by these events and their impacts on the urban development form'. This urban development form may refer to the cityscape, use of event buildings and infrastructure and the long-term effects on urban landscapes. Smith (2012, 11) makes the distinction between event-led and event-themed regeneration. The former means the event itself instigates new growth and infrastructure development, whereas the latter uses the event as part of a wider developmental initiative. Contemporary events management organisations must concern themselves with the physical impact of their event and how it connects to sustainable policies and broader event initiatives. Refer to Chapter 7 for more information about sustainability and technology.

1.4.7 Competitive environment

Competition for services, goods and events in general happens on a local, national and global scale. It is likely that competition to host and manage events will continue as long as there are perceived benefits of hosting. 'Competition from other countries and destinations can take many forms, from higher marketing budgets to greater levels of infrastructure investment, from more client-friendly policies and laws to a more professional and better supported approach to event bidding' (BVEP, 2014, 33).

Different countries bid each year for the right to host a particular mega-event, whether that is the football World Cup, European Capital of Culture or the Olympic and Paralympic Games. Competition is healthy, necessary and useful to assist in boosting the quality standards and professionalism of the events that take place.

Table 1.4 Top international countries for meetings in 2012

Rank	Country	Number of Meetings
1	Singapore	952
2	Japan	731
3	USA	658
4	Belgium	597
5	Republic of Korea	563
6	France	494
7	Austria	458
8	Spain	449
9	Germany	373
10	Australia	287

Source: BVEP (2014, 34)

Table 1.4 shows the top ten countries in the world for hosting international meetings in 2012; these meetings had to be of a certain level and ranking which was set by the Union of International Associations (UIA).

It is important to understand that competition for business and market positioning is not a static discipline but rather requires continuous movement, mobility and flexibility. 'Competitive advantage cannot be gained by only one single improvement, it requires a company to constantly question its strategic position' (Sloan et al., 2013, 29). As stated in the case study at the end of this chapter, the Design Museum uses its dominant social media presence to engage visitors. It is crucial, therefore, that the initial organisational objectives are reviewed and monitored regularly to manage progress and change. Gaining competitive advantage is often about willingness to change, adapt and refresh existing offerings.

Study activity

Think about what the future of the events industry will 'look' like and create an imaginary event that has futuristic characteristics. Be prepared to explain why you have chosen the event features you have, and why you think this event will develop from the current events trends already emerging.

1.5 Conclusion

The relationship between project management and event management is complex to understand and does not offer a universal response. Event management is driven by an event date that all management processes are developed and implemented to work towards. Project management skills and tools are arguably invaluable to the organisation of events, and help to separate small event jobs into projects. Events management is concerned with audience engagement and satisfaction in a unique way, unlike many other sectors. This book will refer to the combination of events and project management techniques as 'event projects' in order to provide a synergy between the two.

The first part of the event initiation process involves understanding the business/event objectives, concept and feasibility of the event. Objective setting is very important to reify the business ethos and also to set targets for the organisation to achieve. Objectives must be SMART and link to the organisation's vision and mission to succeed. The event concept connects to theme, event type, audience profile and overall image for the event; this too must be realistic and appropriate. In order to test whether an event plan/idea will work in practice, a feasibility study is required to investigate the practical considerations involved in making the event a success. The broad themes of pragmatics, facility/venue appropriateness, workforce and expertise, infrastructure, community and legacy will help to guide a useful feasibility study.

When planning event projects strategically it is always wise to consider the current events environment and also potential innovations or changes to the events climate that may occur in the future. A SWOT analysis or situational analysis will help to research potential and future challenges and opportunities. In terms of the external surrounds, Bowdin et al. (2011, 206–207) advise concentrating on the following environments: political/legal, economic, social/cultural, technological, demographic, physical/environmental and competitive industries. The events sector is a dynamic industry that can utilise project management planning techniques effectively to develop and create successful events.

Case study 1: Design Museum, UK

This case study is provided by Paul Gibbons, Head of Visitor Experience at the Design Museum, London.

What type of organisation do you work for and how long have you been there?
The Design Museum was founded in 1989 by Terence Conran as a way of helping everyone understand the value of design in our day-to-day lives. The museum has three gallery spaces which are open seven days a week to the public with a single entry price. There is a very popular shop and café, learning studio and events space. I have been in my role since July 2014.

What does your role involve?
The museum is closing its current site at Shad Thames in June 2016 and reopening in a building three times larger in Kensington in November 2016. My role was created as part of the expansion of the management team in preparation for this move and to professionalise and provide a long-term strategy for the Visitor Experience function in the museum.

At the current site, and as pilot projects for the new museum, I have introduced new initiatives for improved engagement with all audience types. Projects have included introducing volunteer roles in tours and welcoming visitors at the

(Continued)

Case study 1 (*continued*)

entrances, a digital engagement project in the flagship 'Designs of the Year' exhibition, introducing a new Customer Relationship Management and ticketing system, a new website, improved staff and visitor feedback processes, and training and development.

I am also very involved in the detailed planning for the new museum across various large projects including fitting out the public and staff spaces; signage and wayfinding; exhibition programme and design; public, learning and events programming; licensing, emergency and logistical planning; and commercial development, including income from admissions, donations and membership.

What is the vision and mission of your organisation?
The museum's vision is for everyone to understand the value of design. The museum's mission is to be the most exciting, inspiring and engaging design museum in the world. These aims are underpinned by the four key values of being welcoming, collaborative, enterprising and provocative in everything we do.

How do you make sure your organisation's vision is carried out in your day-to-day tasks?
My role is to ensure that visitors have the very best possible experience at the museum, whatever their knowledge of design or their reason for visiting. This responsibility ranges from ensuring that the presentation and maintenance of all spaces is the best it can be to ensuring that the visitor experience team are well briefed, friendly, confident and welcoming, and to maximise income through the ticketing function.

My role is not just about leading my own team but about supporting the other departments in having a clear understanding about their impact on the visitor experience which can be about the design and content in an exhibition; building maintenance, facilities, safety and security issues; the café and shop service; the learning and public programme; IT support; public communication through signage, the website or social media activity.

When launching a new product or event why is it important to consider the feasibility of the task?
The museum has a rigorous business planning process for any new activity that requires expenditure (of budget or time). The museum can only survive if expenditure and income are very tightly balanced therefore any new activity is analysed in terms of cost.

The museum is also about impact and engagement and new activities are not always going to be cost-effective but may still be important to undertake. The feasibility of a new activity will be assessed in all ways to ensure that a piece of activity is sustainable.

Is there rival competition for your business in your sector? If so, how do you strategically plan for this?

The London museum landscape is enormous and we compete for visitor attention with free-to-access collections, paid museum exhibitions and lots of other visitor attractions including tours of historic buildings, rides and experiences, and festivals.

The museum has the largest social media following of any museum in the world and the audience demographic tends to be very engaged in social media. We project our programme as widely as possible through these channels as our traditional marketing budget is relatively small.

Does the wider political and cultural environment affect your business, and if so, how?
The Design Museum has only received public funding in the past year and has always been self-sustaining through its private fundraising and commercial activity. Being a National Portfolio Organisation via the Arts Council and receiving funding through the Heritage Lottery Fund and other high-profile trusts and foundations means that we are now understanding the importance of the political landscape in relation to funding and prioritisation within the sector.

The museum will always be an enterprising organisation and in the new museum there will be lots of opportunity to be commercially minded. However, with a free gallery and an ambitious learning programme, the museum will be seeking support through public funds in the future.

In what way is it important to consider the type of visitor or stakeholder that might engage with your organisation?
It is crucial to understand who our visitors are and what their motivations and expectations are when visiting. Through visitor questionnaires and evaluations we have 'segmented' our visitor types to ensure we can understand the different types of visitor and what their needs might be, as well as the opportunities for engaging them better. This knowledge influences all of our activity, from programming exhibitions and events, to retail products, admission prices and facilities and services.

Does the location of your organisation in the world setting impact upon how the business and culture of the organisation is run?
I only have experience of working in the UK but as a museum based in London we have access to the world's most important designers, architects and partners.

What is your favourite part of your role and working in the events sector?
This role has presented me with the ability to create a vision for visitor experience at the first significant new museum in London for a very long time. I enjoy being able to make important decisions and use my experience to influence other key decisions in the organisation. My role is all about people – visitors and staff – and interaction with lots of different people every day is the best part of my job.

Thank you to Paul Gibbons for sharing his experiences with the authors to formulate this case study.

Evaluative student questions

1 What strengths, weaknesses, opportunities, threats would come from moving a tourist attraction/event to another site?
2 Why is it important to develop new initiatives when focusing on visitor experience?
3 Why should the vision, mission and associated values of an organisation be connected?

Further reading

BVEP (2014) *Events are Great Britain: a report on the size and value of Britain's events industry, its characteristics, trends, opportunities and key issues*. London: BVEP. Available from: http://www.businessvisitsandeventspartnership.com/news/bvep-press-releases/242-bvep-launches-events-are-great-britain-report [Accessed 21 June 2016].

Masterman, G. (2009) *Strategic sports events management*. London: Butterworth-Heinemann.

Smith, S. and Costello, C. (2009) Segmenting visitors to a culinary event: motivations, travel behavior, and expenditures. *Journal of Hospitality, Marketing and Management*, 18(1) 44–67.

References

Andrews, H. and Leopold, T. (2013) *Events and the social sciences*. Abingdon: Routledge.

Bladen, C., Kennell, J., Abson, E. and Wilde, N. (2012) *Events management: an introduction*. Abingdon: Routledge.

Bowdin, G., Allen, J., O'Toole,W., Harris, R. and McDonnell, I. (2011) *Events management*. 3rd edition. London: Butterworth-Heinemann.

Brown, S. (2014) Emerging professionalism in the event industry: a practitioner perspective. *Event Management*, 18(1) 15–24.

BVEP (2012) *About BVEP*. Available from: http://businessvisitsandeventspartnership.com/about-bvep/about-bvep [Accessed 23 February 2016].

BVEP (2014) *Events are Great Britain: a report on the size and value of Britain's events industry, its characteristics, trends, opportunities and key issues*. London: BVEP. Available from: file:///C:/Users/PC/Downloads/events%20are%20great%20report%20final%20version.pdf [Accessed 23 February 2016].

Chan, G.S.H. (2015) Perceived impact of hosting a sport event in a destination: a case study of the Hong Kong Rugby Sevens. *Journal of Management and Sustainability*, 5(3) 49–60.

Cserháti, G. and Szabó, L. (2014) The relationship between success criteria and success factors in organisational event projects. *International Journal of Project Management*, 32(4) 613–624.

DCMS (2016) *What we do*. Available from: https://www.gov.uk/government/organisations/department-for-culture-media-sport [Accessed 23 February 2016].

EMBOK (2016) *EMBOK model*. Available from: http://www.embok.org/index.php/embok-model [Accessed 2 February 2016].

Gezici, F. and Er, S. (2014) What has been left after hosting the Formula 1 Grand Prix in Istanbul? *Cities*, 41(A) 44–53.

Heagney, J. (2012) *Fundamentals of project management*. 4th edition. New York: American Management Association.

Lee, C.-K., Mjelde, J.W. and Kwon, Y.J. (2015) Estimating the economic impact of a mega-event on host and neighbouring regions. *Leisure Studies*, DOI: 10.1080/02614367.2015.1040828

Li, S. and McCabe, S. (2013) Measuring the socio-economic legacies of mega-events: concepts, propositions and indicators. *International Journal of Tourism Research*, 15(4) 388–402.

Lock, D. (2014) *The essentials of project management*. Farnham: Gower Publishing.

McGillivray, D. (2014) Digital cultures, acceleration and mega sporting event narratives. *Leisure Studies*, 33(1) 96–109.

Masterman, G. (2009) *Strategic sports events management*. London: Butterworth-Heinemann.

Maylor, H. (2010) *Project management*. 4th edition. Harlow: Prentice Hall.

Mitchell, H. and Stewart, M.F. (2015) Why should you pay to host a party? An economic analysis of hosting sports mega-events. *Applied Economics*, 47(15) 1550–1561.

OECD (2016) *About the OECD*. Available from: http://www.oecd.org/about/ [Accessed 18 February 2016].

O'Toole, W. (2011) *Events feasibility and development: from strategy to operations*. London: Elsevier.

O'Toole, W. and Mikolaitis, P. (2002) *Corporate event project management*. New York: John Wiley & Sons.

Parent, M.M. and Smith-Swan, S. (2013) *Managing major sports events: theory and practice*. Abingdon: Routledge.

Pielichaty, H. (2015) Festival space: gender, liminality and the carnivalesque. *International Journal of Event and Festival Management*, 6(3) 235–250.

Rio 2016 (2011) *Rio 2016 presents strategic pillars to IOC members in Durban*. Available from: http://www.rio2016.com/en/news/rio-2016-presents-strategic-pillars-to-ioc-members-in-durban [Accessed 2 February 2016].

Rowe, S.F. (2007) *Project management for small projects*. Vienna, VA: Management Concepts.

San Sebastian European Capital of Culture (2016) *Mission, vision and values*. Available from: http://dss2016.eu/en/transparency-portal/mission-vision-and-values [Accessed 2 February 2016].

Sloan, P., Legrand, W. and Chen, J.S. (2013) *Sustainability in the hospitality industry: principles of sustainable operations*. 2nd edition. Abingdon: Routledge.

Smith, A. (2012) *Events and urban regeneration: the strategic use of events to revitalise cities*. Abingdon: Routledge.

Smith, S. and Costello, C. (2009) Segmenting visitors to a culinary event: motivations, travel behavior, and expenditures. *Journal of Hospitality, Marketing and Management*, 18(1) 44–67.

Van Der Wagen, L. and White, L. (2015) *Human resource management for the event industry*. 2nd edition. Abingdon: Routledge.

Chapter 2

Suppliers and supply chains

2.1 Introduction

Every project event team should conduct a feasibility study prior to any sort of implementation phase of an event. The feasibility study should access and research key elements of the project such as funds and budget, staffing, marketing and of course potential suppliers. A supplier is a person and/or organisation which supplies a resource to an event. This resource can be a blend of both goods and services (O'Toole and Mikolaitis, 2002). Visitors to an event may indulge in food and drink, buy a piece of merchandise, or enjoy the live entertainment; without the efficient operation and management of supply chains none of this would be possible. A supply chain can be viewed as the pathway in which that resource is supplied. According to Bozarth, Handfield and Chandiran, (2013, 499), a supply chain is 'A network of manufacturers and service providers that work together to create products or services needed by end users. These manufacturers and service providers are linked together through physical flows, information flows and monetary flows.'

Events are made up of multiple layers of supply chains, and operate by utilising the connections and professionalism of other firms and resources to ensure the event's success. The notion of different flow aspects is important to understand the way events and supply chains interlink. Physical flow can refer to the logistical movement of goods and/or services from one place to another. For example, a porta-loo company will need to transport these facilities to a music festival ready for audience use. Information flow concerns the passing on and dissemination of event messages to suppliers and the event company and other relevant stakeholders. For instance, communication via email, telephones or physical meetings is needed as a way to transfer key narratives from one supplier to the next. Lastly, monetary flows include the pathways the finances take when ordering, paying for and securing supplies. Another flow element that is not already documented, and one that is important here, is that of volunteers as a human resource and therefore a *workforce supply* at events. It is important to think of 'volunteer flow' as a fourth aspect of supply chain management. Volunteer flow describes the assignment of helpers and volunteers at events through direct advertisement, various suppliers or third-party organisations.

Bowdin et al. (2011) acknowledge that specialist event suppliers have emerged in parallel to the growth of such a multi-faceted industry. Some of these include catering, security, legal provision, entertainment packages, health and safety organisations, staging and audio-visual equipment companies. It is therefore more crucial than ever for event organisers of any level to understand the importance of supply chains and the necessary event expertise needed to manage them. Bozarth et al. (2013) explain that supply chain management is an active process that effectively balances competitive needs with customer benefits. This chapter explores in detail the management of supply chains, the role of contractors in events, intelligence gathering, relationship building, venue concerns, contracts and legislation, sustainability of the supply chain, best practice and lastly the review process.

2.2 Supply chain management

A supply chain is the interconnection of an interrelated series of processes through, into and from an organisation (Tum, Norton and Wright, 2011). According to Maylor (2010, 315), 'a project is only as good as the weakest part of the process'. A company may allocate substantial time and resources to make sure that all processes within the organisation run smoothly, but the project outcome will also be dependent on the collaboration and performance of the supply chain. Supply chain management is the synchronisation of an organisation's processes with those of its suppliers and customers in order to match the flow of materials, services and information with demand (Krajewski et al., 2016, 506). The success of an event project depends on four main factors, which include the value of services/products in proportion to the overall value of the project, the relevance and priority of the items being purchased to the project outcome, the time frame and the quality level of the work purchased (Maylor, 2010, 316). Nowadays, considerable amounts of project work can be outsourced and performed by specialist suppliers or contractors. Outsourcing is the means by which a company acquires the processes it lacks or is unwilling to perform. Another approach in which a company purchases the processes it needs is through vertical integration, which implies the formation of businesses at different levels of the supply or distribution chain. For a firm this means investment into either suppliers through *backward integration* – sources of raw materials, parts and services through acquisitions – or through *forward integration*, meaning that the company acquires more channels of distribution (Krajewski et al., 2016). For example, an events company that specialises in organising weddings can invest backwards by purchasing a florist company for quality and flexibility in terms of supplying fresh flowers or invest in an agricultural farm to supply organic products for all the weddings they organise. Likewise, the same wedding organiser can expand through forward integration by purchasing a venue (e.g. a barn for rustic themed weddings) for their own wedding organisation. Some of the main advantages of vertical integration include control over supplies in terms of quality of the goods/services, price, availability, access and ability to reach customers. Horizontal integration refers to a situation when, at the same level in the supply chain, events companies merge in order to remove competition and increase economies of scale. Within the events industry successful supply chain management must prioritise relationship building, trust and commitment. These aspects are acknowledged as having an important impact on developing long-term business relationships (Li et al., 2012).

2.3 Roles and relationships: Contractors/suppliers in the events industry

In order for any event to take place, the event organiser will have to engage the services of a wide variety of contractors and/or suppliers. There are many differing definitions for the terms contractors/suppliers. In the events world, however, they can both be understood in similar ways: they represent a person or company who fulfils a role or provides a service relating to the management or planning of the event for the event organiser. In this book and throughout this chapter the terms will be used together and/or interchangeably because, whichever term is used, the event organiser will need to agree terms and conditions for the role or service provided by a particular supplier. This is further discussed in the chapter case study in relation to a Christmas Market event.

Regardless of terminology, it is more important to recognise that some contractors/suppliers are more significant to the success of an event than others. These can be referred to as 'primary' and 'secondary' contractors/suppliers. Primary contractors/suppliers are those which are fundamental to the implementation and delivery of a safe and successful event, whilst secondary contractors/suppliers can be said to be those which influence the quality levels of the event. Primary contractors can also be referred to as 'critical contractors'. The idea is the same; they are fundamental or crucial to the implementation and delivery of a safe and successful event.

Some contractors/suppliers will always be considered primary or critical, such as health and safety staff or a health and safety company, the medical provider, or any contractors for legal compliance. Some contractors/suppliers will always be secondary ones, such as the merchandising provider, or the catering concessions. Figure 2.1 provides an overview of the 'typical' contractor/supplier categories as a reference point only. It has been created as a Venn diagram to highlight the potential fluidity of some contractors/suppliers engaged at different events. These are contractors who may move between the primary and secondary contractor designation. The middle section of Figure 2.1 demonstrates some of the contractors/suppliers which may be viewed as shifting between the role of primary or secondary contractor/supplier. Note that this is not an exhaustive list. The point at which these contractors become primary and secondary to the event will depend upon a number of factors, and each event will be different and should be treated individually. Primary and secondary contractors/suppliers at one event may not necessarily be the same at another event, even if the providers offer the same service on the same site. Factors that could influence this include weather conditions, the time of year, other events taking place in the area locally or nationally, the time of day, audience profile and type of entertainment.

Study activity

Think of an event that you have been involved in, or will shortly be involved in. Make a list of the different contractors/suppliers that were/are likely to be part of the event. Remember these may be different to those listed under each heading in Figure 2.1. Below are some that may be considered:

- Health & safety; traffic management; event management team; risk assessment
- Landowners; licensing; waste management; security/stewarding; sponsorship
- Ticketing/advertising/marketing; communications/CCTV; temporary structures
- Staging; signage; medical; toilets; entertainment; bar and catering; water
- Hospitality; litter collection; merchandising; lighting/sound; fencing/barriers
- IT; plant; public transport; concessions.

Put them into list form as primary (critical) contractors and secondary contractors. Give reasons why they fall into the particular category for your specific event.

It may also be necessary for event organisers to contract their primary contractors/ suppliers several months or more in advance to ensure the contractor/supplier is aware of what is expected of them and the services that needs to be provided. These items are also in greater demand during the summer months due to the many festivals and other outdoor events taking place generally. Many festivals have clauses in their contracts to prevent acts appearing at their events from performing at other similar events to ensure as much exclusivity as they can. In the case of an air show, it is regular practice for organisers to book static and display aircraft one year in advance

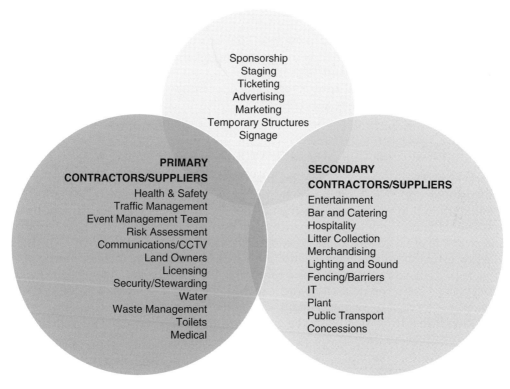

Figure 2.1 Typical primary and secondary event contractors/suppliers

Source: Developed by the authors

which means organisers must plan and commit resources a long time before their events take place. Another added factor is that if these aircraft are military, their availability cannot be guaranteed due to operational requirements that may take precedence.

Many event organisers build clauses into their contractor/supplier contract negotiations to ensure that they are guaranteed to receive what they have ordered or that there are contingencies in place should these companies experience any difficulty in supply. It is reasonable and wise to make sure that in the case of primary contractors to the event, business continuity arrangements and plans have been discussed and included in the successful bids. This should be included in the initial feasibility study for the event and will be included later in this chapter when discussing contracts.

Tip box

It is essential that primary contractors/suppliers are included in the event planning process. This helps to foster trust and relationship building and enables them to understand the event in more detail as well as the role that they will play within it. For this reason, it is also prudent to include them in any exercises that test event management plans and procedures.

Many event organisers will try to use local contractors/suppliers for their events. This helps to build good relationships with local businesses that benefit from money being spent in the local economy, and helps to get the community on side and supportive of the event. The use of local contractors/suppliers can also help to cut down on the carbon footprint of the event.

2.3.1 Relationship building and communication

As previously mentioned, information flow is an important aspect of supply chain management and this is optimised by positive relationship building and effective communication. In traditional investigations of supply chain effectiveness, aspects of operational and economic performance have been prioritised rather than relational and strategic areas (Chelariu, Asare and Brashear-Alejandro, 2014). Event organisers need to establish and manage relationships with various public bodies, mostly at a local level, but sometimes several operational level approvals are needed. Event policy usually has a top-down approach, imposed by laws and regulations established by the government or public bureaux to community level and stakeholders. Event organisers need to comply with the following organisations/guidelines/regulations (Getz, 2012, 350):

- police departments
- fire safety: evacuation procedures, inflammable materials, access to/out of the venue
- health and safety: food safety and security, hazardous materials, licences, electricity

- traffic management: means of access, parking, stewards, control
- consumer protection: loyal pricing, return policy, guarantees, validity
- human resource: working hours, age restrictions, qualifications and certifications, minimum wages
- environmental protection: waste management, emission standards (pollutants, noise), recycling
- inspections: venue and temporary structures building inspection and requirements.

If the event is an annual occurrence or something more frequent it makes good business sense to want to achieve long-term relationships with contractors/suppliers. Atrek, Marcone, Gregori, Temperini and Moscatelli, (2014, 376) established eight elements which contribute to relationship quality between company and supplier:

1 Quality of the products
2 Quality certification for the standard required
3 Flexible and timely services
4 Availability of the salesperson
5 Speed response time to requests of the company
6 Willingness to review economic conditions with the view to develop future relationships
7 Terms of delivery
8 Wide range of materials in stock.

In the quest of relationship building it is advised that the eight aspects are considered when looking for and maintaining business with suppliers. Event managers need to know that the quality of the products being supplied to the event is of a high standard, durable and certified by the appropriate legal systems. Furthermore, suppliers of event companies will need to be even more flexible and available to accommodate the ever-changing and evolving needs that operate within a live event context. O'Toole and Mikolaitis (2002) discuss the need to build a rapport with suppliers, and stress the importance of emphasising this in their business philosophy as well as their products. As an extension to this list, it is proposed that green credentials/sustainability is also an important element of long-term relationship building.

2.3.2 Intelligence gathering, research and reputation

When planning any sort of event it is important that the organiser allows time to consider choice of contractors/suppliers. As in any other industry, some will be better than others, some more reliable and some less expensive than others. The best way for event organisers to achieve satisfactory results is to do some homework. When engaging with contractors/suppliers it can be advantageous to speak with other event organisers that may have used them previously to find out how they performed, and outline any positives or challenges they faced. There are many trade websites and journals full of companies that can supply an event, but firsthand know-ledge and the experiences of others will always make for a better, more informed choice.

In the case of concessions, most will work throughout the same area and region going from event to event. Local councils will be able to provide advice on aspects such as hygiene certificates and related matters, as they all have to be registered with the council in which their business is based. Prior knowledge of pricing at previous events also helps to inform the organiser of what to expect at their event. For example, if the event is taking place on a warm sunny day, a contractor may increase the prices for drinks and ice creams, which will dissatisfy the crowd attending and potentially cause reputational issues for the event. Writing set pricing structures into contracts can eliminate all of this and will ensure the event reputation remains intact. When considering entertainment at the event, it is always wise to contact venues and sites at which they have performed before. This enables the event organiser to consider audience profiles and any additional resources and staffing required for crowd management. For example, crowds attending a rock concert will behave differently and require different management from those attending a classical music concert.

For the event organiser, reputation is of vital importance as it can mean the difference between the event happening again or not. There are many examples of events where incidents or emergencies have taken place, resulting in injuries and worst-case scenario fatalities that have meant the event has been cancelled or would never take place again.

Reputation, therefore, is everything and the event contractors/suppliers can influence this as well. For example, traffic management and efficiency can heavily influence the eventgoers' decision to attend an event again. If there are large tailbacks of traffic both on arrival and again on departure, this affects the attendees' first and last

Table 2.1 Reputation of the event organiser: case study of Love Parade, Germany

Event: Love Parade

Event Location: Duisburg, Germany

When: July 2010

Incident: the first edition of the event was organised in Berlin in 1989. In 2010, over 500 people were injured and trampled as the single entrance to the venue turned into a bottleneck due to the increased number of participants. Duisburg authorities poorly estimated the number of participants.

Result: 21 people were killed and approx. another 500 were injured.

Aftermath: the event organiser (Rainer Schaller), politicians, the local administration and the police force blamed each other. The Cologne police force took over the investigation.

Conclusion: nobody was held responsible for the disaster and German authorities stopped the investigations.

Reaction: Rainer Schaller, the organiser of the Love Parade, cancelled the event after the Duisburg disaster, thus ending the festival.

Class Study Activity: discuss the Love Parade disaster, taking into consideration the fact that the city of Berlin refused to host the parade in the same year due to concerns over estimation of participants' numbers. In 2009, the event was cancelled in the city of Bochum, Germany for similar reasons.

Source: Adapted from Spiegel Online http://www.spiegel.de and DW Online http://dw.com

impression of the event. It is therefore important that the organiser picks an appropriate venue and employs the services of a professional signage and traffic management company to ensure that this is addressed. Security and stewarding is another example of how contractors can be responsible for ensuring that the event organiser's reputation remains intact. These companies are the public-facing element of the event and the point at which people ask for assistance and support. If customers are dealt with in a rude and unaccommodating manner, they will react accordingly, whether via complaint letters, social media or non-attendance the following year.

2.4 Event venues

Event organisers must be aware of the context in which supplies and services are being delivered. Context here can be taken to mean the physical, political, environmental and social environments. Events are not delivered in isolated spaces disconnected from the wider world. This section will be focusing on the physical context and specifically event venues and the logistics of supplying certain services and goods to the venue site. Many factors may limit the type and style of event that can take place, and the following examples do not form an exhaustive list, but do illustrate the common types of issue that may arise.

The location of the venue can cause difficulties in relation to logistics of supply chain management; perhaps it is a park which has only gates that allow pedestrian access. This may cause difficulties in vehicles accessing the site, or may require equipment such as toilets, etc. to be carried across the site. Any event in a location with a poor road network would require significant planning with regard to traffic management in order to avoid annoyance and minimise inconvenience to residents or businesses in the area. Furthermore, appropriate access to the site for contractors/suppliers and visitors is crucial for the implementation of efficient supply logistics. There may be some physical limiting factors to the event logistics such as vehicle weight or width restrictions, and this will affect the type of staging structures or viewing platforms that can be used. For visitors, alternatives such as park and ride or other forms of transport may need to be considered.

For all parties involved in the event management process, the content of the hiring agreement or contract is of great importance. Some venues, particularly heritage sites, will have specific contractors/suppliers that must be used at their location. This may be because the contractors/suppliers have in-depth knowledge of the location, or are competent in using specialist equipment needed there, or because they have a long-standing history of work at this site. It may also be that the venue owner has carried out 'due diligence' checks on the particular contractor, something that is especially relevant where the venue is owned by a public body. In these cases, some venue owners are prepared to allow an organiser to bring in their own contractors, providing that the organiser show proof of 'due diligence' to the satisfaction of the venue, and at the organiser's own cost. Where it is the case that a venue has its own contractors/suppliers, the event organiser will need to consider if this impacts on any of their own contracts.

Some venues will also have permanent facilities which mean they have to have some permanent workers, but these may need to be supplemented for larger-scale events. It will need to be agreed between the venue and event organiser who is responsible f procuring these additional staff and for any necessary training. Where an event o iser is free to bring in their own contractor/supplier, that is, where a venue d have pre-existing arrangements, it is still important that the organiser carries out the 'due diligence' checks on the competency of their contractor/supplier, and is prepared to provide the venue with full details. Most venues will also require the organiser to share copies of the contractor/supplier's safe systems of work, their method statements, risk assessments and insurance.

Organisers must remember that, although the site may be hired from a venue, the venue always retains some level of responsibility for the safety of visitors to their site. It is likely that the venue would be sued along with the organiser if an incident were to occur at the event. It is very important, therefore, that there is a clear agreement or contract between the venue and the organiser; it is all too easy for the legal representative of a claimant to play one off against the other if there are gaps in the planning arrangements, or lack of clarity as to which organisation is responsible for what. This will be a productive relationship if contractors/suppliers are managed effectively and the supply chain is monitored throughout the process.

2.5 Supply contracts for events

Contracts for events may be of several types.

For events that take place across multiple locations, it is often the case that some contractors/suppliers take part for the duration of the tour (e.g. the staging contractor). These events will also have smaller local contractors in use, required either by local legislation to provide jobs for those businesses or by local agreements regarding knowledge of the area/country. These can sometimes be referred to as 'local crew'. This mix of contractors/suppliers means that communication must be clear and unambiguous in both verbal and written agreements to ensure the safety and success of the event. Likewise, the terms and conditions of any contract must be clear and easily understood so as to avoid conflict and misunderstanding. It is worth noting that different companies may require a contract to be determined under a particular country's legislation (e.g. an American company operating in the UK may have its contract determined by US legislation).

Before selecting a contractor/supplier, consider what is needed for the event (e.g. do not select a contractor based upon the latest design of stage if the event does not need a stage). If possible, use event trade shows as a means to view what options are available in the market place, and what particular contractors have available for hire. Discuss the event needs with the contractor/supplier to ascertain if they can provide and meet the event requirements. A competent contractor/supplier will know their equipment and be better able to provide equipment appropriate to the needs of the organiser if they are able to discuss the event with the organiser. Furthermore, take references from a contractor/supplier and investigate them – many organisers do not take or check references, citing reasons such as lack of time or appearing to mistrust the contractor/supplier. Many good contractors/ eferences as part of their quotes, and will expect them to be

ll be able to provide details of their corporate CV as well as h and safety information such as method statements and safe eir appropriate insurance to cover the risks, as well as records of petency to carry out the necessary tasks. Take or keep records of ntractors provide, as well as noting any information about the equipment and its use. All of this provides a good audit trail for the organiser to ensure the contractor and equipment are appropriate for the event needs, as well as giving evidence of 'due diligence' to an organiser's insurance company and any future court or judicial investigation. As well as providing physical information, this level of checking also illustrates the good intent of any organiser in ensuring the health, welfare and safety of their public.

2.6 Responsible and sustainable sourcing and resourcing

In this section we discuss sustainability and how this connects to events and resourcing. It is discussed in this chapter because contractors/suppliers, and indeed supply chain management, are pivotal to sustainable development. Sustainability is viewed as a buzzword in contemporary society and for the past two decades the United Nations, governments, national government organisations and private companies have sought to engage with social responsibility concerning sustainability. One of the outcomes of the Rio+20 Conference was the production of 'The Future We Want', which states the sustainable development goals (SDGs) that need to be addressed by an 'inclusive and transparent intergovernmental process open to all stakeholders' (United Nations, 2012, 47). The principles of sustainable development were first set out in the 1987 Bruntland Report of the United Nations:

> Sustainable development requires meeting the basic needs of all and extending to all the opportunity to satisfy their aspirations for a better life [. . .]. A world in which poverty and inequity are endemic will always be prone to ecological and other crises.
>
> (World Commission on Environment and Development, 1987, 41–42)

> Sustainable development meets the needs of the present without compromising the ability of future generations to meet their own needs.
>
> (WCED, 1987, 41)

In 1992, at the UN Conference on Environment and Development in Rio de Janeiro, Brazil, sustainability was seen as the guiding principle for long-term global development, and sustainable development was defined as consisting of three main pillars: economic, social and environmental. Sustainability represents a balance in which consumption and renewal of resources are in harmony, and the optimal conditions for human survival can be maintained for ever (Holmes, Hughes, Mair and Carlsen, 2015). The equilibrium of the three dimensions of sustainability is of utmost importance as events, by their nature, produce both positive and negative impacts and are organised in resource-intensive economies, something that applies pressure in terms of achieving profitability and growth (Bladen et al., 2012). Consequently, sustainability plays a vital role in contemporary events management and also future event planning and execution. Sustainability in relation to event projects can be defined as the successful management of event projects in a way that consciously values the current and future economic, social and environmental factors affecting the planning, promotion and hosting of events in relation to local, regional, national and inter-national communities.

For the past three decades, a global movement towards sustainability has taken place and the future of events management is greener than it has ever been before. Yeoman (2012) envisions a future with a fast growth in green designs and green technologies which will allow events destinations to undertake sustainable design initiatives which will ultimately reduce the impact on the natural environment. Implementing sustainable design facilities, however, needs the support of govern-ments to change the supply side through legislation and conservation measures and approve higher costs than normal (Yeoman, 2012, 169). Environmental laws and regulations have been implemented by governments worldwide to address these global changes and a good example illustrating the case is the New Zealand environ-mental legislation approved by Parliament in 1991 – the Resource Management Act. Starting with this key environmental act, New Zealand set the ecological impact assessment as an integral component of the entire planning and approval process. The act was seen as both revolutionary and controversial for its time, revolutionary as it gave a new direction and philosophy for the country that benefited several businesses and even set the ground for New Zealand's tourism brand – '100% Pure NZ' – but was disputed due to high costs, delays and limiting property rights. Bosselmann (2010) argues that the act did not limit the widespread environmental degradation, and the current environmental crisis that society faces emerged out of a severe imbalance of economic, social and environmental aspects. According to Dernbach and Mintz (2011, 532), environmental law is an essential element of sustain-ability, but only a part of the necessary legal framework as a range of different laws, regulations and government structures are needed. Sustainability challenges can be addressed by encompassing the idea of governance for sustainability. But what does governance for sustainability mean? And can it applied in an events context? Bosselmann, Engel and Taylor, (2008) conclude that governments, political parties and the media are driven by the global market ideology and what may have started with great plans and promises has been compromised or lost on the way because the demo-cratic institutions are fixated on economic growth. The concepts of sustainability and democracy are imperative and fundamentally linked and, thus, sustainable governance is defined as:

> the set of written and unwritten rules that link ecological citizenship with institu-tions and norms of governance, the emphasis being on the 'link' as no form of governance can succeed if there is no common bond between those who govern and those who are being governed.
>
> (Bosselmann et al., 2008, xiv)

In the connected interdependent society of today, governance must be embedded glocally in the transformation and restructuring of social spaces. Building on the same concepts, Foley, McGillivray and McPherson, (2012) review politics and policy in an event's context, stating that hallmark, special and mega-events are focused around urban environments and an integral part of the refashioning of urban governance. A decisive element of this reshaping is the growth in public–private part-nerships that enable publicly funded entrepreneurship to develop and grow. Nowadays, cities around the world are involved in inter-urban competitions that require proactive and innovative city-branding and specialisation in order to attract private investment in the area and inbound visitors (Foley et al., 2012, 65). Following on the previously discussed brand narrative of New Zealand's '100% Pure NZ', in a period of urban entrepreneurial governance, cities must identify and exploit their unique assets, as they are competing at an international level. Under the umbrella and sustainable objectives of New Zealand's destination brand, in 2008 the city of Auckland revised its strategic plan and published a document that prioritised events. The document, 'Positioning Auckland as a Major Events Destination', was focused on aligning Auckland's brand, values and strategic objectives with the national equivalents, increasing the number of visitors and bringing economic benefits with minimal negative environmental, social and cultural impacts (Foley et al., 2012, 82).

With the rapid change of the events industry towards sustainability, a demand loop in event management has been established. Governments are regulating events by imposing new rules and regulations upon them in relation to their environmental processes and at the same time participants are more aware of sustainability issues and arguably now expect event practices to be aligned with these expectations. In the same vein, the event organiser can be viewed as the customer of those who supply products and services for and to events and can impose new rules in terms of green practices. According to Krajewski, Malhotra and Ritzman (2016, 599), there are three elements in the sustainability of the supply chain: firstly, the *financial responsibility* which addresses the financial needs of all stakeholders (e.g. owners, employees, customers, business partners, financial institutions and community) that supply the financial means (capital) for the production of goods or services; secondly, the *environmental responsibility* that focuses on the one hand on the current global ecological challenges and pressures, and on the other on the internal management of natural resources used in the production of goods and services; and thirdly, the *social responsibility* which encompasses the moral, ethical and philanthropic expectations that society has of an organisation. Along the same line of thought, Schneider and Wallenburg (2012) consider that a focus on the three sustainability dimensions of the sourcing process (economical/financial, environmental and social) can be achieved in practice in two ways: firstly, by increasing the number of sustainability criteria looked at in the sourcing process, and secondly, by developing the number of sourcing activities of the company. Depending on the attention and commitment placed on the economic, environmental or social dimension, a sustainable sourcing pattern should be utilised. Hence, in order to meet its sustainability goals, an event must purchase ethically and socially responsible goods/services. Jones (2010) recommends some general rules that can be followed in terms of production and contractor/supplier purchasing for an event, as highlighted in Table 2.2.

So with new legislation and pressure from stakeholders, event companies are trying to increase their environmental practices. Martínez-Jurado and Moyano-Fuentes (2014) are creating connections between lean management and environmental sustainability, stating that the principles and practices of lean management can be implemented in the supply chain in order to optimise activities with little or no waste. The concept of lean thinking was initially implemented by manufacturing companies that aimed at improving quality, flexibility and customer response within a dynamic business environment (Fullerton, Kennedy and Widener, 2014). Nowadays, lean thinking is implemented in manufacturing, distribution, design and customer service industries. In the events industry, the principles of lean management are applied by adopting a holistic approach that encompasses the integration of a series of prac-

Table 2.2 Production and contractor purchasing for events

Purchasing Policy	• Make a commitment to work only with suppliers that are able to provide environmentally products • Make sure that the production office only purchases the ethically preferable products • Make agreements with contractors that they will follow the same principles and policies • Make a pledge that the event will only use ethically produced and environmentally responsible merchandise
Fair-trade Products	• Garments • Merchandise • Fabric • Electronics • Consumer products
Environmentally Friendly Products	• Timber, paint, stationery, office supplies, printed promotional materials
Sanitation Products	• Phosphate and solvent free • Completely biodegradable • Made out of natural ingredients • Biological rather than chemical
Merchandise	• Raw materials sustainably produced (fair-trade label attached) • Garments/ merchandise manufactured in a fair labour environment and with the necessary certification • Reduced packaging • Offset transport of merchandise if sourced overseas
Materials	• Timber to be sustainability sourced and certified • Paint to be non-toxic, solvent free, water wash-up and low or zero VOC

Source: Jones (2010, 282)

tices such as: reduction of costs, waste management and constantly improving the quality.

2.6.1 Best practice and industry standards

Due to increased environmental issues and consumer pressure, various standards, certification, laws and regulations have been developed worldwide for the better planning and management of sustainable events. The developing bodies of these guides vary from government-led to industry-driven or developed by non-governmental organisations, but the common element is that generally all take into consideration the three pillars of sustainable development and depending on the geographical location, type, scale and focus of each event, stakeholders are in the position of making or influencing policy decisions (Holmes et al., 2015). Jones (2010) believes that developing the sustainability policy of an event is an essential element as it indicates the event's commitment to sustainable management, and details the pathways to sustainability. There are different guides that should be followed as government policies and some general guidelines and models of best practices that could inform event practice.

In order to help with the planning and running of sustainable events, some standards and certifications have been developed. The International Standard for sustainable events (ISO 20121) emerged from the need to make events more sustainable, and it represents a comprehensive and detailed guide to organising events by evolving a system of continuous development aimed at reassuring stakeholders that the event is addressing environmental and social risks and still being profitable. The standard can be applied to any event-organising company that is aware of the impacts of its operations on the environment. Companies that organise more sustainable events can make higher profits because of reduced costs and bigger audiences. Another UK standard relating to all aspects of organising sustainable events which is BS8901, which aims at providing a benchmarking process for sustainable events practices (Bladen et al., 2012), from basic information on effective standard implementation to measuring performance. Only a few events, however, are actually able to meet the standard in all its three phases of planning, implementation and monitoring as the sector continues to be an ad hoc field of delivery. Last but not least, the 'Sustainable Events Guide', developed by the Department for Environment Food and Rural Affairs (DEFRA, 2007) can assist with the planning of sustainable events. Furthermore, a series of toolkits, awards, guidelines and good practice guides have been developed in different regions. The authors, however, claim that the best way of understanding, implementing and adapting sustainable policies for an event is by being aware of the methods and best practices in events across the globe. One of the most iconic examples in terms of sustainable practices and innovative ways of greening the supply chain is the Roskilde Festival in Denmark, which undertakes several green initiatives towards sustainability such as waste management, recycling, container deposits for beer cups, energy management, and influencing suppliers and contractors to make a shift towards fair trade and green products (Jones, 2010, 44). Not as famous and emblematic in terms of sustainable green practices, Rowmania Fest is nevertheless an event that can be showcased to demonstrate good practice in terms of building relationships with contractors and suppliers, and encouraging them to drive their products towards environmental friendliness.

Taking into consideration consumers' sustainable demands, greater connectivity than ever with contractors/suppliers as well as the globalisation of the industry is required. According to Butner (2010), the supply chain of the future will be more instrumented, interconnected and intelligent. Firstly, it will be more instrumented because information is increasingly processed by machines instead of people (e.g. sensors, bar codes, meters). Secondly, it will be an interconnected system because companies are linked to a worldwide network of supply chains, which permits flexibility in terms of availability, diversity of products/services and choice of providers. Finally, it will be intelligent, as preformat systems support decision makers in evaluating alternatives against a diverse range of constraints and risks. Event organisers can be connected to complex networks of global capabilities and have to think strategically in order to be players in the global arena.

An event can be evaluated throughout its life cycle; however, usually within a month after the close-down of an event, the event organisers should organise a meeting to review the entire event process (please refer to Chapter 12 for more

Table 2.3 Supplying locally: case study of Rowmania Fest events, Romania

---

Event: Rowmania Fest

Event Location: Tulcea, Romania

Organisers: 'Ivan Patzaichin – Mila 23' Association

When: yearly event organised in late August for one weekend.

Event's Mission: to promote the Danube Delta region through a sporting competition aimed at raising awareness of a fragile ecosystem.

Participants and the Audience: the event is aimed at bridging the local community with the national and international participants/and audience. More than 100 international participants from Tour International Danubien (TID)[1] attend the rowing competition.

Umbrella Event: the rowing competition is the main highlight of the festival, but several other small events aimed at raising awareness on sustainable practices are organised during the weekend: an urban adventure competition, an eco-craft local fair and a photography exposition, music concerts and an academic/practitioners' conference – 'Black to Black – Cooperation from the Black Forest to the Black Sea'.

Green Footsteps: sustainable transport, waste management, recycling.

Contractors/Suppliers: instead of changing contractors/suppliers, Rowmania decided to keep local links and to conduct a campaign and programmes (e.g. including applying for government and EU funding) that will help the local contractors/suppliers to swap to sustainable choices.

Results: the festival is supplying locally to support the community and to reduce the transport impact of purchasing.

Conclusion: with the tenacious aim of supplying locally and sustainably, the Rowmania Fest organisers managed to influence the supply chain by making it greener each year.

Class Study Activity: Debate on the future of events management and the role of sustainable practices in organising events. In small groups, students are asked to develop three different scenarios on the topic.

Source: adapted from www.rowmania.ro, www.tour-international-danubien.org, and an interview with the event organiser (data collected in June 2015).

[1] Tour International Danubien (TID) – started in 1969 in Germany and has been organised, following the same route from Ingolstadt, Germany to Austria, Slovakia, Hungary, Croatia, Serbia, Bulgaria and Romania, up to the present day. Participants row between 40 and 60 km per day regardless of weather conditions. The final contest terminates in late August/early September in Sfantul Gheorghe, Romania after approximately 2500 km. The tour is the longest trip for canoes and rowboats linking all the Danube countries.

detail). Depending on the scope, size and frequency of the event, information will be collected and stored for future planning and organisation of the same event or similar ones. With the advancements in technology, most event companies keep a computer database of event information and contacts (e.g. contractors/suppliers, clients, sponsors, volunteers). According to Shone and Parry (2010), contractors/suppliers play a major role in the preparation, opening and running of an event as flexibility in delivery and respecting deadlines depends mainly on them. That is why the review process and an online database is essential when it comes to contractors/suppliers. A general list of reliable contractors/suppliers evolves from one event to the other and is usually adapted according to the individual needs of each event. Lessons learned from each event will be adapted for improving future practices.

2.7 Conclusion

This chapter has defined supply chains and supply chain management in the context of the fast developing global events industry. Throughout the chapter, event contractors/suppliers have been analysed by discussing the main challenges and opportunities applied to the particularities of this dynamic sector. The chapter begins with the aspects of project work that could be performed by specialist contractors/suppliers and then distinguished between primary and secondary contractors/suppliers depending on external factors that could influence an event's decisions and processes. Furthermore, the discussion continued around the direct connection between the performance of contractors/suppliers and the event organiser's reputation. Subsequently, the three dimensions of sustainability were introduced, along with how the sourcing process can achieve them. Finally, some specific sector guidelines and standards of sustainability were highlighted, followed by examples of best practice. To conclude, it can be argued that there is a global trend of implementing sustainable practices and policies in events, and, further, that there are a growing number of examples where events are positively influencing the entire supply chain.

Study activity

Choose one of these types of events: Christmas market, street festival, agricultural show/state fair or music festival and devise a blueprint/diagram/chart/model of all the different suppliers and contractors of the event by employing measures that would green your supply chain and make the event more sustainable. The following points could be taken into consideration:

- Instead of changing your suppliers, can you work with the current ones after revising their green practices? Is it more sustainable in the long term?
- Can you align your event's strategies to the ones of your company and to those of your suppliers? If yes, what are the challenges in achieving this?

Case study 2: Lincoln Christmas Market, UK

Lincoln Christmas Market is a well-established event, having grown extensively over the past 30 years from a small-scale local German-style Christmas Market to a very large four-day event attended by visitors from both the UK and Europe. The event takes place in the historic area of the city, at the top of Steep Hill. The primary areas are Castle Square, Lincoln Castle, Cathedral and Bailgate. Significantly, all of these areas are residential, feature many local businesses and are popular with tourists.

Approximately 250,000 people attend the Christmas Market over the four days during the first week of December each year. The Christmas Market hosts a mix of Christmas themed craft stalls and local food delicacies alongside festive entertainment. The event is organised by the City of Lincoln Council and is calculated to bring in over £10 million annually (Thompson, 2015) to the local economy. As such, staging the event has become one of the council's top priorities during budget setting. It also receives cross-party political support from the council's elected members. Governance of the event requires officers responsible for its organisation to report at regular intervals to the Corporate Management Team, the Performance Scrutiny Committee and other, full Committee meetings. Following the event, reports are also presented to these committees covering matters such as finance and inconvenience to any local residents and permanent businesses.

The council has a dedicated event team, who work all year round on the planning and execution of the event. Through experience they have learnt that all contract/supplier tendering and any change of contractor/supplier must take place at the same time, as many contract/supply activities are interlinked. Contracts are awarded on a three-year basis; this facilitates relationship building between contractors/suppliers, local residents, businesses and the council. These contracts apply to all City of Lincoln Council events (Remembrance Day, Christmas Light Switch On, Lincoln 10k), which allows for better value for money contracting, as well as making the contract more valuable (attractive) to companies who may wish to submit a tender. The council's health and safety and procurement officers are also involved in the tendering process and contractor/supplier compliance is built into the successful tender and monitored throughout the event.

If contractor performance is below that expected, a default notice is served similar to a yellow card system; after three default notices the contracts may be terminated. Removing a company is always a worst-case scenario and the council prefers to communicate and discuss concerns or problems in order to resolve matters; this can be particularly important if the default of a primary contractor comes in the final weeks before the event. Contractors/suppliers are paid after delivery of their services at the event; this differs from stallholders/concessions that pay for their 'pitch' before the event.

The council's definition of a primary contractor/supplier is one that is critical to the event proceedings and one that cannot easily be replaced at short notice. For example, a toilet contractor/supplier letting the council down prior to the event would not pose a great problem because in December there are many other contractors available who could be called upon. This, however, would not be the case if the event were to take place in the summer months, in which many more events take place. In contrast, a stewarding contractor/supplier or a traffic management contractor/supplier not able to perform their role would pose a serious threat to the event; the numbers of stewards required/road closure and diversionary signage specific to the event would make it very difficult to obtain a new contractor/supplier with sufficient capability and experience to perform the necessary tasks at short notice. Other examples of primary contractors/suppliers for this event include electrical suppliers, CCTV suppliers and coach/park and ride sites and operators. The council also recognises that the time of year an event takes place can influence how contracts are placed (i.e. whether all are renewed at the same time or in stages), and also that different contractors may be of primary/secondary importance.

An alternative definition of a primary contractor/supplier for the City of Lincoln Council is one who, being public-facing (such as the stewarding contractor), may pose a risk to the reputation of the council or the event. It is understood that this contractor/supplier will be seen as the 'face' of the council, as people attending the event will gravitate to the stewards for assistance or information in the first instance. If members of the public are dealt with inappropriately, it is the council's

Figure 2.2 View of Lincoln Castle Grounds during Lincoln Christmas Market, taken from the Castle Walls, Lincoln, UK

Source: ©Ian Reed

(Continued)

Case study 1 (*continued*)

Figure 2.3 View of Lincoln Cathedral and Castle Square during Lincoln Christmas Market, taken from the Castle, Lincoln, UK

Source: ©Ian Reed

reputation on the line. For this reason, importance is also given to local knowledge and staff training ahead of the event.

The council commences its planning cycle immediately after the end of the previous event; a debrief takes place in January which looks at all aspects of the event both from a council and contractor perspective, as well as from a multi-agency perspective. This involves a review of what worked well and what could have worked better. It also identifies any changes or amendments that need to be incorporated into future event planning. In addition, it ensures that matters such as the coach bookings are available to coach companies at an early point in the year. This is designed to maximise bookings in relation to competition, as well as to allow for 'early bird' fees. It has the added bonus for the council of being able to commit more time to other planning aspects of the event throughout the year: for example, the Safety Advisory Group and writing the event management plan and appendices.

Thank you to City of Lincoln Council for granting the authors permission to use this case study.

Evaluative student questions

1   What are the main factors influencing the selection of the primary and secondary contractors/suppliers for Lincoln Christmas Market each year? Can these factors differ from one year to the other?
2   How important is the need for strong collaboration and communication between the event organiser, City of Lincoln Council, and contractors/suppliers?
3   Could you provide some examples of primary/secondary contractors/suppliers that through their performance could damage the reputation of the City of Lincoln Council?

Further reading

Butner, K. (2010) The smarter supply chain of the future. *Strategy & Leadership*, 38(1) 22–31.
Krajewski, L.J, Malhotra, M.K. and Ritzman, L.P. (2016) *Operations management: processes and supply chains*. London: Pearson.
Schneider, L. and Wallenburg, C.M. (2012) Implementing sustainable sourcing: does purchasing need to change? *Journal of Purchasing & Supply Management*, 18(4) 243–257.

References

Atrek, B., Marcone, M.R., Gregori, G.L., Temperini, V. and Moscatelli, L. (2014) Relationship quality in supply chain management: a dyad perspective. *Ege Academic Review*, 14(3) 371–381.
Bladen, C., Kennell, J., Abson, E. and Wilde, N. (2012) *Events management: an introduction*. Abingdon: Routledge.
Bosselmann, K. (2010) Losing the forest for the trees: environmental reductionism in the law. *Sustainability*, 2(8) 2424–2448.
Bosselmann, K., Engel, R. and Taylor, T. (2008) *Governance for sustainability: issues, challenges, successes*. IUCN – The World Conservation Union, Environmental Policy and Law Paper No. 70. Bonn, Germany. Available from: http://cmsdata. iucn.org/downloads/eplp_70_governance_for_sustainability.pdf [Accessed 22 March 2016].
Bowdin, G., Allen, J., O'Toole,W., Harris, R. and McDonnell, I. (2011) *Events management*. 3rd edition. London: Butterworth-Heinemann.
Bozarth, C.C., Handfield, R.B. and Chandiran, P. (2013) *Introduction to operations and supply chain management: international edition*. London: Pearson Education.
Butner, K. (2010) The smarter supply chain of the future. *Strategy & Leadership*, 38(1) 22–31.
Chelariu, C., Asare, A.K. and Brashear-Alejandro, T. (2014) 'A ROSE, by another name' . . .: relationship typology and performance measurement in supply chains. *Journal of Business and Industrial Marketing*, 29(4) 332–343.

DEFRA (2007) *Sustainable events guide*. London: DEFRA. Available from: http://webarchive.nationalarchives.gov.uk/20130402151656/http://archive.defra.gov.uk/sustainable/government/advice/documents/SustainableEventsGuide.pdf [Accessed 1 April 2016].

Dernbach, J.C. and Mintz, J.A. (2011) Environmental laws and sustainability: an introduction. *Sustainability*, 3(3) 531–540.

Foley, M., McGillivray, D. and McPherson, G. (2012) *Event policy: from theory to strategy*. Oxon: Routledge.

Fullerton, R.R., Kennedy, F.A., Widener, S.K. (2014) Manufacturing and firm performance: the incremental contribution of lean management accounting practices. *Journal of Operations Management*, 32(7–8) 414–428.

Getz, D. (2005) *Event management and event tourism*. New York: Cognizant Communication.

Getz, D. (2012) *Events studies: theory, research and policy for planned events*. Abingdon: Routledge.

Holmes, K., Hughes, M., Mair, J. and Carlsen, J. (2015) *Events and sustainability*. Abingdon: Routledge.

Jones, M. (2010) *Sustainable event management*. London: Earthscan.

Krajewski, L.J, Malhotra, M.K. and Ritzman, L.P. (2016) *Operations management: processes and supply chains*. London: Pearson.

Li, L., Ford, J.B., Zhai, X. and Xu, L. (2012) Relational benefits and manufacturer satisfaction: an empirical study of logistics service in supply chain. *International Journal of Production Research*, 50(19) 5445–5459.

Lincoln Council (2013) *City Council budget*. Available at: http://www.lincoln.gov.uk/your-council/news-and-media/latest-news/city-council-budget/115479.article [Accessed February 2016].

Martínez-Jurado, P.J. and Moyano-Fuentes, J. (2014) Lean management, supply chain management and sustainability: a literature review. *Journal of Cleaner Production* 85 134–150.

Maylor, H. (2010) *Project management*. 4th edition. Harlow: Prentice Hall.

O'Toole, W. and Mikolaitis, P. (2002) *Corporate event project management*. New York: John Wiley & Sons.

Resource Management Act 1991 (n.69). Available from: http://www.legislation.govt.nz/act/public/1991/0069/latest/DLM230265.html [Accessed 22 March 2016].

Schneider, L. and Wallenburg, C.M. (2012) Implementing sustainable sourcing: does purchasing need to change? *Journal of Purchasing and Supply Management*, 18(4) 243–257.

Shone, A. and Parry, B. (2013) *Successful event management: a practical handbook*. Andover: Cengage Learning.

Thompson, C. (2015) *Christmas Market 2014 financial outturn report*. Performance Scrutiny Committee, 19 March. Available from: https://democratic.lincoln.gov.uk/documents/s16342/Christmas%20Market%202014%20Financial%20Outturn%20Report.pdf [Accessed 22 March 2016].

Tum, J., Norton, P. and Wright, J.N. (2011) *Management of event operations*. Oxford: Elsevier.

United Nations (2012) The future we want: outcome document of the United Nations Conference on Sustainable Development. *Rio+20 United Nations Conference on Sustainable Development,* Rio de Janeiro, 20–22 June. Available from: https://

sustainabledevelopment.un.org/content/documents/733FutureWeWant.pdf [Accessed 22 March 2016].

United Nations Conference on Environment and Development (UNCED) (1992), *Agenda 21 – program of action for sustainable development: Rio declaration on environment and development*, United Nations Conference on Environment and Development, Rio de Janeiro, United Nations, New York.

Yeoman, I. (2012) *2050: Tomorrow's tourism*. Bristol: Channel View Publications.

World Commission on Environment and Development (WCED) (1987) *Our common future: the Bruntland Report*. Available from: http://www.un-documents.net/our-common-future.pdf [Accessed 22 March 2016].

Chapter 3

Stakeholder relationships

3.1 Introduction

The importance of stakeholder relationships within the events industry cannot be overlooked. Traditionally, business scholarship concentrated on the role of *shareholders* within business models and the connected organisational behaviour. Stakeholders, however, is now a more preferable way to describe and account for the multiple parties who have an investment and/or interest in a particular business (Newcombe, 2003) or indeed event. The 'stakeholder concept' (Brown, Bessant and Lamming, 2013, 116) concerns the wider organisations involved in the business supply chain. Freeman (1984) pioneered the stakeholder approach within strategic management and argues that it is useful for understanding the complexities and variables of business. He argued that the following 'stakes' can be classed as stakeholders: owners, financial community, activist groups, customer advocate groups, unions, employees, trade associations, competitors, suppliers, governments and political groups. Success of mega-events is not so much connected to the effectiveness of the organising committee but their ability to keep each stakeholder group satisfied (Parent and Swan-Smith, 2013). That said there is a scarcity of literature surrounding mega-events in connection to one key stakeholder, namely the community (Lamberti, Noci, Guo and Zhu 2011). As Bowdin et al. (2011, 79) comment, 'events do not take place in a vacuum' and therefore the significance and impact events have on their surrounding landscapes, communities and political spheres can be extensive and significant. This chapter will focus on sponsorship, media relationships and local stakeholders.

3.2 Sponsor stakeholders

Sponsorship has been defined as 'a business relationship between a provider of funds, resources or services, and an event or organisation which offers in return some rights and an association that may be used for commercial advantage' (Sleight, 1989 as cited in Brown, 2000, 72). Sponsorship needs to be researched and understood from different angles as it associated with stakeholder management, strategic planning, risk management, financial control, legal aspects, marketing, communication and branding (Getz, 2012). Sponsorship has become a primordial issue for most events and a main concern for event managers (Brown, 2000). This section will review and discuss the position sponsors have as an event stakeholder.

For events seeking sponsorship, the assembling of the sponsorship proposal is vital and constitutes the backbone of the sponsorship pitch (Cornwell, 2014). The sponsorship proposal needs to be regarded as a business proposal as companies arguably sponsor events with the intention of making a return on their investment (ROI). An events project manager needs to have a planned approach on how to gain access to companies that will be the *appropriate* sponsors. This is the reason why the event project manager needs to have the necessary set of skills to develop not only the initial proposal stages of the plan but also the entire sponsorship strategy. In events project management the planning of the 5Ws (who, what, where, why and when) is essential and most of the time events managers work backwards from the scheduled date of the event in order to plan deadlines effectively (Bowdin et al., 2011). The Gantt chart is a project management tool that helps with managing deadlines; this is referred to in more detail in Chapter 5. The steps used in creating a Gantt chart will be applied to sponsorship planning in order to illustrate the importance of project management and techniques at all project levels. The work of Bowdin et al. (2011, 273) with reference to Gantt chart planning has been here adapted by the authors in relation to sponsorship planning:

- *Tasks*: break down the work involved in the entire sponsorship plan into manageable tasks and activities. One of the tasks can be the initial proposal/pitch to sponsors. This can be further broken down into target markets, benefits for each of the sides, creating sponsorship packages, resources, the marketing plan and audience profile. All tasks and responsibilities need to be identified for a good sponsorship pitch.
- *Timelines*: the times for each task need to be set. The most important factors to take into consideration are the starting and completion times. Other factors that need to be looked at when dealing with the relationship between time and sponsors are availability, sponsorship costs, cash or in-kind, tiered packages.
- *Priority*: the priority of sponsors and sponsorship tasks needs to be set. What tasks need to be completed before sponsors can be approached? Elements such as brand identity, audience, business benefits and prices need to be defined before the first meeting. The more a sponsorship proposal will be tailored to the needs and interests of the business, the more effective the approach will be.
- *Grid*: a horizontal bar corresponding to each task will be drawn in the grid. Tasks are dependent upon each other. For example, making an approach to sponsors is dependent on the previous research conducted on companies that would be appropriate to sponsor the event.
- *Milestones*: 'sponsorship charts' can be used for monitoring the progress of the deals; tasks of main importance are called milestones and highlighted on the chart. For example, securing a media sponsor can act as a trigger in securing other sponsorship contracts.

Bryde (2008, 801) discusses the concept of a project sponsor as 'being used to describe either an individual/person or a body/group with a particular role in a project environment'. The project sponsor is usually part of the middle or senior management position within the client's company and has the responsibility to oversee the development of the project (Bryde, 2008). This knowledge is useful and can be used by the event's organisers when seeking to secure sponsorship deals. Each event that receives benefits/revenues from sponsorship deals can delegate *an event project sponsor* who will be responsible for effective collaboration with sponsors. This would be beneficial especially in event management companies where several events are being arranged/prepared/overseen at the same time and a number of sponsors are secured for each of the events. Event managers tend to focus on the next event, and sometimes securing and developing the relationship with sponsors can fall at the wayside and can ultimately be detrimental to organisational activities.

The main role of the event project sponsor would be to optimise the relationship with sponsors and make sure that sponsors are satisfied throughout the process. An element to consider is that the sponsor's expectations may have increased due to increased spending allowances within events; therefore, in order for event managers to gain a competitive advantage, their focal point needs to be directed towards these heightened expectations (Masterman, 2009). Sponsorship can be used as a strategic business tool which directly links to the growing share of marketing budgets worldwide (O'Reilly and Horning, 2013). Fruitful collaboration between the event manager and the event project sponsor is imperative. In addition, the event project sponsor should make sure that both the event's interests and the sponsor's interests and expectations are fulfilled. This role of event project sponsor, even if working within the events company, creates an extra element of security for the sponsor. It is a positive for any sponsor to know that they have a person in charge of the sponsorship, and a plus point in terms of sealing the deal. O'Reilly and Horning (2013) suggest that a unique sponsorship strategy is one that presents and compares the reality and the current situation of the organisation with potential business scenarios (objectives, competitive position/brand equity, past sponsorship efforts).

Jackson (2013) states that event organisers tend to direct their attention and focus towards the people who pay to attend the event (the external consumers), but that the internal consumers (such as sponsors, suppliers, staff members and volunteers) should not be ignored as they too are consumers in their own rights and, furthermore, influence external consumers. A sponsor's image is directly affected by the event image, event–sponsor fit and sponsorship exposure. Companies should direct their sponsorship budgets towards events that share either a functional or an image fit. An appropriate fit between the sponsor's image and the event is beneficial even for the 'less involved' consumers (Grohs and Reisinger, 2014). Sponsorship programmes should have a degree of flexibility in order to adapt to the latest emerging trends such as social media and causes (O'Reilly and Horning, 2013). Sponsorship exposure occurs at the event or in the mass media potentially before, during and after the event.

On a practical basis, one of the more difficult aspects for the event organiser may be retaining hold of or maintaining the direction of their own event when working with sponsors. This may occur if the 'appropriate fit' has not been effectively determined. If the sponsors available, or those who have been brought on board, are not an ideal fit for the event and the event team, then the event organiser may be put under pressure by the sponsor. It is extremely important for the event organisation to prioritise working with sponsors who share their values, objectives and strategies.

Tip box

Take advice from a specialist before signing or agreeing any contracts with sponsors to ensure that you know exactly what you are agreeing to, and what the sponsor will be providing. It is likely that a sponsor may be better informed about these matters than you will be, as this is more likely to be a 'normal' way of conducting business for them.

This pressure can manifest as a request to alter certain aspects of the event to make it more successful, or it can be pressure to alter aspects of the event to better promote the sponsor. Whilst both of these suggestions may seem to be innocent and positively intended, they may also cause the event organiser to feel pressurised to amend their event in ways in which they are not comfortable. In extreme situations, an event organiser that has not agreed clear parameters with their sponsor(s) may find that there is no alternative but to change aspects of the event against their wishes. The alternative for the organiser may be the loss of the sponsor(s), which may stem from a breakdown in the relationship between organiser and sponsor. Depending on the agreement between event organiser and sponsor, a breakdown may be a contractual breach that may have other consequences. It is clear from this section that the sponsor as a stakeholder can have a great deal of influence on the success of the project event. The next section focuses on the potential impact that media stakeholders have on the event and event relationships.

3.3 Media stakeholders

Katz (as cited in Bladen et al., 2012, 387) defines the media as 'any communication medium that is designed and managed by an owner with the aim of informing or entertaining an audience'. As indicated by the phrase 'informing or entertaining an audience', it is clear to see how events and the media closely align; both seek to reach out to an audience with a specific focus. The media must always be seen as a stakeholder in events. For some event organisers, this relationship with the media might be an uncomfortable one due to the uncertainty about what will be reported. The savvy event organiser, however, will realise that working with the media can provide more positive feedback or advertising about the event, and ignoring them or failing to engage with them may lead to challenges.

In recent years, the media and media consumption have evolved rapidly, something that will be discussed in more detail in Chapter 6. Earlier forms of the media could be described as being limited by choices such as national, regional or local printed newspapers, trade or interest-specific magazines, and national, regional or local television. Contemporary media now has a very wide appeal and usage across multiple platforms with far-reaching sources and engagement levels. The media platforms available now are arguably more impactful and it is possible that a small-scale localised story may become an internet sensation. Consequently, for an event organiser there are many decisions to be made about the use of the media. These should be considered in conjunction with other parts of this book that assist in identifying the target audience.

The organiser of a small event aimed at local community engagement may not be able to afford full-page advertising for their event; however, it is extremely likely that they will have a social media presence on which to provide details of their event and raise its profile, or give information relating to the activities or latest booked attractions. The organisers may also be able to engage with the local print media and the local television and radio stations. In the current financial climate, all organisations will be focusing on how to use their resources in the most effective and efficient way. Journalism and the media are no different, and if an organiser can 'feed' stories to the different forms of media for print or broadcast, then this has less cost attached to the media company and provides them with information to fill their printed edition or their broadcast slot. Clearly, there are practicalities to be considered in this method. The media will want new angles for each story; they will not want to repeat the same narrative. For the organiser, it may turn out that the media do not use the piece to communicate the point that the organiser was trying to make. After all, the organiser's purpose in sharing its event in the media is to advertise the event to make it more successful, whereas the media's agenda may be to make the story cover as many column inches or broadcast minutes as possible. It is worth investing time and effort in developing a strong and reliable relationship with media stakeholders to limit miscommunication and ensure both parties get the outcome they require.

Large-scale events may have a dedicated media relations manager or officer in place to oversee and monitor the media stakeholder. Typically, this will be someone who has knowledge of the media and how it works, as well as knowledge of the event world and its requirements. This may well be someone who used to work in the field of journalism and the media and may still have contact with different outlets or publications. Getz and Fairley (2004) focused on five case studies from the Gold Coast, Australia: the Gold Coast Airport Marathon, the Pan Pacific Masters Games, the Australian and New Zealand Police (and Emergency Services) Games, Honda Indy 300 and lastly the Quicksilver Pro. They found, across all five events, there was a 'need for a more coordinated and focused strategy for co-branding and media management' (Getz and Fairley, 2004, 135–136). Implications of this research concern the need to work together with other local offerings to optimally promote the destination and image of the event setting.

Many large-scale events, depending on their target audience, will use social media platforms to promote their event. This is available to smaller-scale events, but it may be that the organising group lack the expertise to make the maximum use of this phenomenon. Clearly this method has low-cost implications for an organiser, as the use of social media is largely free and can be seen to be an electronic form of 'word of mouth', referred to as e-WOM (Shalom and Yaniv, 2015). Social media, however, does rely on the event: its concept, its promotional material and the continuation of new attractive messages to engage and excite the different types of user. The importance of using platforms such as Twitter for stakeholder engagement is significant because organisations can 'build information communities by using hashtags' (Lovejoy, Waters and Saxton, 2012, 316).

The level of engagement from different aspects of the media will be very dependent on the size, style and aim of the event. In the same way as each event will need research to identify its target audience, it will also require research to identify its target media. This may be the target media for facilities at the event such as concessions or contractors/suppliers, or it may be the target media for ticket selling. As previously noted, the media must be seen to be stakeholders in the event, regardless of whether there is any explicit arrangement in place between organiser and media provider. An event organiser that does not recognise the media as a stakeholder will run the risk of the media reporting their own version of a story. In the same way as social media can work for the organiser, it can also work against them. Social media makes it very easy for a disgruntled visitor to an event to report and publish a very honest account of the event in a rapid way. If this negative comment is then picked up by a 'traditional' media outlet, what was originally one visitor's unhappy experience will potentially be shared across an untold number of potential visitors. On such trivial happenings reputations can be won and lost.

It can be argued that event organisations that have actively sought out media opinion and buy-in from an early event planning stage will have created a more effective and lasting relationship. This can have very practical implications and the media can be of very significant use if an incident has occurred at an event. In this circumstance, the event organiser is likely to have provided a point of contact for the media at the event, perhaps also facilities and a location for them to report from. At a time when the organiser is dealing with an incident situation, the media arrangements already in place may mean that there is one fewer aspect for them to consider.

Arguably, the ultimate media–stakeholder relationship is when a particular media agency has sole rights of access to performers or activities in the event, in return for their free promotion of the event. This has clear positive results in that the amount of event publicity is very great, but it can have a negative impact on other stakeholders. It may limit the way in which other sponsors can achieve publicity so they may be less likely to become involved, and it may limit the way in which an organiser can promote the event through other media outlets. This means that it is crucial to identify the correct media stakeholder to achieve the best event publicity before signing any contracts. A media agency may have rights to an event or to a venue, or they may have rights to competitors or a sport. An example of a collaboration between a media outlet and a sport is the relationship between Sky and British Cycling. This commenced in 2008, in the wake of the Beijing Olympics and is set to end in 2016, although Sky will still retain its Team Sky cycling team (Cary, 2015).

Study activity

Make a list of current or previous events which have been linked to media, and consider the benefits and drawbacks for each stakeholder in those relationships, including appropriate fit of media relationship for events.

3.4 Local relationships

Each event is different, and different event organisations will prioritise or establish stronger and/or weaker stakeholder relationships with some parties as opposed to others. Arguably, however, the relationships with those local to the event are highly significant to the impact and success of the event in question. Ensuring that local stakeholders are satisfied and informed about the event at each stage of the project management process is critical for success. This section discusses in further detail the various local relationships involved in event planning.

3.4.1 Land and venue owners

Most event organisers will not have the luxury of owning the land or venue on which their event is to take place. Usually event organisers identify a location they feel is particularly appropriate for their event (e.g. a historical re-enactment event which will take place at a relevant heritage site). Alternatively, an event organiser may be approached by a venue, and asked to bring their already established event to a new site (e.g. a music event such as 'Proms in the Park'). Those event organisers who do use land or a venue owned by someone else are usually required to pay a hiring fee, and to sign or agree a contract of hire or hiring agreement.

There are a variety of factors to be considered in this arrangement, both for the organiser and for the land or venue owner. For the organiser, they may wish to build up a long-term relationship with the location owner, allowing for the event to have a stable base from which to operate, and perhaps (having contracted the location for some time) on more favourable terms than would be achieved by an individual event contract. The venue may have particular aspects that the organiser wishes to take advantage of, such as already having facilities built which keep costs down for the organiser, or good transportation links that make a highly successful event more likely. For the venue owner, the particular event being held on their site may raise the venue profile and bring in further business, or (again with a longer-term contract) may provide some financial stability or long-term income. It may equip them with a direction for their own business (e.g. if they have a successful relationship with one vintage vehicle company, they can market this to attract other vehicle events). It is a minority of event organisers who will be using their own land or venue. It is therefore worthwhile investing time and resources into the necessary research to find a suitable venue and to build a relationship with the land/venue owner as well as to ensure an appropriate contract/agreement of hire.

3.4.2 Statutory agencies

The first point to consider is 'what is meant by the term *statutory agency*?' One way is to use the following definitions:

- an agency with obligations about public safety placed upon them by legislation (e.g. transportation or emergency planning)
- an agency that you would expect to deal with or respond to emergency situations (e.g. police, fire, ambulance)
- an agency with a responsibility to deliver/maintain a service required to live safely (e.g. the different departments of local authorities).

Having identified the agencies from the above definitions, an event organiser may well be reluctant to build a relationship with them, fearing they would want to prevent the project being run, or that they would place challenges and extra costs in the way. These fears are often misplaced because local stakeholders typically realise that events can be good for local economies and for local communities, and so these agencies are more likely to be in favour of events, provided they are organised properly and safely.

Such agencies also have many positive aspects that can assist you in your event project:

● They have local knowledge about many factors which will be relevant to your event.
● They have expert knowledge and expertise within their own field.
● They already have working relationships with each other.

In working with the event organiser, to ensure that the event is safe, the agencies minimise the need for them to respond in an emergency. This is a positive point for them, as it safeguards the local community from any costs associated with responding to the incident, as well as reassuring the community that the incoming event will not bring them danger. For the event organiser this support can be invaluable in helping build a good reputation for events and, if the worst were to happen, it is likely that the impact of any incident would be minimised by the advice and guidance already received. It is also quite likely that the relationships that have been built up over the planning phase will stand the organiser, and the agencies, in good stead in dealing with an incident.

One model used to form relationships with agencies in planning for events is the Safety Advisory Group (SAG) system. This can be viewed as a meeting where all the relevant agencies meet the event organiser and, having heard the event overview, the agencies give advice and guidance relevant to the safety of the event in this particular location. It is usual that the meeting will take place local to the event site; this is to ensure that the staff from the agencies who attend are those who regularly work in that area. If it is not a purpose built venue and not in regular use as an event site, it can be an advantage to visit the site, or hold the meeting there, assuming there is a suitable place. A meeting such as this may last more than an hour, but it is time well invested to build the relationship and to explore safe event solutions. A case study which features the SAG system can be found at the end of this chapter and more information is also available in Chapters 4 and 11 due to the importance of SAGs to the events management environment.

Agencies and event organisers should always remember that these meetings aim to provide advice and guidance on safety matters; the agencies are not likely to be experts on commercial success and they should not expect to exert influence outside their knowledge area. They are also unlikely to be able to recommend individual contractors/suppliers, but they will have guidance on what questions to ask and how to take references in order to ensure the contractors are appropriate to the event. There are many positives for an event organiser in engaging in the SAG system:

● They can meet all the different agencies in the same place at the same time. This can save repeated journeys to the same area and the repetition of information such as the event overview.
● The agency staff are competent in their field and knowledgeable about the particular area, and are likely to have a wealth of past experience which can be used by the event organiser.
● The agencies are used to working together, so will be giving 'joined-up' information, advice and guidance.
● Statutory agencies receive updates in legislation and good practice as well as information alerts and incident reports/lessons learnt. This is information that may

be less readily available to event organisers, however professional; a SAG meeting allows for any relevant information of this type to be exchanged.

Similarly, for the agencies, there are also several positives of engaging with an event organiser:

- The agencies can obtain first-hand knowledge of the event which is to take place.
- They can use this knowledge to allow them to consider any action they may need to take in ensuring they can continue their daily business.
- This knowledge can also be used in the planning of their other activities (e.g. road works).
- The agencies can also help organisers engage with and reassure the local community, particularly in cases where there is conflicting or negative comment or concern about a forthcoming event.

For both event organiser and agency, the SAG system can only work if all information is shared without reservation. All attendees must have a clear and transparent view of the reason for the meetings, commonly called the terms of reference, and these should always be agreed at the first meeting, and adhered to thereafter. It is also crucial that members of the agencies who are involved in the SAG are trained, experienced and knowledgeable about their agency and what the SAG is or is not able to do as well as having a full knowledge of the way that the SAG system works in their local area. A successful SAG system is one in which all events are dealt with in a consistent manner, and where event organisers are provided with up-to-date, accurate and consistent advice and guidance whilst still allowing them to retain responsibility for their events.

Study activity

Identify an event known to yourself, not necessarily of national or international scale, and consider which agencies or organisations you would like to be present at a SAG meeting. Discuss the different needs or aspects that each agency or organisation has, in terms of their individual specialisms (i.e. what questions will they be likely to ask, what information can they give you.)

3.4.3 Local residents and businesses

All events involve a community, whether that is a local, international, cultural or business community (Raj, Walters and Rashid, 2009). Community can be defined as a collection of people, ideas or shared beliefs in relation to a certain key focus, such as an event. For the purposes of this book, community will be taken to mean a group of people within close proximity to and/or who will be impacted upon by a specific event. According to Raj et al. (2009), communities are a key component of event objectives and come under the scope of people, place and purpose of event rationale and implementation. It can be argued that most events will have some sort of economic and social impact on their local community due to their close proximity to the event site or possible access and egress issues. It is therefore especially important that event organisers engage and consult with these communities regarding any potential issues that may affect them during all stages of the planning process. It is known that 'The community wants to have its say in the event, they want it to be accessible, and they are concerned about the quality of the event as it can reflect back on them' (Parent and Swan-Smith, 2013, 184).

As a stakeholder group, then, communities can be very demanding and outspoken due to the personal nature connected to event hosting in their locality. It has been found that certain events can strengthen 'community identity' (Butch, Milne and Dickson, 2011, 325) as well as foster a sense of community cohesion, pride and togetherness. It is clear, therefore, that communities must be consulted with and considered when hosting and designing an event project.

The support of the local community cannot be underestimated. Event organisers should always engage with local community leaders and groups such as parish councils, chambers of commerce, residents' associations and any other groups that may be impacted upon by the event. This liaison should take place during all operational and planning stages. The importance of community consultation has been acknowledged in previous research (Derrett, 2012) and this is especially important if the organiser is planning the event for the first time and hoping that it will become an annual event or if the area is not used to events taking place. If the local community is not on board and has been affected in any negative way, the chances are it will not support the event's return the following year.

The widest breadth of research around communities and events relates to the staging of mega-events and their associated host communities. Cashman (2002) describes the often limited community consultancy between Olympic organisers and the host community due to the fast-paced nature of infrastructure construction and the colossal task at hand. Furthermore, Cashman (2002) explains that any community benefits from hosting the Olympic Games are often vague and difficult to pinpoint reliably. In relation to the World Expo in Shanghai, Lamberti et al. (2011) discovered community stakeholder engagement involved in educating community members rather than allowing them to be part of the decision-making process. This approach, however, may not always work in some areas or for some type of events: ultimately the local community wants to be involved and aware of events taking place in its locality.

It is logical to suggest that events may bring significant benefits to the local economy and have the potential to leave a lasting legacy if planned and managed in the right way. Local businesses such as hotels, restaurants, cafés, pubs and shops all benefit from the increased footfall and business from those people attending. For example, the impact of the Grand Depart for the Tour de France in Yorkshire in 2014 was reported to have brought £102 million into the local economy, with one local business selling ice creams reportedly doing a whole year's business in one day (Leeds City Council, 2014). It is likely that visitors to a host event destination will increase before and during event time. Many people attending the event may not have visited the area before and may return on subsequent occasions to visit other attractions that they have become aware of and then in turn later introduce to others. This can lead to businesses expanding and new businesses opening in the area, creating additional employment opportunities for the local community. The relationship, therefore, between the event organisers and the local community stakeholders must be positive and have longevity. More information and detail about event legacy and impact can be found in the final chapter of this book.

Other practical and logistical aspects should also be considered when viewing community relationships. Road closures and traffic regulation orders can have a significant impact on the local community. Local residents and local businesses will need normal access to their homes and places of work for the duration of the event, as will carers and delivery vehicles supplying those businesses. This will require careful management, especially if any vehicle movements are to take place through or near crowds. The use of traffic regulation orders for the same area or stretches of roads should also be closely monitored. This is especially important for iconic or historic venues and areas of towns and cities. The local community may raise objections if events are impacting excessively on their daily lives because of the frequency with which they take place.

When looking for venues or event sites, audience profile should be taken into consideration. If the event organiser researches and monitors audience profile effectively, this will positively affect reputation, event success and community relationships. Knowing the target audience and conducting some intelligence gathering around behaviours and past experiences of similar events and acts can help to decide on site and venue suitability. It is always prudent to research the entertainment act and talk to people that have staged similar events to establish what went well and what did not, and to find out any learning points and best practice. Listed below are several types of audience profile in relation to a live music events and some common characteristics that can be expected from them. This list is not intended to include all characteristics as there may be more that are exclusive to the event or entertainment that is being staged. It is merely a guide for use as part of planning assumptions.

- *Teenage audiences*: very knowledgeable about the act(s), tend to be in groups and can arrive early. They are excited and emotional and when the doors open, will run for the front-of-house barrier to establish the best viewing positions. Depending on the act, they may come over the front-of-house barrier. Once they have their place they tend not to move. Increased medical provision may need to be in place and arrangements made for pickups and drop offs.
- *Classical audiences*: these are audiences who are attending classical music events, such as Proms-style, operas or orchestral renditions. They have a bigger footprint due to picnics, tables and chairs, etc., they tend to be older and will be more compliant, and there are fewer alcohol issues. Will arrive and leave according to event timings.
- *Dance audiences*: tend to be issues around alcohol and recreational drugs so therefore require experienced medical provider that can recognise and deal with these when presented. Mostly made up of a mixture of teenage and twenty-somethings but expect under-age attendees. There may need to be some post-event provision.
- *Child audiences*: age of admission restrictions may apply and children may only be admitted with responsible persons. Provision should be made for lost children, staffed by competent people that have been through the 'disclosure' process. Organisers may wish to use wristbands for the audience. There may also be a requirement for a crèche, again staffed by appropriate people.
- *Assisted needs audiences*: disabled ramps, disabled toilets, clear signage and evacuation strategy should all be considered. Thought should also be given to ratio of carers per person allowed to use these facilities, as this can sometimes be a challenge.

- *Festival audiences*: made up from a mixture of all the previous audiences. There will be issues around alcohol, recreational drugs and petty theft. They will be there for longer, sometimes arriving the day before and leaving the day after, camping arrangements permitted. As they may be camping, they are likely to be exposed to the elements and may require some support if the weather becomes extreme, both hot and cold. Toilets at festivals are infamous and will require regular servicing on a 24-hour basis. Additional infrastructure such as security, lighting, post-event activities, medical provisions (pharmacy), campsite (shop) should all be considered.

Event organisers should consider all of the mentioned audience profiles before deciding upon a suitable site and entertainment. Different entertainment, acts and audience profile can all impact on the local community, resulting in the potential for public disorder, petty crime and drunkenness, waste management and noise-related issues. If the event is to be staged in a residential area, then a suitable curfew should be agreed and the noise levels regularly monitored.

It is always better to involve the local community in the pre-event planning process as experience shows they can provide much local knowledge and intelligence useful to the event organiser, and without their support the event may not receive a licence and therefore not take place. The event organiser must be aware that meaningful consultation and communication with the stakeholder community is needed. In the past, community collaboration has been overlooked in order to fast-track decision making and used merely to inform rather than create a relationship with the community. This was arguably the case in Rio for the 2016 Olympic Games as it was argued that 'there was no community involvement at any stage of the decision-making process (apart from constant requests for public support via the media) or open discussions about the proposal for hosting the Games' (Reis, de Sousa-Mast and Gurgel, 2014, 449). Community consultation, engagement and communication across all project stages of event management will have positive repercussions for the sense of ownership and pride in relation to the event.

3.5 Conclusion

Events are not isolated affairs but rather involve the guidance, assistance and investment of other organisations, people, groups and agencies. Managing stakeholder engagement and developing fruitful, cooperative and sustained relationships is the key to successful long-term event management. This chapter has focused on three key areas of stakeholder relationships, namely sponsors, media and local stakeholders. There are many other organisations and groups which can be considered event stakeholders but it is beyond the scope of this chapter to include more. The relationship with sponsors is a crucial one and ensuring the fit is appropriate between sponsor and event from the outset will help to alleviate any future issues. Media organisations can also be viewed as event stakeholders, and establishing positive media relationships at an early stage will be useful in promoting the event and associated event messages to the audience. Lastly, engaging with local partners and community members is paramount to event success. Taking the time to listen to and address community ideas and concerns will help to develop and maintain positive local connections.

Case study 3: Lincolnshire Event Safety Partnership (LESP), UK

Lincolnshire Event Safety Partnership is a multi-agency organisation working within the county of Lincolnshire, UK. It is made up from suitably qualified and competent members of the three emergency services, emergency planning officers and the county and district councils, and aims to give accurate and consistent advice to event organisers in putting on a safe event within the county. The group actively encourages and promotes new events and event organisers bringing their events to the county, because it recognises their importance for tourism and the local economy. It believes that by working with event organisers in staging their events, the 'them and us' attitude that can sometimes exist is avoided, and events can take place in a safe manner for both those working at and attending them.

The partnership is a part of the Local Resilience Forum, a multi-agency body enshrined in the Civil Contingencies Act 2004 with a responsibility to plan for foreseeable emergencies that may require a response from the statutory agencies. The agencies, known in the legislation as Category One Responders, reasoned that if the law required them to produce a local risk register and plan for foreseeable emergencies, such as floods or explosions at oil or gas installations, then it must also be common sense and good practice to make plans to deal with an emergency that may arise at a location where a different activity from the norm may be taking place, and with additional people present – an event.

Having a well-established system to deal with their largest event, the agencies adopted this method for other events within the county. In 2004, the Lincolnshire Event Safety Advisory Group (LESAG) was born and became the strategic organisation to ensure consistent advice and to oversee or 'set the rules' as to how SAGs should work in Lincolnshire (e.g. what types/sizes/risk levels of events should be invited to attend a SAG). Renamed in 2010 as Lincolnshire Event Safety Partnership (LESP) this group's current criteria or rules regarding which events should use the SAG system are set out here:

- events of an unusual nature
- events with significant numbers of attendees
- events with a significant or an unusual level of risk
- new venues/events/event organisers.

LESP does also allow that a SAG may consider small, low-risk events if an event organiser requests it to do so and resources permit. In addition to this, the SAG may also identify a need to carry out a debrief of events, if necessary, to ensure continuous improvement. It is the responsibility of the event organiser to undertake the debrief.

The group created documents to give information to event organisers, whether they were of sufficient size to need to work through the SAG system or smaller. They worked with course providers to deliver specialist training to local organisers and agencies at cost-neutral prices. A website was developed and now acts as a central point of information and advice for event organisers before they attend SAGs. Lincolnshire Event Safety Partnership also set criteria relating to the knowledge, experience and qualifications of the members of the agencies who sit on the SAGs, thus ensuring that event organisers are given accurate, up-to-date and consistent advice and guidance.

In order to cover the wide range and number of events (in excess of 300 each year, several with attendances of more than 50,000 people) and to make best use of agencies' and organisers' time, the SAGs work over the local authority areas and have monthly meetings arranged a year ahead. The Chair and Secretariat of the different SAGs ensure that organisers are given dates for the meetings and time slots if their attendance is required. Consideration is given to the need for commercial sensitivities; it may not be appropriate for details of an event to be overheard/listened to by other organisers and therefore all events are discussed by agencies privately, and the ensuing minutes are redacted to ensure confidentiality. Depending on the type, size and arrangements of the event, as well as the experience of the organisers and their home base, it may not be necessary for them to attend the meetings in person. In these cases, events may be discussed by email discussions, or by technical equipment (e.g. video conferencing), though none of these methods will be allowed to affect the quality of the relationship between the organiser and agencies.

References

Bladen C., Kennell J., Abson E. and Wilde N. (2012) *Events management: an introduction*. Abingdon: Routledge.

Bowdin, G., Allen, J., O'Toole, W., Harris, R. and McDonnell, I. (2011) *Events management*. 3rd edition. London: Butterworth-Heinemann.

Brown, G. (2000) Emerging issues in Olympic sponsorship: implications for host cities. *Sport Management Review*, 3(1) 71–92.

Brown, S., Bessant, J.R. and Lamming, R.C. (2013) *Strategic operations management*. Abingdon: Routledge.

Bryde, D. (2008) Perceptions of the impact of project sponsorship practices on project success. *International Journal of Project Management*, 26(8) 800–809.

Butch, T., Milne, S. and Dickson, G. (2011) Multiple stakeholder perspectives on cultural events: Auckland's Pasifika Festival. *Journal of Hospitality, Marketing and Management*, 20(3/4) 311–328.

Cary, T (2015) Sky to split with British Cycling but stick with Team Sky. *The Telegraph*, 1 July. Available from: http://www.telegraph.co.uk/sport/othersports/cycling/11709551/Sky-to-split-with-British-Cycling-but-stick-with-Team-Sky.html [Accessed 24 January 2016].

Cashman, R. (2002) *Impact of the Games on Olympic host cities: university lecture on the Olympics*. [online] Barcelona: Centre d'Estudis Olímpics. Available from: http://ceo.uab.cat/lec/pdf/cashman.pdf [Accessed 5 February 2015].

Cornwell, T. B. (2014) *Sponsorship in marketing: effective communication through sports, arts and events*. Abingdon: Routledge.

Derrett, R. (2012) Festivals, events and the destination. In: Ian Yeoman, Martin Robertson, Jane Ali-Knight, Siobhan Drummond, and Una McMahon-Beattie (eds), *Festival and events management*. Abingdon: Routledge, 32–50.

Freeman, R.E. (1984) *Strategic management*. Boston, MA: Pitman Publishing.

Getz, D. (2012). *Events studies: theory, research and policy for planned events*. Abingdon: Routledge.

Getz, D. and Fairley, S. (2004) Media management at sport events for destination promotion: case studies and concepts. *Event Management*, 8(3) 127–139.

Grohs, R. and Reisinger, H. (2014) Sponsorship effects on brand image: the role of exposure and activity involvement. *Journal of Business Research*, 67(5) 1018–1025.

Jackson, N. (2013) *Promoting and marketing events*. Abingdon: Routledge.

Lamberti, L., Noci, G., Guo, J. and Zhu, S. (2011) Mega-events as drivers of community participation in developing countries: the case of Shanghai World Expo. *Tourism Management*, 32(6) 1474–1483.

Leeds City Council (2014) Three inspirational days: impact of the UK stages of the Tour de France 2014. Leeds: Leeds City Council. Available from: http://www.leeds.gov.uk/docs/141203%20THREE%20INSPIRATIONAL%20DAYS%20FULL%20FINAL.PDF [Accessed 24 April 2015].

Lovejoy, K., Waters, R.D. and Saxton, G.D. (2012) Engaging stakeholders through Twitter: how non-profit organizations are getting more out of 140 characters or less. *Public Relations Review*, 38(2) 313–318.

Masterman, G. (2009) *Strategic sports event management*. Olympic edition/2nd edition. Oxford: Butterworth-Heinemann.

Newcombe, R. (2003) From client to project stakeholders: a stakeholder mapping approach. *Construction Management and Economics*, 21(8) 841–848.

O'Reilly, N. and Horning, D. L. (2013) Leveraging sponsorship: the activation ratio. *Sport Management Review*, 16(4) 424–437.

Parent, M.M. and Swan-Smith, S. (2013) *Managing major sports events: theory and practice*. Abingdon: Routledge.

Raj, R., Walters, P. and Rashid, T. (2009) *Events management: an integrated and practical approach*. London: Sage.

Reis, A.C., de Sousa-Mast, F.R. and Gurgel, L.A. (2014) Rio 2016 and the sport participation legacies. *Leisure Studies*, 33(5) 437–453.

Shalom, L. and Yaniv, G. (2015) How credible is e-word of mouth across digital-marketing channels? *Journal of Advertising Research*, 55(1) 95–109.

Sleight, S. (1989) *Sponsorship: what is it and how to use it*. London: McGraw-Hill.

Chapter 4

Structures and teams

4.1 Introduction

> One of the greatest challenges faced by an event manager is creating effective 'team(s)' capable of achieving an event's objectives.
>
> (Bowdin et al., 2011, 355)

A significant aspect of successful project management is the ability for a team or workforce to complete a set task to time. Event management utilises many different project management tools and approaches in order to plan, organise and execute a successful and safe event. Part of this measurement of success is based around the ability of event teams and individuals to work effectively with one another. The events industry is a unique sector which demands a different and unusual approach to human resource management (HRM) due to its changing short- and long-term needs. This chapter will focus on the various aspects of structures and teams that contribute to the organisation of event projects. Firstly, event teams and their connection to employees and HRM will be reviewed and analysed specifically for the events field. Secondly a look at leadership will be discussed before a focus on event volunteers, their motivations and needs, because, after all, volunteerism is a crucial part of event success. Lastly, group psychology will be highlighted as an important consideration for understanding the complexities of group work and team cohesion.

4.2 Event teams

Event teams will be constructed based upon the type of events organisation in charge and also external factors such as the annual events cycle, political factors, economic considerations and social and cultural ties. Arguably, there are three types of organisation: the flexible organisation, functional flexible organisation and lastly the numerical flexible organisation (Raj et al., 2009). The flexible organisation encapsulates the notion of a 'pulsating' structure which is so prevalent within the events industry (Hanlon and Cuskelly, 2002). The flexible organisation, therefore, expands and contracts in a reactive manner in relation to the annual events cycle. The functional flexible organisation is one which allows employees with a diverse range of skills and abilities to take on multiple roles within the organisation. Lastly, the numerically flexible organisation uses outsourced or agency staff for their actual events. In reality, events organisations may demonstrate one, two or all three of these organisational types simultaneously or individually throughout the year. It is important for event managers to assess, monitor and arrange event teams appropriately to match the organisational structure.

Tip box

Every events team will vary in size, and some events organisers will not have the luxury of a large team to assist them. If you are involved in a small event team, make sure you utilise local expertise to assist you in making decisions and planning for the event.

According to Parent and Swan-Smith (2013, 74), there are five different types of workforce within the events industry:

1 *Employees*: these are regular, paid, full-time staff members.
2 *Consultants*: these operate flexibly (short-term, long-term, full-time or part-time), paid members.
3 *Contract workers*: these are short-term, paid members.
4 *Secondees*: these are short-term or long-term members of the workforce but are 'on loan' from other organisations and therefore are paid directly by the other organisation.
5 *Volunteers*: can be short-term or long-term members but are unpaid workforce.

The events sector is a dynamic, changeable and fluid industry and likewise its workforce must be able to move, shift and accommodate the associated ongoing developments. Event teams can be broken down into more specific sub-teams to allow for greater productivity. This is especially important when considering the vast number of tasks per event-specific project which need to be completed in order to host a successful event. It is acknowledged that 'the success of an event often depends upon the effective delivery of "wow" factors that require a level of expertise that is rarely found within the skill set of the general organisational team' (Bladen et al., 2012, 125).

These 'wow' factors are considered to be the memorable and exciting elements of an event that are likely to get the event noticed by the media and also increase the satisfaction levels and therefore repeat visits of the audience members. The general organisational team, or core events team are those which are classed as the 'employees' when thinking about Parent and Swan-Smith's (2013) five modes of workforce. It is acknowledged that an expanded workforce for the approach and duration of event time is required to support and create the development and implementation of 'wow' factors.

Due to the sometimes fragmented but often fluid nature of event teams, it is important that group cohesiveness is a priority for event managers. Group cohesiveness can be thought of as 'the way "it hangs together" as a tight knit, self-contained entity characterised by uniformity of conduct and mutual support between members' (Hogg and Vaughan, 2005, 291). This can often be very difficult for an event manager to achieve given that the event manager may be from any one or more of the five categories of workforce. Which one they come from will depend on the type of event which is taking place, as well as on matters such as the financial aspects of the event (e.g. an event which has a very tight budget may not be able to afford to bring in an event manager at an early stage). The event manager is therefore joining an already established event team, with its own group cohesiveness.

4.3 Human resource management

Traditionally, the concept of personnel management was used to explain and present event teams and staff roles, but more recently human resource management has been used to encapsulate the philosophy and complexity of contemporary event workforce and team strategies (Bladen et al., 2012). Human resource management can be defined as 'the process of organising and effectively employing people in pursuit of organisational goals' (Raj et al., 2009, 51). The objectives and vision of the events organisation must be considered when hiring new employees or shaping and re-shaping the organisation's workforce structures. It must be noted that in the events sector how human resources operate for events is vastly different from other commercial sectors; therefore, it follows that the management of employees is also different (Bladen et al., 2012). Hede and Rentschler (2007) acknowledge that recruitment, development and people motivation are central in order to achieve festival success. The case study at the end of this chapter also identifies the components of success linked to teams in the wedding industry. It is very important to understand the ways in which the events sector and human resource management interlink: 'Essentially, the biggest difference between the management of an event and the management of an ongoing business enterprise is that the event is generally intangible, untested and there is only one chance to get it right' (Van der Wagen and White, 2015, 5).

The pressure, therefore, on the event team and the human resource management is intense and it is very important to get the staffing and management of the event right. As well as the notion of the event being an 'untested' phenomenon, the structure and recruitment of event staff can also present challenges. Getz (2012, 297) refers to the 'pulsating' nature of event organisations by which the size of the event team expands on the approach to an event and then contracts back to its core team after the event is over. This pulsating structure will repeat constantly throughout the year to mirror the events schedule of that specific organisation. Due to this pulsating event team structure, there will be staff members on different types of contract (e.g. permanent, fixed term, short-term, volunteer capacity). Managing and encouraging cohesion within the events setting of these different types of people is a difficult task but one which can be effectively carried out if human resource management processes are transparent and fit for purpose. Additional difficulties in management connected to events come from the exciting and potentially celebrity-filled nature of events. In 2014 during the Commonwealth Games in Glasgow, a member of the security staff was dismissed because he took a 'selfie' of himself with Usain Bolt (Lydall, 2014). It was expected in this situation that security staff would maintain a professional and focused approach to their work at all times and not become star struck by seeing their favourite athletes train.

This chapter will also discuss the roles and responsibilities of those teams involved in the events setting. A role is a behavioural and social descriptor ascribed to a person; it is not a person directly (Hogg and Vaughan, 2005). This section will concentrate on the roles assigned to organisations, groups and individuals in order to ensure the smooth running of event projects and operations. The very nature of human resource management is created and based on roles and responsibilities, and therefore understanding how these impact on the events environment is essential. Roles and responsibilities must be clear, exacting and well managed in order to prevent any slippages in performance, neglect and/or lack of attendee satisfaction.

4.3.1 Using work breakdown structures (WBS)

Event managers can help to visualise organisational structures and roles by using a work breakdown structure. This is an example of the connectivity between project management, and event organisation. A WBS involves a visual mapping of tasks and roles to the workforce teams. In project management it is common to use the organisational structure as a starting point in which to attach a WBS and from there devise the associated tasks and responsibilities (Bowdin et al., 2011). The benefits of using a WBS and more examples of how to use them can be found in the next chapter on 'Event Management Project Tools'. It is important to mention it here as a way to visualise how event teams may operate and exist. The example in Figure 4.1 represents a generic structure of a community sports organisation. Each employee on this organisational structure will have their own roles and responsibilities which they must fulfil in order to comply with the company's objectives. Take the role of the Events Manager, for example; some of their tasks may include the following:

- organise and host the major events in the company's annual calendar
- guide and manage the Events Officer
- work with volunteers to staff the events
- build up relationships with local suppliers and sponsors
- find sponsors to support the local events
- work closely with the Fundraising Officer to generate income for events
- liaise with the Communications Officer to ensure the events are publicised.

4.4 Planning events and preparing for emergencies

There are several 'teams' that may work together to plan event projects and the following roles and responsibilities group list are centred on the need to do this in a safe and professional manner.

4.4.1 Governing bodies

In terms of events, governing bodies are groups of officials who draw up the rules and formulate policy that govern the direction, actions and conduct of a body organisation, for example in sports. They also ensure that these rules and policies are followed, applied and implemented when necessary. This can also apply to other areas such as universities and schools, and so if organising a charity or fundraising event, the governing body may require consultation to ensure that what is planned is acceptable.

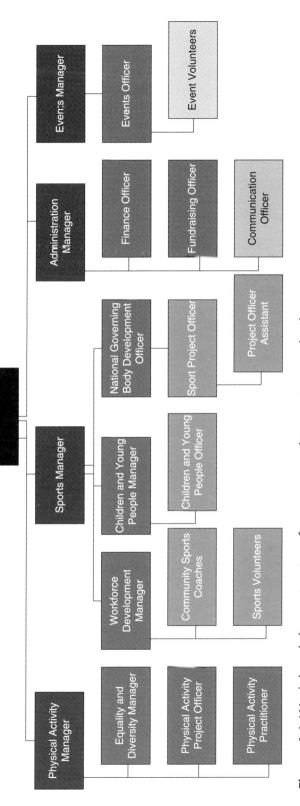

Figure 4.1 Work breakdown structure for a community sports organisation

A sporting governing body is a sports organisation that has a regulatory or sanctioning function. They come in various forms, and have a variety of regulatory functions. This can include disciplinary action for rule infringements and deciding on rule changes in the particular sport that they govern. Governing bodies have different scopes. They may cover a single sport at an international level, such as the Fédération Internationale de Football Association, (FIFA) or the World Boxing Organisation (WBO). They may also cover a range of sports such as the International Olympic Committee (IOC) or the International Paralympic Committee (IPC). Governing bodies also cover single sports at a national level, such as the Rugby Football League (RFL). National bodies may or may not be affiliated to international bodies for the same sport. If sporting competitions are being organised, these should always be in accordance with the relevant governing body's requirements and recommendations.

4.4.2 Safety Advisory Group (SAG)

Safety Advisory Groups have been in existence for many years now and a key example is their role in relation to football events. The *UK Good Practice Guide to Working in Safety Advisory Groups* (Griffiths, Woodham and Stuart, 2015) gives the history of Safety Advisory Groups as originating from Lord Wheatley's report into the Ibrox Disaster of 1971. SAGs were given more weight in Lord Justice Taylor's report on the Hillsborough Stadium Disaster, where in the recommendations, paragraph 31, he suggested that:

> to assist the local authority in exercising its functions, it should set up an advisory group (if this has not already been done) consisting of appropriate members of its own staff, representatives of the police, of the fire and ambulance services and of the building authority. The advisory group should consult representatives of the club and of a recognised supporters' organisation on a regular basis. The advisory group's terms of reference should encompass all matters concerned with crowd safety and should require regular visits to the ground and attendance at matches. The advisory group should have a chair from the local authority, and effective procedures. Its resolutions should be recorded and it should be required to produce regular reports for consideration by the local authority.
>
> (Home Office, 1989, 192)

It must be remembered that SAGs are *advisory* in their capacity. There is no legal requirement to form a SAG for any event, but if an event, like a football match, involves the gathering of large crowds, then it is encouraged. It is a foreseeable risk that incidents and emergencies could occur when large numbers of people gather together in the same place, and this could result in death or serious injury. There have been many cases over the last few years of near misses or incidents at events across the world and this continues to be the case. Ruth Shaw, Chief Executive of Sports Grounds Safety Authority, explains 'it is important that everyone involved in delivering spectator events understands the roles, responsibilities and liabilities' (Griffiths et al., 2015, 5).

The SAG should be formed to eliminate the 'them and us' attitude that can some-times exist between the event organiser and the local authorities and emergency services. All agencies should be aware of the importance to the local economy of events taking place in their area, and it is good practice to foster good working relationships between all agencies in the planning, delivery and aftermath of any event. This can be achieved by agreeing a clear set of terms of reference for the group at the initial meeting. Successful multi-agency planning ensures that the event takes place in a safe manner, not only for those attending but for those working there as well.

Whilst SAGs are not statutory bodies, the individual agencies belonging to them do have statutory powers, and if problems occur during the planning process it should be these agencies that make representations. Any event organiser would be unwise to ignore the collective advice of any SAG membership and as a result may not be able to acquire insurance for their events. As recommended in Lord Justice Taylor's report (Home Office, 1989, 192), all SAG meetings should be accurately recorded by a competent person and these records will become public documents in the event of any enquiry into an incident that may occur at the event.

There are no set requirements for a membership of SAG. Membership should include representatives from organisations appropriate to the safe delivery of the individual event. It is always important to ensure that members have the appropriate skills and training, experience and competencies to make informed decisions on behalf of their organisation. Core SAG membership organisations are illustrated in Figure 4.2 and their roles and responsibilities later outlined in the following sections.

Figure 4.2 Various members of a Safety Advisory Group

4.4.3 Event organisers

The event organiser's responsibilities include all health and safety matters related to the organisational delivery and breakdown of the event. They should ensure that safe systems of work are applied as they have a duty of care towards their employees and those attending. Risk assessments should be undertaken with clear method statements and health and safety policies. Risks should be monitored and audited, and a system should be put in place for record keeping pertaining to any incident or significant occurrence taking place for the duration.

The event organiser is also responsible for writing the event management plans. This should include the event risk assessment, a separate fire risk assessment, a traffic management plan, crowd safety planning, management and evacuation procedures, details of stewarding and security arrangements, medical and first aid provision, communication and welfare arrangements, licensing, safety certification, insurance and any other statutory requirements. They are also strongly advised to liaise and cooperate with the SAG.

4.4.4 Local authorities

Local authorities are an important member of any SAG and in most instances it will provide the SAG chair role. Local authorities are known as a Category 1 Responder under the Civil Contingencies Act 2004 and as such have duties to plan for and respond to emergencies. In some cases it may be that the local authority is the event organiser or the venue owner of an event. The local authority may have a number of officers representing it at any SAG. For example, it will be the local authority that issues, reviews and enforces safety certification at sporting venues with regulated stands under the Safety of Sports Ground Act 1975. It is one of the agencies that will issue, review and enforce licences under the Licensing Act 2003. It will provide environmental health officers to monitor and enforce any environmental health incidents. It may be responsible for highways management and maintenance and potentially for granting any traffic regulation orders and road closures.

4.4.5 Police

The police are also Category 1 Responders under the Civil Contingencies Act. The police have statutory powers relating to many acts of parliament, too many to list or identify here, as they will vary greatly depending on the type of event. Their main responsibilities include crime prevention and detection, dealing with public order, intelligence gathering and coordination of emergencies. They will also respond to incidents where appropriate, and they may provide community policing, if applicable, for an event. If special policing, known as Special Policing Services, is required at the event, there will normally be a charge and this varies depending on the type of event, as well as the location in which it is being held. A commonly held belief is that the police will provide staff to undertake traffic management. These staff may be police officers, police community support officers or Community Safety Accredited Stewards (CSAS). The CSAS are staff members who have received training in traffic management and are employed by a traffic management company that has been accredited for traffic management by the Chief Constable of the police area in which it operates. Not all police services in England and Wales have taken on Community Safety Accredited Stewards (they can also be known as Police Authorised Traffic Officers), for traffic management; it is at the discretion of the service as to whether they wish to use this system. In 2015 it was usually not the case that police services would take on traffic management for events. There were two main reasons for this: the legal powers available to them are limited and specific, and in many of the different areas of the UK there are insufficient police staff to carry out those roles as well as their core activities.

4.4.6 Fire and Rescue

The Fire and Rescue Service is a Category 1 Responder under the Civil Contingencies Act. It has statutory powers under the Regulatory Reform (Fire Safety) Order 2005 and the Fire Safety and Safety of Places of Sport Act 1987. It can provide guidance on fire safety related concerns and can assist with advice about the compilation of a fire risk assessment. It will also respond to incidents where and when appropriate. Like the Police Service, and Ambulance Service It is possible to ask the local authority Fire and Rescue Service to act as fire marshals at an event; however, they are likely to charge for this service.

4.4.7 Ambulance Service

The Ambulance Service is a Category 1 Responder under the Civil Contingencies Act. Whilst it may not be the medical provider for the event, it can provide advice and guidance to the event organiser if private companies are being used. It will respond to incidents and emergencies. It can also advise the event organiser in calculating the level of medical cover required at the event.

4.4.8 Venue/operator

Even where the owner of the land or premises is not the event organiser, they will still have allowed the organiser to hire or use their site, and this means that they still have responsibilities with regard to the use of the land and should therefore be invited to participate in the SAG. They will need to ensure that appropriate insurance cover is in place, must be aware of the licensing requirements and make sure that the condition of the land or premises does not cause danger to users and/or visitors.

4.4.9 Critical (primary) contractors/suppliers

Contractors/suppliers may also be invited to SAG meetings, as organisers cannot be expected to be experts in all aspects of their event. The decision to invite a critical contractor/supplier to a SAG meeting must be for the event organiser, as there will undoubtedly be cost and contractual implications. The teamwork ethos, however, will be enhanced if organisers, contractors/suppliers and agencies meet and work together to resolve issues in advance of the event taking place. (See Figure 4.3.)

Study activity

Discuss and list other agencies or organisations who may be involved in the Safety Advisory Group process.

Figure 4.3 Safety Advisory Group meeting for 2012 Olympic Torch Relay through Lincolnshire, UK

Source: © Vanessa Mawer

4.5 Leaders and leadership

As already discussed, there are many complexities to the running of teams in relation to events management. The 'pulsating' event structure and the different stakeholders involved means that strong and effective leadership is paramount. According to Van der Wagen and White (2015, 257), leadership can be defined as 'the ability to inspire confidence and support among people who are needed to achieve organizational goals and it is about the capacity of an individual to inspire and motivate'. The key words here are those of 'inspire', 'achieve' and 'motivate' which present leadership in a positive and influential light, as a quality possessed by people who seek to encourage and enthuse others to succeed. The leadership of the event organisation will impact upon the event itself and the 'project culture' of which the event is a part (Bladen et al., 2012, 31).

There are many characteristics that can make up the concept of 'leader'. As identified by Van der Wagen and White (2015, 258), they are known for 'exerting influence, having followers, lifting people to a new level, persuading others to act towards achieving a common goal and leading by example so that others follow'. Other scholars have developed their own interpretation of leadership, including Pendleton and Furnham (2012, 47), who refer to the Primary Colours Model of Leadership. This model can be separated into three domains, the strategic domain, the operational domain and lastly the interpersonal domain. They argue that leadership is formed by the abilities connected to each of these domains. The first connects to the leader's ability to think strategically about the organisation and act in ways that advance the company. The operational domain refers to the practicalities of leadership, the doing, ensuring goals are reached. Finally, the interpersonal domain refers to emotional intelligence and the ability of the leader to create, build and sustain relationships useful to the organisation. 'Leadership has been described as a mixture of art, craft and humanity' (Taylor, 2011, 342). It is vital for event managers or leaders to showcase abilities in each of these domains in order to effectively run more complex event projects. Taylor (2011, 344) outlines a leadership styles grid (Figure 4.4), illustrating the four leadership styles of supporting, coaching, delegating and directing. Leadership style and potential impact depends on the strength of the leader's directive or supportive behaviours.

Due to the dynamism and change of the events industry it would be foolish to think one leadership style will be effective in all situations. Rather, a proactive leader is one who is able to change their style depending on context, timing and situation. Intelligent leadership is about 'reading' a situation and responding to it with the most appropriate and relevant type of action; we will refer to this new definition as 'context intelligence'. For example, needing to mentor new event volunteers would involve adopting a 'coaching' style, but at the same event the leader may also need to show a 'delegating' style to give existing colleagues the freedom to operate efficiently. The event coordinator or manager will need to express leadership capabilities in some capacity, and these must be based on effective communication and context intelligence.

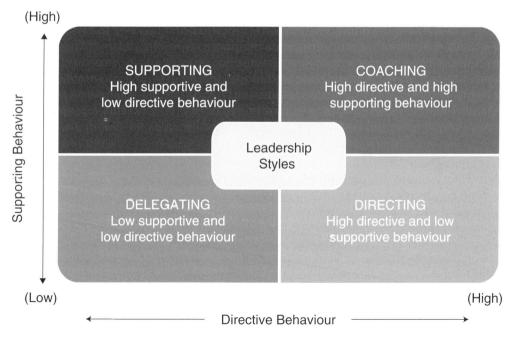

Figure 4.4 Leadership styles

Source: Taylor (2011, 344)

4.6 Event volunteers

Volunteers are a crucial part of the events management workforce, and recruiting, managing and maintaining quality volunteers is critical for event success. Events are increasingly reliant on the use of volunteers, and the act of volunteering can be viewed as an 'economic activity' (Barron and Rihova, 2011, 202). They can also be referred to as the fourth aspect of supply chain management as 'volunteer flow' in terms of the supply need for them to help run an event. According to the Community Life Survey 2014–2015, 69 per cent of people in England had volunteered at least once within the year (Cabinet Office, 2015), demonstrating the close relationship society has with volunteerism. It is acknowledged that volunteers are an integral part of the organisational structure of delivering successful events (Bang, Won and Kim, 2009). 'The activities that volunteers engage in are as varied as the volunteers themselves and their value to the events that contribute to society as a whole remains immeasurable' (Surujlal, 2010, 460).

The commitment and dedication offered by volunteers to the events industry remains the foundation for success and for reinforcing positive societal values. Event volunteers provide 'a crucial source of labour and support' (Alexander and Kim, 2015, 1), which is one reason it is important to delve deeper into the minds and activities of volunteers.

This book argues that volunteer flow should be considered a fourth aspect of supply chain management and that the movement and allocation of volunteers is paramount to event success. As part of the 2002 Commonwealth Games in Manchester, the event organisers used a third-party group, Manchester Event Volunteers (MEV) to supply volunteers for the event. In a report by Nichols and Ralston (2011) this was found to have both advantages and disadvantages for the event organisers. An advantage was that MEV staff helped and encouraged event organisers to lead and manage volunteers in relation to best practice. As a result of using a third-party organisation, however, the event organisers did not have a great deal of prior knowledge about the volunteers due to inclusivity policies, which may limit advanced strategic planning. A very interesting report finding was the importance of the 'psychological contract' between the volunteers and managers whereby mutual respect was offered and received (Nichols and Ralston, 2011, 16).

Tensions, however, can be present between paid staff and volunteers within event teams (Parent and Swan-Smith, 2013). An explanation of this might be the difference in status between volunteer and full-time paid employee. Some roles are more valued than others, involving greater levels of respect and imparting status to the role holder (Hogg and Vaughan, 2005). In addition, Kim, Kim and Odio, (2010) have noticed that a great deal of attention is paid to volunteer recruitment instead of on effective volunteer management in relationship to job satisfaction. One of the main sources for stress at work is frustration with poor management (Randall, 2013) and therefore event teams must be directed, trained and managed efficiently throughout the events cycle. It is important that volunteers are 'tied by a shared set of values' (Nichols and Ralston, 2011, 17) to their volunteer organisation, and this acknowledgement may help in the better management of potential workplace tensions. If volunteers are value driven then the event managers need to ensure these values are met, achieved and reinforced within the volunteers' set tasks.

4.6.1 Volunteer motivation and recognition

There are multiple reasons for individuals and teams to be motivated and rewarded within the events industry. In their study on student volunteers at events, Wakelin (2013) found that 389 students provided 495 reasons for volunteering. In a different study focusing on volunteer motivations, Barron and Rihova (2011) discovered that volunteers have moved away from altruistic reasons for volunteering towards more utilitarian motivations, such as personal gains. The top motivation for their volunteer sample group was that of work experience to improve their curriculum vitae. Whereas, Surujlal (2010) found that volunteers' main reason for participation was to ensure the event was a success and to contribute to the community, and less than 20 per cent expected to be rewarded.

In their study on volunteer motivation in the Expo 2012 Yeosu Korea, Lee et al. (2014) explained that motivators of patriotism and intrinsic reasons affected volunteer satisfaction. As the event was promoted by the Korean government, a sense of community spirit and civic pride were important factors for the volunteers. In addition, the intrinsic focus of it being interesting, engaging and fun was also significant to volunteers' motivational reasons for getting involved. According to Treuren (2014, 61–62), event volunteers can be segmented into six different categories based on their motivations for getting involved:

1   The instrumentalist: the volunteer who is motivated by freebies such as the free ticket and T-shirt for taking part.
2   The obliged volunteer: the volunteer who feels that they should get involved in volunteering.
3   The very keen enthusiast: this volunteer loves the event and everything about it, enjoys all the benefits involved and wants to volunteer again next time.
4   The semi-keen enthusiast: this volunteer is supportive, getting involved feels good and they think it will be good for their careers.
5   The associative/supportive enthusiast: this volunteer is happy to support their colleagues and the group to put on a successful event.
6   The habitual but not very interested volunteer: this volunteer has been helping over the long term but does not have very strong connections to the event.

The equally highest ranked volunteer types were the very and semi-keen enthusiasts who were motivated by the love and enjoyment of the event. A side to event volunteer motivations that is not often documented is that of tourism – those who want to travel and take part in different cultures through the medium of volunteering. Jarvis and Blank (2011) discovered that a large proportion of volunteers considered themselves to be tourists during the volunteering period and wanted to take part in tourist activities as well as volunteering. Furthermore, they discovered that the volunteers also perceived themselves to be 'spectators' (Jarvis and Blank, 2011, 144) which adds an additional layer of complexity to the role and position of an event volunteer. They explain that their findings should be considered when event managers are planning how to utilise and reward volunteers strategically. Tourist activities and spectator passes on their free days may be useful rewards for volunteers to help further increase motivation and engagement.

For an event manager, it is important to consider how these volunteer segments may operate on the event site. Imagine that the 'very keen' or 'semi-keen' volunteer is working as a steward at an event in which they are particularly interested in the sporting team, competitor or act involved. They will be very engaged, enthusiastic and animated and will undoubtedly present a very positive and welcoming face to the event. It is, however, important to think about the concentration levels and professionalism of volunteers faced with their favourite band or athlete. This may result in the kind of issue presented in section 4.3 in relation to the 'selfie' with Usain Bolt. A potential solution to this dilemma is to assess the tasks that need to be carried out and allocate the volunteer to an appropriate task that will not be too distracting. Depending on the scale of the event, it should be possible both to allocate tasks and take advantage of the positive vibe these volunteers will bring to the event.

Another consideration with volunteers, perhaps more relevant to those who fit into category 6, 'habitual but not very interested', is that of reliability. Some volunteers may be seen as 'fair weather' volunteers. They may not be committed to the event, or attached to it or interested in it in a meaningful way; they may literally check the weather forecast before deciding whether to complete their voluntary role on that day. Other examples of reasons that volunteers fail to attend an event at which they have promised to help centre around them being required to attend their paid work or to care for an ill relative or dependant. It is common for many of the events that use volunteers to find that at a crucial time they do not have the required number of staff present to carry out the necessary tasks. This lack of staff to fill all the roles required may have a significant impact on the event. It may mean that insufficient ticket booths can open, resulting in a longer queue for visitors arriving at the event, which in turn may result in negative publicity about the event as visitors voice their complaints. It may mean that bins are not emptied as often as required, or litter is not picked up. Whilst neither of these examples directly impacts upon the safety of the event, each may impact on the reputation of the event and its organisers, which is also of significance.

Tip box

Before finalising staffing decisions, assess roles that need to be filled and be clear about the most appropriate type of staff to carry out the task. If it is a role that is to be carried out by a volunteer, make sure that a risk assessment has been conducted for the suitability of the volunteer to carry out this task and that there is a fall-back position if the volunteer should fail to attend for some reason.

Solutions to a shortage of volunteers at events includes booking more volunteers than are required for the tasks. Some organisers may book up to 50 per cent more than required. If more attend than are needed, shorter shifts can be worked amongst them. The reassurance of this method is that it is usually able to ensure that there are sufficient numbers present to carry out the tasks required. Another solution often employed by festival organisers is to require a volunteer to pay for their ticket to the event. The volunteer is then given a 'loyalty card', which is stamped or marked every time they attend their rostered shift. Once they have completed their required shifts or tasks, they are given a refund on their ticket fee. Both of these methods work well to resolve issues relating to attendance.

4.7 Psychology of event teams

The way in which groups, and indeed teams, socialise, communicate and behave has been of interest across many different disciplines including anthropology, business and psychology. This section will specifically focus on the application of psychological approaches to teamwork which can help event project managers to understand the way in which groups may think and behave. In 1913 Ringlemann, an agricultural engineer, observed that individual input was higher than overall group input when people were asked to pull on a rope (Simms and Nichols, 2014). This observation has had a lasting effect in psychology and organisational behaviour. What's now termed the Ringlemann effect is the discovery that individual input and effort for team tasks reduces exponentially with the increase in team size. In other words, 'individual effort on a task diminishes as group size increases' (Hogg and Vaughan, 2005, 286). This concept could have a significant effect on the way in which event teams and organisations are structured and managed. It follows then that during the pulsating periods of event management, event teams that increase in size can be potentially detrimental to individual effort. Motivational strategies and techniques, therefore, will be of the utmost importance to event organisers to ensure morale, effort and commitment are high.

Teams are powerful, and individuals who operate within a team environment may act differently or make different decisions than they may make alone, separate from the group environment. It is important to address the concept of *groupthink* here, which was first developed by Janis (1982) in connection with decisions made by American governments in relation to policy fiascos across previous decades. Groupthink is described as a psychological team motivation for agreement and consensus that may override other more favourable decision options.

> Over and beyond all the familiar sources of human error is a powerful source of defective judgement that arises in cohesive groups – the concurrence-seeking tendency which fosters overoptimism, lack of vigilance and sloganistic thinking about the weakness and immorality of out-groups.
>
> (Janis, 1982, 12)

Managing event projects is all about getting the best out of the full events workforce in order to meet both short-term and long-term strategy goals. Groupthink as a concept has been used widely since the 1980s and has been applied to all types of groups and teams, not just those that have political power. Groupthink in simple terms can be described as a collective, taking an easier decision in order to maintain cohesion and keep all parties happy and on side. In the events industry this can relate to decisions made behind closed doors in a planning meeting or on the ground during the event itself. It is important that the workforce is managed in a way that allows for employees to feel confident to speak out against any decision they may not be satisfied with or one they believe will be detrimental to the events organisation. Creating transparent and simple modes of communication across all layers of the workforce will enable groupthink to be managed effectively.

4.7.1 Audience 'teams'

One final type of 'team' which is often not recognised, yet may be said to be the most important team of all when planning an event, is that of the audience: 'audience team'. Those who attend an event do so because of their common interest in whatever the subject of the event is. For example, if the event is a car show then all visitors will have an interest in motor vehicles. If the event is a music event then typically visitors will have an interest in one or all of the bands playing. If an event is a success and takes place with no major issues, then the audience team may be *invisible* to the event organiser. This will be largely due to the fact that they do not need to show themselves in the form of a team. The 'team' will still be there, but it is a happy and satisfied team and, even though invisible, can act in a positive way to reflect the event and enhance the reputation of the organiser.

If there is an issue at an event then the 'team' which is made up of the visitors or the attendees may very quickly become *visible* and powerful. For example, the attendee of a music concert who has paid a significant amount of money for the ticket will want to ensure their experience lives up to their high expectations. If the sound quality is poor or their view is obscured for some reason, this may have a negative impact upon their satisfaction levels. Undoubtedly, the event attendees will be disappointed that their enjoyment has been spoiled and may feel aggrieved about the amount of money paid for the ticket. It is likely that other attendees will have the same feelings and this will be communicated amongst each other; perhaps by mutterings in the toilet queue or just amongst the audience in between the songs. It may become visible to the organiser by 'heckling' (shouting out of negative comment or even abuse) or by direct complaints to stewards or other staff. As the swell of discontent in the audience increases, so may their cohesion as a team and their power to influence the event organiser's response. If that 'team' unites behind a charismatic person, their power is even greater. They are now not just all members of a team with similar issues; they are members of a team united in their issues and direction. The potential of group cohesion and teamwork and team vision must be effectively surveyed, monitored and managed by event organisers.

4.8 Conclusion

The way in which an event organisation creates its structures and teams will have significant impact on the effectiveness of their event delivery. Due to the 'pulsating' structure of the events sector, teams must operate and gel under complex and challenging situations. It is important to understand that their leadership in the events world is connected to influence, inspiration and motivation. This chapter argues that effective leaders must be 'context intelligent' and demonstrate varying capabilities across multiple settings and scenarios within the events environment. Volunteers play a crucial role in the success of the events industry and must be motivated and rewarded for their efforts. It is volunteers that often form the backbone of the events structure and therefore time should be spent on recruiting, retaining and successfully managing these event volunteers. Finally, the psychology and traits of teamwork and team operations should not be overlooked; group cohesion is a powerful concept and should be considered in event project planning.

Case study 4: Structures and teams in the wedding industry, Croatia

This case study is an interview with Kristina Skvrce, who is a Wedding Planner and Coordinator in Dubrovnik, Croatia.

Please provide a summary of your current job role and what it entails.
I currently work as a Wedding Planner and Coordinator, which involves communication with clients and suppliers through all steps of the wedding planning

process and on the day of the wedding itself. It is important that I am visible and present on site so I can coordinate many of the different teams/suppliers I work with on that day.

Geographically, where is your business based and what are the benefits to working in your current location?
My business is located in Dubrovnik (Croatia) and its region (islands, Cavtat and the coast). There is a great balance of natural beauty and rich historical heritage which makes this region ideal for events. I'm very familiar with this region since I grew up here and have been always active in the area and know lots of local people, which is very helpful in my industry.

How long have you worked in the wedding sector? Has it changed a lot over that time, if so in what way?
I have worked in the wedding business for the past eight years. It's an emerging market here in Dubrovnik. I have noticed, though, as the wedding events market has grown, so has the number of suppliers available, venue spaces, and along with this prices have increased too. It is very important to work with the different teams and staff members in the venues and across suppliers, especially when needing to negotiate prices and requirements.

What type of customers do you get and where are they from?
I mainly work with couples from the UK (80 per cent), some from the US (10 per cent) and other customers come from either Norway, Australia or Ireland (combined 10 per cent). When thinking about our customer demographics, about 90 per cent of couples are from middle-class backgrounds, 5 per cent upper-class and for the remaining 5 per cent of couples we manage events on a budget.

Please describe the key component linked to a successful wedding event.
Reliability counts the most. There is only so much information that can be included in written contracts and agreements; the most essential aspects are trust and giving your word. This is of paramount importance when dealing with both customers and suppliers.

Do you work on your own or do you have a team of people who help you? If so, who (roles) makes up this team?
I have a team of staff that work with me for events; without them it would not be possible for me to run the weddings effectively. For each event I organise, two to three wedding coordinators/assistants join me. I have another team of three planners who are office based and help me in the planning phase dealing with contracts, emails, payments, etc.

In your experience how do you make sure your clients are satisfied with the service you provide?
Satisfaction comes from clear communication with couples and with a lot of quality control on the suppliers' side. Each wedding is covered by at least 10–20 services.

(*Continued*)

Case study 4 (*continued*)

If any of these are not delivered exactly as it was earlier communicated, I consider the whole event incomplete.

Please can you provide an example when something has not gone to plan and how you have managed to resolve the situation?
This has happened many times. Some things are really beyond our control. Unstable weather usually causes some decisions to be made at the last moment (or even ten minutes after that!). In another example, we often organise post-ceremony cruises of one to two hours in length. The cruises include a cocktail, music, canapés, etc. This wedding day event is planned on its own in communication with a couple that need to decide budget, type of boat, food/drinks and the rest. In the planning phase we agree upon the right set of services for the event through the process of timing – budget – number of people – services. Two years ago, after one such cruise was carefully planned and all the goods where delivered on board (and catering staff were there), the engine had a failure so the boat wasn't able to get to the meeting point. Usually the boat sails out from another harbour and picks up people in the, more romantic, central, ancient harbour. This happened 30 minutes before the expected pickup. I needed to first find a replacement boat. I had to deal with last-minute booking and a negotiation for the price in relation to the couple's expectations and budget. Another thing I had to solve was finding transport for caterers, assistants and goods and have them transported to another boat. On top of this I needed to stay perfectly calm while talking to my couple (who were getting married for the first time and it's supposed to be the happiest day of their life). A reasonable delay was not possible to avoid so I needed to figure out entertainment for the couple and their guests so they would not get annoyed.

The aspect which made it all the more difficult was the fact that it was high season in Dubrovnik and most of the boats were sold out months in advance so I absolutely had no clue if an available boat could be found. A few things helped me to solve the problem that day:

- Luckily, I have been in similar (or worse) situations before.
- I'm from Dubrovnik and if anyone can find a boat that's a good match and could be used straight away, I can.
- Local people I knew were willing to help.

In your opinion why is it important to work successfully with other organisations in the events business, i.e. caterers, hospitality managers, hotel venues, etc.?
We all share the same bread. We'll meet sooner or later at a common event and we need to continue to build great relationships with one another in order to manage future challenges together. One person/company is nothing. Only a group of people working together as if we were from the same company and delivering different services together, at the highest level, will assist in creating and developing new leads.

Figure 4.5 Boat trip as part of a Dubrovnik wedding package

Source: © Hanya Pielichaty

What skills and characteristics must you possess to be successful within the events industry?
1   Communication (client and suppliers)
2   An eye for detail
3   Experience (knowing people on site – very important).

(Continued)

Case study 4 (*continued*)

Figure 4.6 Boat trip as part of a Dubrovnik wedding package

Source: © Hanya Pielichaty

Thank you to Kristina Skvrce for sharing your experiences with the authors to formulate this case study.

Evaluative student questions

1 Is the wedding industry different from all other event types in relation to structure and teams?
2 What are the important messages communicated by Kristina Skvrce in this case study?
3 In what way is working with others crucial to success in the events industry?

Further reading

Griffiths, B., Woodham, R. and Stuart, E. (eds) (2015) *The UK good practice guide to working in Safety Advisory Groups*. Norwich: Stationery Office.
Treuren, G.J.M. (2014) Enthusiasts, conscripts or instrumentalists? The motivational profiles of event volunteers. *Managing Leisure*, 19(1) 51–70.
Van der Wagen, L. and White, L. (2015) *Human resource management for the event industry*. 2nd edition. Abingdon: Routledge.

References

Alexander, A. and Kim, S.-B. (2015) Segmenting volunteers by motivation in the 2012 London Olympic Games. *Tourism Management*, 47 1–10.
Bang, H., Won, D. and Kim, Y. (2009) Motivations, commitment, and intentions to continue volunteering for sporting events. *Event Management*, 13(2) 69–81.
Barron, P. and Rihova, I. (2011) Motivation to volunteer: a case study of the Edinburgh Magic Festival. *International Journal of Event and Festival Management*, 2(3) 202–217.
Bladen, C., Kennell, J., Abson, E. and Wilde, N. (2012) *Events management: an introduction*. Abingdon: Routledge.
Bowdin, G., Allen, J., O'Toole, W., Harris, R. and McDonnell, I. (2011) *Events management*. 3rd edition. London: Butterworth-Heinemann.
Cabinet Office (2015) *Community life survey: 2014–2015 statistical bulletin*. London: Cabinet Office. Available from: https://www.gov.uk/government/uploads/system/uploads/attachment_data/file/447010/Community_Life_Survey_2014-15_Bulletin.pdf [Accessed 24 March 2016].
Civil Contingencies Act 2004 (c.36). London: HMSO.
Fire Safety and Safety of Places of Sport Act 1987 (c.27). London: HMSO.
Getz, D. (2012) *Event studies: theory, research and policy for planned events*. 2nd edition. Abingdon: Routledge.
Griffiths, B., Woodham, R. and Stuart, E. (eds) (2015) *The UK good practice guide to working in Safety Advisory Groups*. Norwich: Stationery Office.
Hanlon, C. and Cuskelly, G. (2002) Pulsating major sport event organizations: a framework for inducting managerial personnel. *Event Management*, 7(4) 231–243.
Hede, A. and Rentschler, R. (2007) Mentoring volunteer festival managers: evaluation of a pilot scheme in regional Australia. *Managing Leisure*, 12(2/3) 157–170.
Hogg, M.A. and Vaughan, G.M. (2005) *Developmental psychology*. 4th edition. Harlow: Pearson Education Limited.

Home Office (1989) *The Hillsborough Stadium disaster 15th April 1989: Inquiry by the Rt. Hon. Lord Justice Taylor final report.* Available from: http://hillsborough.independent.gov.uk/repository/docs/HOM000028060001.pdf [Accessed 24 March 2016].

Janis, I.L. (1982) *Groupthink.* 2nd edition. Boston: Houghton Mifflin Company.

Jarvis, N. and Blank, C. (2011) The importance of tourism motivations among sport event volunteers at the 2007 world artistic gymnastics championships, Stuttgart, Germany. *Journal of Sport and Tourism*, 16(2) 129–147.

Kim, M., Kim, M.K. and Odio, M.A. (2010) Are you proud?: the influence of sport and community identity and job satisfaction on pride of mega-event volunteers. *Event Management*, 14(2) 127–136.

Lee, C.-K., Reisinger, Y., Kim, M.J. and Yoon, S.-M. (2014) The influence of volunteer motivation on satisfaction, attitudes, and support for a mega-event. *International Journal of Hospitality Management*, 40 37–48.

Licensing Act 2003 (c.17). London: HMSO.

Lydall, R. (2014) Commonwealth Games security staff sacked for taking selfies with Usain Bolt. *Standard*, 31 July. Available from: http://www.standard.co.uk/sport/athletics/commonwealth-games-security-staff-sacked-for-taking-selfies-with-usain-bolt-9639451.html [Accessed 18 February 2016].

Nichols, G. and Ralston, R. (2011) *Manchester Event Volunteers: a legacy and a role model.* Sheffield: Sheffield University. Available from: http://www.shef.ac.uk/polopoly_fs/1.227269!/file/MEV_2012_with_cover.pdf [Accessed 25 July 2016]

Parent, M.M. and Swan-Smith, S. (2013) *Managing major sports events: theory and practice.* Abingdon: Routledge.

Pendleton, D, and Furnham, A. (2012) *Leadership: all you need to know.* Basingstoke: Palgrave Macmillan.

Raj, R., Walters, P. and Rashid, T. (2009) *Events management: an integrated and practical approach.* London: Sage Publications.

Randall, C. (2013) *Measuring national well-being – what we do – September 2013.* London: Office for National Statistics.

Safety of Sports Grounds Act 1975 (c.52). London: HMSO.

Simms, A. and Nichols, T. (2014) Social loafing: a review of the literature. *Journal of Management, Policy and Practice*, 15(1) 58–67.

Surujlal, J. (2010) Volunteer motivation in special events for people with disabilities. *African Journal for Physical, Health Education, Recreation and Dance*, 16(3) 460–474.

Taylor, P. (ed.) (2011) *Torkildsen's sport and leisure management.* 6th edition. Abingdon: Routledge.

The Regulatory Reform (Fire Safety) Order 2005 (n.1541). London: HMSO. Available from http://www.legislation.gov.uk/uksi/2005/1541/contents/made [Accessed 4 March 2016].

Treuren, G.J.M. (2014) Enthusiasts, conscripts or instrumentalists? The motivational profiles of event volunteers. *Managing Leisure*, 19(1) 51–70.

Van der Wagen, L. and White, L. (2015) *Human resource management for the event industry.* 2nd edition. Abingdon: Routledge.

Wakelin, D. (2013) What motivates students to volunteer at events? *Event Management*, 17(1) 63–75.

Chapter 5

Event management project tools

5.1 Introduction

As in any profession or workplace there are always tools and resources available to assist employees with their day-to-day activities, and project management is no different. There are specific training courses for aspiring and experienced project managers to attend. The most established is called PRINCE2. PRINCE is an acronym for **PR**ojects **IN C**ontrolled **E**nvironments and was launched in 1989, whereas PRINCE2 arrived in 1996 (PRINCE2, 2015). The main features of this training course involve guiding and supporting organisations and individuals to develop their project effectiveness. Furthermore, there are computer software programmes available to assist with project management planning and implementation, such as Microsoft Project or StageIT. These software programmes are designed to speed up and simplify the planning, distribution and sharing of project stages and tasks. Project management can be understood in relation to control – controlling time, money, resources and tasks. Of particular importance in this chapter is control of time; the way in which time is established, maintained and manipulated is of significance to the project manager. It is argued that 'Management is continually seeking new and better control techniques to cope with the complexities, masses of data, and tight deadlines that are characteristic of highly competitive industries' (Kerzner, 2013, 597).

The events industry can be considered to be highly competitive and one which is inextricably tied to an end deadline date (the event itself) like no other sector. The control techniques and project management tools endorsed and utilised within the events industry must be able to cope with the complexity and dynamism of the sector. Bowdin et al. (2011, 268) refer to the *project management cascade*, a suggested order in which to plan and implement events. The order of the cascade is as follows: project definition, scope of work, work breakdown structure, task analysis, schedule, Gantt chart/critical path. These connect to responsibility in relation to activity sheets and work packages. It is not surprising that project management practices have been absorbed by events management, as previously acknowledged:

> The need for thorough accountability to stakeholders, risks, complexity, rules and regulations affecting events, cross border status, increasing size, number and

economic importance of events are factors that create the need for a systematic and accountable approach to the actual management of events.

(O'Toole, 2000, 86)

This chapter is about the use of project tools and resources, and therefore more emphasis will be placed on the scheduling tools and work structures that assist event managers to successfully embed project tools within their planning stages. Using tools such as work breakdown structures, Gantt charts, activity-on-node analyses and critical path analyses effectively will assist with the planning and, indeed, delivery of an event.

5.2 Work breakdown structures (WBS)

It is important to discuss work breakdown structures again in this chapter because they do provide much cross-over within the different areas of project management. Work breakdown structures are used widely in human resource management as well as project management to illustrate how a project or organisation can be structured to meet its delivery objectives. This type of structuring involves dissecting all of the tasks or job roles of a project in order to understand and visualise how the overall project may be managed and realised. Lock (2013, 176) describes it as a 'logical, hierarchical tree of all the tasks needed to complete a project'. At the top of this tree will be the general task or area of expertise, which will get increasingly more detailed as the tasks are identified moving downwards along the tree structure. Work breakdown structures illustrate the dependency or relationship between one employee and another or one task and another. This allows for efficient problem solving on the part of the project manager, who can quickly see who has line management responsibility in which broad employee/volunteer area.

The work breakdown structure used in Figure 5.1 demonstrates the general holistic role of Event Coordinator at the top of the structure, who oversees the work carried

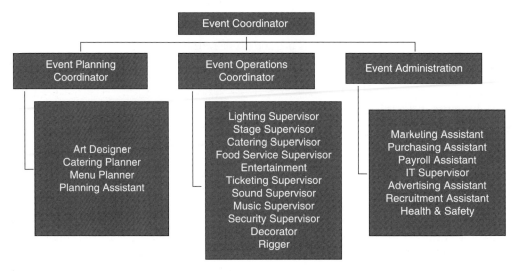

Figure 5.1 Example of a work breakdown structure organised by event employee roles

Source: Bowdin et al. 2011, 29

out by the Event Planning Coordinator, the Event Operations Coordinator and the Event Administration team. It is, however, the responsibility of the three areas along the second tier of the structure to manage the delivery outputs of their more specialist employees and tasks. A work breakdown structure can also be understood as a jigsaw puzzle, where 'every piece put in its right place and with no piece missing' (Lock, 2013, 177) is necessary for project management success.

Due to the complexity of the events sector and the widespread variation in what an event is and how events can be managed, traditional work breakdown structures may need adapting. Event projects which are stand-alone projects with no tangible outcomes or necessity for project handover are referred to as 'management projects' (Lock, 2013, 180). The main example of this used by Lock (2013) is that of a large, high-profile wedding project, and he develops the two work breakdown structures illustrated in Figures 5.2 and 5.3 to highlight this. One is a functional structure, the second a structure based on physical locations.

The work breakdown structure illustrated in Figure 5.2 would allow for specific managers to take control of the tasks related to their expertise, whereas the work breakdown structure in Figure 5.3 would require managerial cross-over work and the conducting of tasks by several teams within the various locations. It is important that the event project manager designs an appropriate work breakdown structure for their own event in relation to the event's/organisation's needs. The senior management team on the event should create the work breakdown structure and relevant key milestones in the first instance (Parent and Smith-Swan, 2013). On some occasions it may be more logical to identify tasks and roles on the basis of physical place, whereas at other times separating tasks by roles and functions will be more appropriate. The arrows used in both of these examples demonstrate the continuation of the task or role at hand; there may be other functions and roles to consider beyond what is displayed.

Tip box

Whichever work breakdown structure is being utilised by the event organisation the key to effective cohesion between tasks and roles is communication. The project manager must communicate the structure of the project and the rationale behind it to all of those involved.

5.3 Gantt charts

Gantt charts are named after their originator, Henry Gantt, an American industrial engineer (1861–1919) (Lock, 2013). A Gantt chart allows project managers to collate the entire project tasks within one document in a manner that measures the tasks to time frames. Gantt charts or an equivalent measure are frequently used within the events industry to structure and organise events effectively in order to monitor the overall project and keep to deadlines. Microsoft Project or StageIT (see Figure 5.4) are examples of dedicated computer software programmes used to assist project managers

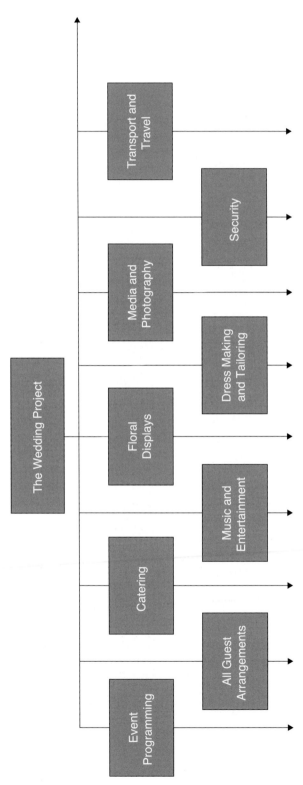

Figure 5.2 Example of a work breakdown structure for a high-profile wedding organised by event functions

Source: Lock, 2013, 181

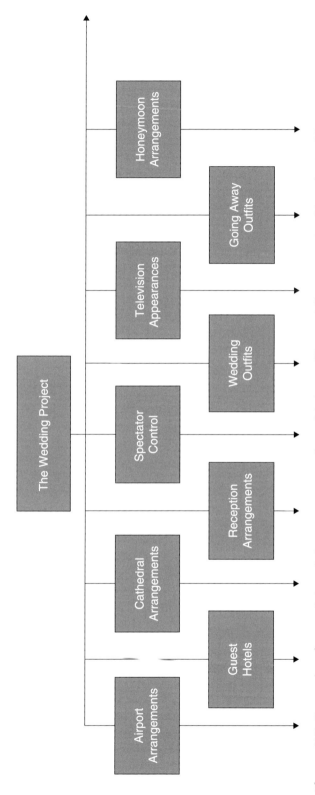

Figure 5.3 Example of a work breakdown structure for a high-profile wedding organised by physical locations

Source: Lock, 2013, 181

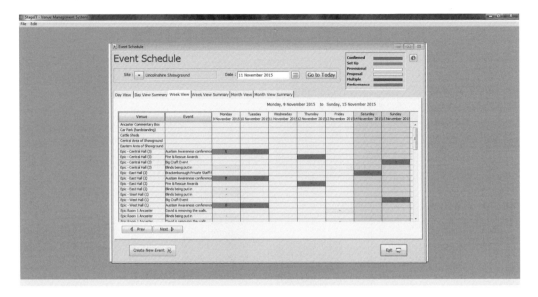

Figure 5.4 Example of an event schedule created using StageIT

in designing and implementing Gantt charts for their various projects. There are other programmes available that are used in the industry and this section is not a recommendation for either programme, but simply connects to the case study at the end of this chapter.

Accessible programmes such as Microsoft Excel can also be used to provide the framework for creating Gantt charts. An example of this is shown in Figure 5.5, a Gantt chart illustrating the activities and responsibilities for a sports awards evening. This Gantt chart provides both functional and physical place indicators under the 'description' tab with then more detailed tasks under the 'activities' tab. Furthermore, employees are allocated dedicated activities and their progress is documented under the 'complete' tab which allows for easy visual acknowledgement of project progress.

Each activity is given a time frame in which to start and complete the task. These time frames are indicated by the black, blocked out spaces on the Gantt chart, which show both a start and finish date as well as specifying the estimated duration of the task. Gantt charts are useful for providing a visual tool highlighting both the holistic project view as well as detailing specific tasks. Furthermore, using software such as Microsoft Excel is potentially a cheaper alternative to investing in project specific software if the event is short on finances.

In general, the main advantages for using Gantt charts within the events industry are as follows:

- it allows large, complex projects to be broken down into specific tasks
- members of the workforce can be allocated responsibility for tasks
- it provides a holistic and micro view of the project
- time frames allow task start and finish times to be illustrated
- it provides an account of task durations.

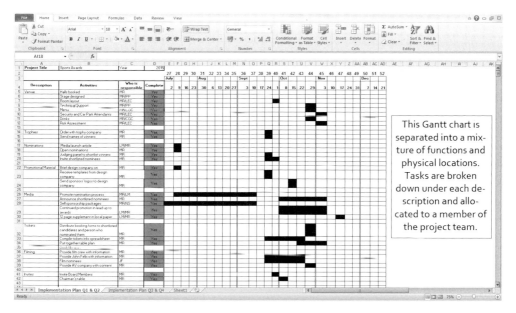

Figure 5.5 Example of a Gantt chart used for sports awards evening

The main issue, however, with using Gantt charts is their inability to 'show all the complex interdependencies that exist between the different tasks in most projects' (Lock, 2013, 197). Within the events sector it is important to understand the relationship between one task and the next, and the relevant knock-on effects of delaying a task or finishing one early. For example, if the marketing team have delays receiving their advertising posters because the printing company they are using is under-staffed, the team must be aware of subsequent follow-on tasks and their time frames in order to not impact upon the entire project completion time (i.e. event day). These challenges will be addressed in the next section, which focuses on network analysis.

Study activity

Using the Sports Awards Gantt chart for guidance, create your own retrospective Gantt chart for an event you have recently been involved with, or create one in preparation for an event you will be involved with soon.

5.4 Network analyses

The use of network paths to assist in scheduling within project management was developed in the 1950s with a focus on time and resource scheduling (Maylor, 2010).

Unlike a Gantt chart, networks create links and connections between one task and another to illustrate their interdependency. Network analysis, therefore, within a project management context refers to the structure of all tasks in relation to one another, bound by their own project network. Logic and logical thinking is at the heart of network analyses in terms of creating a critical path and also implementing it. According to Verhaar and Eshel (2013), network planning is advantageous because it allows for transparency in complex projects and highlights the relationship between different tasks. Event challenges can be effectively managed by using these planning techniques because a holistic view of the project can be visually interpreted and monitored.

As sourced from Kerzner (2013, 600) networks represent:

- interdependencies of activities
- project completion time
- impact of late starts
- impact of early starts
- trade-offs between resources and time
- "what if" exercises
- cost of a crash programme
- slippages in planning/performance
- evaluation of performance.

This list highlights the advanced nature of network planning as opposed to the more isolated Gantt chart. Network planning provides event project managers with both a relational view of project tasks as well as a scheduling framework incorporating instances of delay and budgetary concerns. Logical sequencing is highlighted as significant by Silvers (2012, 46), who notes 'there will be a natural and a necessary order in which the various event elements (and the tasks associated with them) will have to be chronologically organized'. The concept of logical sequencing formulates the basis for this chapter and underpins the rationale for using project tools. This section will first look at the basic principles of network analysis in relation to the activity-on-node technique before moving to more complex critical path analysis.

5.4.1 Activity-on-node

The basic step to constructing a time plan around project tasks is to develop a network using the activity-on-node (A-on-N) technique. An A-on-N diagram is useful because it separates project tasks into dependency between one another and is measured by task duration. For example, if Activity A takes 15 days to complete and must be finished before Activity B starts, which takes 22 days to complete, then the overall project time will be 37 days. Activity A and B are dependent upon one another; in this scenario Activity B cannot start until Activity A has been completed. For example, Activity A, the sourcing of funds for an event, must come before Activity B, which is the negotiation of payments and contracts with the venue. It would be foolish to start discussing finance in Activity B before the acquisition of funds is completed as per Activity A. There are four versions of network connectivity which are associated with the A-on-N technique: Finish-to-Start, Start-to-Start, Finish-to-Finish and, lastly, Start-to-Finish (Maylor, 2010, 136–137).

To make this clearer the four versions can be applied to the events sector using the below examples:

- Finish-to-Start
  - Decorating the set cannot start until the stage has been built.
- Start-to-Start
  - Cannot seek sponsorship investment until the company directors approve the sponsorship policy.
- Finish-to-Finish
  - Cannot close the case of the assault during the community event until the police have finished their investigation.
- Start-to-Finish
  - The people working on the turnstiles cannot leave work until the football match has started.

Some events organisations may not physically use the A-on-N technique to project manage their events. Consciously or subconsciously, however, they are likely to use the rationale and philosophy behind the technique. Project managers need to know how the duration and complexity of an individual task interrelate to other tasks around it. Event project managers must use logical thinking and logical sequencing (Silvers, 2012) to work out how to prioritise and implement tasks to specific time frames in order to complete projects to time. Critical path analyses extend the methods of A-on-N techniques to incorporate detailed time estimates that will be reviewed in the next section.

5.4.2 Critical path analyses

It can be argued that 'critical path networks provide the more powerful notation needed to show all the logical, interdependencies between differing jobs' (Lock, 2013, 198). In its simplest form, path networks are the set of tasks that need to be carried out in the right order for the overall project to be successful. Durations and time frames can be allocated to these tasks so the project manager is able effectively to calculate how long the entire project and component tasks may take. Knowing this information is valuable in terms of communicating with key stakeholders about project progression and success, as well as keeping the event workforce on track. It is sensible to expect some tasks to take longer than others and therefore tasks conducted along a network path will have varying durations as well as varying start and finish times. The simplified network path shown in Figure 5.6 provides an example of a family clothes shopping trip.

The word 'predecessor' means to come before, so the activity 'Travel' comes before the activities Coat, Shoes and Trousers as listed in the table and shown in the network diagram. The diagram highlights that the tasks Travel and Home can be carried out in parallel and will work simultaneously in order to complete separate tasks to ensure the project is completed. The duration in this example is in hours, but time durations in critical path analysis diagrams can be in hours, days or months, depending on the project. The easiest way to digest the information presented in Figure 5.6 is to imagine the project 'family clothes shopping' in which you and two members of your family 'travel' two hours to spend the day shopping for clothes. Your brother has decided to stay at 'home' to repair his old clothes instead of buying any new ones (parallel activity). When out shopping, you are in search of a new winter 'coat', your mother is in need

Task/ activity	Predecessor	Length in time (hours)
Travel	-	2
Home	-	1
You coat	Travel	2
Mother shoes	Travel	3
Father trousers	Travel	5

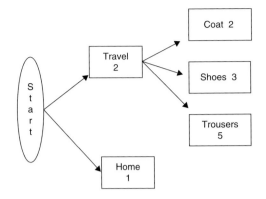

Figure 5.6 A network path for 'family clothes shopping'

of a new pair of 'shoes' and your father is looking for a new pair of 'trousers'. It only takes you two hours to find a new winter coat but unfortunately it takes your mother an hour longer to buy shoes and your father three hours longer to find some trousers. Even though you completed your activity in the quickest time, this does not mean that the project is finished because you must wait for both your mother and father to complete their tasks before you can all travel home together. The total project time, therefore, for this example is seven hours, because your father's trouser buying is the longest task and this signifies the *critical path* of the network, or in this case the clothes shopping project. *An important thing to remember is that the critical path through any project network is the one which takes the longest time to complete.*

The way in which critical network path analysis can be conducted is through compartmentalising tasks into earliest start times (EST) and latest start times (LST), duration and slack time. These terms and abbreviations are demonstrated and utilised by Maylor (2010, 138) through an activity task box whereby the EST features in the top left and LST features in the top right of the task box. It is important to list the event or project task in the middle of the task box before stating the duration and slack time, (Maylor (2010, 138) refers to this as 'total float') in the bottom left and right accordingly. This is further demonstrated in Figure 5.7 with regard to 'making breakfast'.

All activities within a critical network must be completed in order for the overall project to be successfully finished. In order to complete a critical path network the project manager first needs to have a list of all of the tasks within the project and the duration (estimated) of each task. This information can then be used to populate a table similar to that in Figure 5.6 to work out the dependency of one project task on the next and how long each will take to complete. It is at the point that this has been completed that a critical path network can be worked out, but it is a logical process and must be completed in a certain order:

1   All of the task durations should be entered into the task boxes (bottom left corner).
2   The earliest start times (EST) can be added (top left corner) – these are calculated by adding the EST of the previous activity to the duration of the previous activity (go through the diagram forwards – left to right).
3   The latest start times (LST) can be added (top right corner) – these are calculated by subtracting the latest start time of the current activity with the duration of previous activity (go through the diagram backwards – right to left).

4 Slack time (bottom right corner) can be understood as the contingency time in a project and is calculated by subtracting the latest start time by the earliest start time of the current activity.

In order to demonstrate how this works in a very simple way, the example of making breakfast (boiled egg, toast and a cup of tea) will be explained. Firstly, a critical network table (Table 5.1) has been created to highlight the tasks involved and their estimated durations.

There are some considerations to take into account when creating a critical network path diagram. Firstly, the start box is always filled with zeros for the EST, LST, duration and slack time, and this is the same for the finish/final box with respect to the duration and slack time. In addition, the numbers in the EST and LST for the finish box will be the same because this box documents the end of the project which has the same completion time. In Figure 5.7 it is apparent that the 'plate up' task is approached by two tasks: which EST should therefore be used? This task is dependent on all previous tasks being completed first and must allow for the longer tasks to be finished. When faced with multiple task options for the EST, always chose the highest option: in this case it was 'eggs in water' which was 5 (EST) + 4 (duration) = 9 minutes. This is also true of the 'eat' task, which should use the EST based upon the highest option from the previous connected tasks. Alternatively, when faced with multiple options for working out the LST, always choose the lowest option (this scenario does not feature in Figure 5.7). As Lock (2013, 210) explains, 'where more than one path exists, the longest must always be chosen so that the result after subtraction gives the smallest remainder (earliest time)'. In order for the project deadline to be met, the LST of this task must not impact on the LST of any of the next tasks.

Slack time can be understood as the contingency or spare time available to use if a particular task overruns. Slack time, however, is limited, so if a task goes over the spare time available to it this will have a direct impact on the overall project completion time, affecting the critical path. Every event manager should have a contingency plan for their event in relation to the event overall and all of the different project tasks involved. Contingency planning is crucial to event success and is about planning and managing challenging situations within the events sector. Dugalic (2013) endorses the use of critical network planning for sports events, and argues that using models such as this will help to resolve organisational issues linked to complex sporting and special events. There may be some events organisations or project managers who do not use critical path analyses to organise and time plan their project tasks. The essence,

Table 5.1 Critical network table for making breakfast

Activity	Predecessor	Duration (minutes)
Kettle	–	3
Boil water	–	5
Slice bread	–	2
Brew tea	Kettle	2
Eggs in water	Boil water	4
Toast bread	Slice bread	2
Add milk/sugar	Brew tea	1
Plate up	Eggs in water and toast bread	2

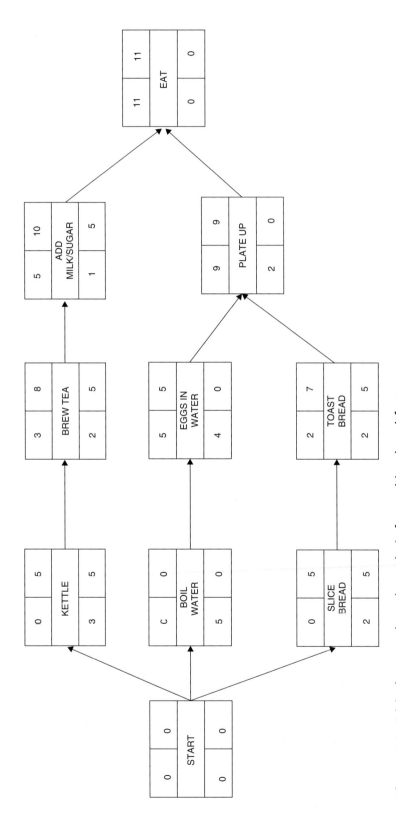

Figure 5.7 Critical network path analysis for making breakfast

however, of the critical path analysis in relation to logical thinking, time planning and pragmatic awareness of the overall project is instrumental to success. It is important to understand the basic structure and framework of these project tools in order to comprehend task dependency, time restrictions and critical paths.

Study activity

Take one element of event management, such as 'event staffing', 'marketing and promotion' or 'financial planning', and draw up your own network path table and then a critical network diagram. Remember, there is always more than one way of creating and delivering critical network path diagrams so be prepared to justify and evidence the decisions you have made.

5.5 Event planning and design

The event planning stages should also incorporate event design and venue design to encourage synergy between project organisation and creativity. In order to know how to budget for certain events and understand the requirements of both staff and resources for particular event bookings, computer programmes such as StageIT are used. StageIT is a multi-faceted software programme which brings together a variety of key information for event organisers, such as:

● contact details of organisation or client
● event purpose and event details
● event resource requirements in terms of equipment, tables, seating, audio-visual requests.
● timescale for event setup, event and also event breakdown
● catering details
● event budget and invoicing information and facilities.

Figure 5.8 illustrates the overall event information available using StageIT; start and end dates, event notes and allocated staff members are used here to inform users of the event specifications. The case study at the end of this chapter further illustrates the importance and value of these software programmes as perceived by the Front of House Manager at Lincolnshire Showground events venue.

According to Wates (2008, 48) 'skilful and imaginative timetabling' is one of the best ways to plan and deliver successful events. The schedule and the timetable for the event itself will be easily prepared if the initial planning stages are undertaken using a programme such as StageIT or a Gantt chart. The schedule for the event for employees and volunteers may include setup time, meeting points and an event shut-down and debrief, this is sometimes known as a run-sheet or running order of the day. The agenda or schedule (if appropriate) provided for event attendees, however, will be focused on arrival time, event content, refreshment and lunch breaks, and event finish. An example of a schedule for an academic conference can be viewed in Table 5.2, which indicates the key start and finish times for each session the delegate is expected to engage with.

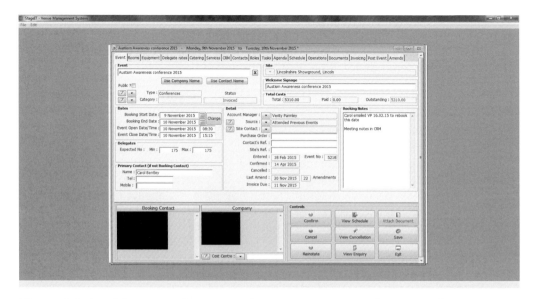

Figure 5.8 Booking page for an Autism Awareness Conference using StageIT

Table 5.2 Schedule example for an educational conference

Time	Activity
8–9am	Conference registration desk opening
9–9.20am	Conference opening and welcome
9.20–9.50am	Plenary sessions
9.50–10.20am	Refreshment break
10.20am–12pm	Parallel sessions
12–12.50pm	Lunch break
12.50–2.30pm	Parallel sessions
2.30–2.45pm	Refreshment break
2.45–3.15pm	Poster presentations
3.15–3.20pm	Session transition
3.20–5pm	Parallel sessions
5–5.30pm	Conference closing

Tip box

When planning for a conference style event be mindful that delegates will arrive at varying times and therefore it is useful to have 30 minutes to an hour arrival time factored in to your schedule to allow flexibility for delegates.

Much like critical path analysis, which includes slack time, event timetables must also include flexible tasks and timing to allow for technical issues, over-running breaks and other routine event challenges. Furthermore, the inclusion of a 'session transition' is useful when the venue space is large or complex and involves movement from one place to another.

The project tools we have focused on so far have allowed the event manager to control time, resources, staff and event tasks. The visual importance, however, of event design and planning is of paramount significance in the current eventscape. 'As participant antecedents and expectations change and the competitive event marketplace intensifies, event creators must respond with insightful experience design' (Crowther and Orefice, 2015, 123).

With information and entertainment now so freely available, event attendees arguably have higher expectations than ever in pursuit of quality and enjoyable entertainment. The design and success of events is therefore directly connected to attendee satisfaction. Events are creative, artistic and imaginative in their very nature and so being able to visually plan and manage an event venue can be valuable to a project planner. Venue and room layout and design is crucial to event success and often involves improvisation with the space provided (Wates, 2008). The role of the event project manager, however, is to limit the amount of improvisation needed by effectively planning and designing event spaces prior to the event.

Computer project software programmes such as Room Arranger allow event organisations to visually construct both 2D and 3D representations of the venue space in relation to their client's requests, as illustrated in Figure 5.9. This also features in the case study at the end of this chapter in relation to real-life event management examples.

These mock-up visualisations should be to scale where possible and allow the project manager and colleagues to imagine how the event space will be fitted and look on the day of the event. The benefits of using a programme such as this are to alleviate any challenges before the event takes place, such as potential issues around crowd flow and movement as well as the use of space in compliance with health and safety guidelines. This type of event design can also be done manually through drawing the event space and taking photographs and videos to build up a picture of the venue prior to the event. It must be noted that not all events will use design software such as this, but it is important to use visual imagery such as video, photos and mock-up diagrams as a practical way to assess the venue space, and to seek out potential challenges and opportunities presented by the space on offer. 'Events do not just happen; they are carefully crafted to weave narratives (content) into places (context) through processes of experience design' (Richards, Maques and Mein, 2015, 1).

In order for the event project manager to create a successful experience design, this must be imagined and engineered at the very start of the project, and planned for meticulously using project tools and resources. Successful event design also facilitates audience interaction with an emphasis on event socialisation (Nordvall, Pettersson, Svensson and Brown, 2014). In their research looking at the event design and socialisation of audience members at a Swedish music festival, Nordvall et al. (2014) highlight the importance of programme planning, area planning, social spots and meeting points as important aspects (amongst others) of successful event design. These can be planned for by the event project manager using site design tools, visual methods and prior market research into audience and stakeholder expectations.

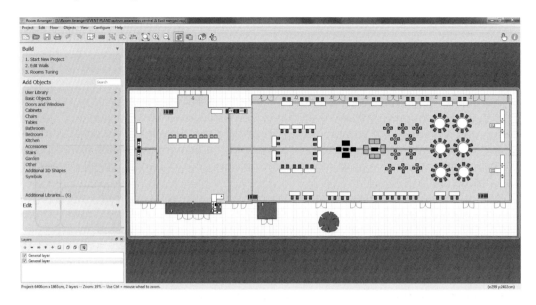

Figure 5.9 Examples of a clothing sale exhibition venue design with Room Arranger

5.6 Challenges to using project tools in events management

It was mentioned earlier in this chapter that project tools must be comprehensive enough to accommodate the complexity and diversity of the events industry. The use of standard project management tools within the events sector has, however, previously been criticised. Project management tools such as scheduling devices or critical networks can sometimes create confusion and add complexity to very large, global events such as Olympic Games (Bowdin et al., 2011). It was only in 2002 that the International Olympic Committee introduced a feedback loop into their event planning system that allowed the event hosts to view evaluative reports (Masterman, 2009). This meant that host nations and organising teams were able to assess the information evaluating the success of their event.

Arguably the biggest challenge connected to the application of project tools in the events sector is the potential mismatch between using a streamlined and rigid approach of project management within the more flexible, creative industries. Marcella and Rowley (2015) explored the ability for creative industries to adopt project management tools and techniques in their planning phases. Challenges and resistance to using project tools came from the apparent lack of flexibility within them, as well as the lack of space for reflection. They found that the 'fast-paced, change-orientated nature of the fashion industry makes it more difficult to carefully plan as there is a need to be more open and reactive to opportunities' (Marcella and Rowley, 2015, 743). These findings have implications for the events sector, an arguably creative industry that is dynamic, fluid and complex. An event itself, however, is benchmarked to strict time pressures and has to be delivered on the set date, so the rigidity of project tools will have some usefulness in this sense. Each event manager must be aware of the strengths and weaknesses of project management tools for planning and hosting an event. Tools of this kind can be used effectively to draw up roles, event tasks, time schedules and task dependency models. Due to the importance of stakeholders in relation to events and the varying needs of these various stakeholders, it is to be expected that times will change, tasks will alter and flexibility will be needed. Events management is a unique sector, characterised by change, intense demands and stressors to which project managers must adapt.

5.7 Conclusion

Project management tools have a place within the events management sector and can often provide practical event planning guidance to new and experienced event managers alike. Different project tools can be accessed via computer software packages or created manually. The overall aim of project tools in general is to document the planning of project tasks and key milestones within a specified event time frame. Work breakdown structures are useful to show task and role dependencies within events planning but do not offer information about timing and durations. Gantt charts create a holistic view of event tasks and associated responsibilities against the backdrop of time, though they do not embed the complexities of events planning within their structure because they do not demonstrate the interdependencies between tasks. Critical path analysis successfully binds event tasks and their interdependencies to others using detailed time frames and durations to ensure the project runs to time overall. It may be argued that event teams and organisations do not always use these project tools within event planning, but the logical rules and methods implied within these tools are useful and valuable to the events industry.

Sometimes overlooked, the design and layout of the event venue should also be considered within the event planning stages, and project tools can be utilised for this. In addition to booking information, run-sheets and planning schedules, an understanding of venue design and layout will assist in the delivery of project mapping.

Being aware of venue layout and design will have a direct impact on tasks and responsibilities set aside within work breakdown structures or Gantt charts. There are some challenges to the use of project tools within the events industry, such as their inflexible nature and (in)ability to align to the dynamic and creative environment of events. Event managers must balance the planning and implementation of event ideas in ways that are strategic, logical, clear and adaptable to change. How they do this is up to them and their organisation, but using project tools at some point along the way, to some degree, will assist in the success of their event.

Case study 5: Project management and tools in action

This case study is an interview with Verity Parmley, who is the Front of House Supervisor at the Lincolnshire Showground, UK.

What does your role involve at Lincolnshire Showground?
My role is rather varied and covers quite a wide list of duties. My desk is based in the main reception area of the building so I am usually the first person someone sees when they enter the building. Whilst at my desk, I am required to sign for deliveries, greet visitors who come for meetings, and provide them with refreshments and answer the phone. I will also provide refreshments for any internal meetings or meetings with clients. I am responsible for keeping stock of all the essentials that I need such as tea, coffee, cups, sweets, pens, paper and even lids for the bottles I fill with water for conferences. All equipment that is used for events I am responsible for cleaning, maintaining and re-stocking. I am also responsible for ordering all the décor for our Christmas parties, the crackers and candles and even decorating the big trees we have! Anything that requires the "Front of house/First impressions" touch falls under my remit. If it needs cleaning, I clean it (within reason)!

The facilities team are responsible for setting up a room to the client's specifications but I am then required to add the additional extras. For example, if they have booked a day delegate rate package, I need to ensure they have pens, paper, flip chart, sweets, cups and water and event signage to put around the building to direct people to the right room.

For each event I have to prep. This involves completing a checklist which I put together to help me ensure I cover everything and nothing gets missed. The checklist covers the basic checks on the building before I open up each day. I always arrive half an hour before the client is due to arrive to ensure I have time to carry out these checks prior to them arriving. I ensure all the doors to the building are open, the toilets are clean and presentable, the music and slideshow presentation in the reception area are on, that the room is set as per the contract, and then when the client arrives, I check the timings for the day, run through general housekeeping and fire procedures and get the client to sign the checklist once they are happy with everything. This ensures that the client is happy with the initial setup and they are equipped with everything they need to start their event. I also provide them with a feedback form so they can leave us any feedback at the end of the day.

I am always then on hand for the client if they need me for anything throughout the day. This can be anything from as little as providing extension leads or table-cloths to setting up additional AV support such as microphones and projectors if required. I refresh their bottled water at lunch-time and then on quiet days I will restock the bottled water. I have a dishwasher to sterilise the bottles and new lids and a filter machine which allows me to fill the bottles with still and sparkling water ready for the next event. They are stored in crates and then moved to the big refrigerator where they are kept overnight to chill. I normally calculate how many I will need for the week and make sure I have spare, so depending on how busy we are, I may need to redo this during the week

Evening events are slightly different in that I still need to complete my checks, but I have to ensure the lights are on around the building and car parks so that evening events are well lit. I check all timings and I also have to log in any security we have on an event and provide radios. I will also brief the security staff on duty with details of the event and what I require them to do. Sometimes we contract in someone to provide a cloakroom service for large events but I do this too if it's smaller. I am also First Aid trained so should anyone require any first aid I am required to give it. Normally, if someone spills a drink or is sick during an evening event, I have a special kit which allows me to clean up waste in a safe manner so I am protected. This can be quite frequent when alcohol is involved.

I am also a licence holder so I am responsible for ensuring that guests drink responsibly and are not under age. I work with the bar staff to ensure they are abiding by the law. So there tends to be added pressure and greater responsibility when we have events that require a bar and more people in the building. Should there ever be a fire during an event I am the fire safety marshal so I need to be able to report to the fire department should we ever need them, so it's important I know how many people are in the building and where they are.

My working hours vary each day and I will always fit these around the events we have on. Any quiet days I will use to catch up with admin. Every Wednesday we hold an operations meeting which I run with the rest of the team. It normally involves me putting together sheets which list all the events we have on for the forthcoming fortnight with details for each event. I will produce an agenda sheet for the meeting, minute the meeting and follow this up with an email to everyone confirming everything we discussed. After this meeting I then produce the cleaning rota for our cleaning contractors and provide them with the list of events and the rota so they know when we require them to come in. Other admin involves making staff parking passes, producing log sheets and check sheets for various things, and updating any booking forms or templates for things that are event related.

As I mentioned before, I also produce the signage for each event and try to include their logo to personalise the sign as an added touch. For some events I am required to attend client meetings prior to the event, especially if they require me to help out for any reason. This mainly applies to weddings where I have to be a little more hands-on. I look after the family and bride and groom, ensuring they are happy; timing for events on the big day is so important to stick to. Like I say, it's a very varied role!

(*Continued*)

Case study 5 (*continued*)

What kind of things can go wrong when working on event projects and how do you manage these challenges?

So many things can go wrong, and they often do! Some things can be our fault and other times things can go wrong but are either out of our control or not necessarily our problem. However, we make it our problem because the impact it can have on our venue/reputation is far greater, so if we can fix it or solve it, then we will! It may require a phone call to someone we know who can help or it might be that as a team we just get stuck in and sort it out. But this is where planning comes into it. We plan and prep for every event and cover all eventualities where possible, which is why our operations meetings and client meetings are so useful, so we can cover everything. Larger events require big event plans which are run past the Safety Advisory Group meetings. They cover wider things such as car parking, first aid and emergency exits, table-top exercises, etc. These kind of events have plans in place should anything go wrong so they are covered on a larger scale.

On the smaller scale of things, we can often be faced with a supplier turning up late. Things can get forgotten due to human error, for example wine not being on the table or someone being missed off the list for dinner, but we always have spare and backup. Table plans can be wrong, but again they are quickly adjusted and staff rally round to put out another chair and place setting, etc. It's never too difficult. The power can often go, shutting down the lights and the ovens and music, etc., but we have a back-up generator which kicks in. So there is always a backup plan and we can generally work with the client or work as a team to solve things.

Are there any specific project tools or computer software programmes you use to plan events?

We use a system call Room Arranger which is a great tool for us! It's new to us and we are finding it so useful. Before we had this system, we used Paint Shop Pro to draw out room plans, which wasn't ideal because it was never 100 per cent accurate or to scale. Room Arranger allows you to build each room/hall to scale and create a library of equipment and furniture that you can then just drag and drop into the room you want and start building your plan. It's so simple and quick to use and can be viewed in 3D so you can almost do a virtual tour around the room and show clients how it will look once complete. Which is great for us and for the client.

Another system we use is StageIT. This is our booking system, which stores all our client information and their events. It allows us to add lots of information about the event, including costs and income, so you can view profit margins, and allows us to attach documents to the booking such as contracts and room plans. The system does have its limitations because the system is built for many types of companies to use and not just ours so there are some elements we would like to change or alter; however, on the whole it's a good system and works well for us. The system allows us to record the rooms and layouts for each event and the equipment that needs to be set up in each room. The number of people attending an event and whether or not they are on a particular package deal and all their catering requirements are recorded too.

What are the advantages of using these software programmes?
Using a purpose-built programme to manage your events is extremely beneficial. You can safely store all your clients' details, and their event information. Everything is in black and white and all can be transferred to a contract. One thing to bear in mind with events is that things can change all the time on a daily basis, so it's important to be flexible as a lot of the information you record can quickly change. Having a system that records all the changes and allows you to update everything is crucial to running an event on the day. If it's not kept up to date then this is where problems can occur with missing information. Communication is key in this industry! It can also be accessed by all members of staff so should anyone be off sick or on leave, someone else can pick it up and continue with the booking. Which again is a reason why keeping everything up to date is so important.

Are there any disadvantages to using these software programmes?
There are very few disadvantages really. The main thing is ensuring that all users of the system are fully trained and know how to use the system to its full advantage. If people don't know how to use it or don't use it to its full potential by recording everything, it can lead to missing information, which can result in things being forgotten and cause problems on the day.

As I mentioned before, the system can't be fully tailored to your business. For example, there are some things we don't use anymore or sometimes we would like to update certain lists, but you can't delete the old ones because they are stored in the history. The inventory for some things can be so long because we have years worth of things stored. Different menus, wine choices, etc. – they change each year but once you have entered something, it can't be removed when you no longer need it in your list, which can be frustrating.

What is the best piece of advice you can give to someone who wants to run events in the future?
Never underestimate how much work is involved in running an event! Events or wedding planning or working on concerts are all deemed to be glamorous and exciting jobs . . . and yes, they can be. But be prepared for early mornings, late nights, long shifts and on-the-spot problem solving! Be prepared to deal with complaints and be prepared to produce event plans – very detailed ones to cover every eventuality – especially when the public are involved. Public liability insurance is a must have! However, this mainly applies to people who actually want to start up an event from scratch. If you work for a hotel or a venue, like I do, the previous still applies, but aside from any negative points, the job itself is highly rewarding and the passion comes from the rewarding feeling you get when you complete each event and everyone goes home happy. Even overcoming any issues is rewarding. Being recognised for your efforts can make it even more so!

(Continued)

Case study 5 (*continued*)

I always find that whatever effort, time and energy you put in to the event, you generally receive back by the rewarding feeling event success brings at the end of the day!

Thank you to Verity Parmley for sharing your experiences with the authors to formulate this case study.

Evaluative student questions

1   What are the limitations of using project tools software programmes?
2   What other 'project management tools' are mentioned by Verity in this case study, not necessarily computerised in format?
3   What skills are needed to be a good project manager?

Further reading

Mantel, S.J., Meredith, J.R., Shafer, S.M. and Sutton, M.M. (2011) *Project management in practice*. 4th edition. Hoboken: Wiley, pages 155–158.

Maylor, H. (2010) *Project management*. 4th edition. Essex: Prentice Hall, pages 138–142.

Vaidyanathan, G. (2013) *Project management: process, technology and practice*. Boston: Pearson, pages 350–360.

References

Bowdin, G., Allen, J., O'Toole, W., Harris, R. and McDonnell, I. (2011) *Events management*. 3rd edition. London: Butterworth-Heinemann.

Crowther, P. and Orefice, C. (2015) Co-creative events: analysis and illustrations. In Richards, G., Marques, L. and Mein, K. (eds), *Event design: social perspectives and practices*. London: Routledge, 122–136.

Dugalic, S. (2013) Management of activities in the opening of sporting events through the techniques of network planning. *SportLogia*, 9(2) 118–138.

Kerzner, H. (2013) *Project management: a systems approach to planning, scheduling, and controlling*. Hoboken: Wiley.

Lock, D. (2013) *Project management*. Surrey: Gower Publishing Limited.

Marcella, M. and Rowley, S. (2015) An exploration of the extent to which project management tools and techniques can be applied across creative industries through a study of their application in the fashion industry in the North East of Scotland. *International Journal of Project Management*, 33(4) 735–746.

Masterman, G. (2009) *Strategic sports event management: Olympic edition*. 2nd edition. London: Butterworth-Heinemann.

Maylor, H. (2010) *Project management*. 4th edition. Essex: Prentice Hall.

Nordvall, A., Pettersson, R., Svensson, B. and Brown, S. (2014) Designing events for social interaction. *Event Management*, 18(2) 127–140.

O'Toole, W. (2000) Towards the integration of event management best practice by the project management process. In: Allen, J., Harris, R., Jago, L.K. and Veal, A.J. (eds), *Events beyond 2000: setting the agenda*. Available from https://www.uts.edu.au/sites/default/files/Eventsbeyond2000.pdf [Accessed 6 November 2015].

Parent, M.M. and Smith-Swan, S. (2013) *Managing major sports events: theory and practice*. London: Routledge.

PRINCE2 (2015) What is PRINCE2? Available from https://www.prince2.com/uk/what-is-prince2 [Accessed 4 November 2015].

Richards, G., Maques, L. and Mein, K. (2015) Introduction: designing events, events as design strategy. In Richards, G., Marques, L. and Mein, K. (eds), *Event design: social perspectives and practices*. London: Routledge, 1–13.

Silvers, J.R. (2012) *Professional event coordination*. 2nd edition. New Jersey: John Wiley and Sons.

Verhaar, J. and Eshel, I. (2013) *Project management: a professional approach to events*. 3rd edition. Portland: Eleven International Publishing.

Wates, N. (ed.) (2008) *The community planning event manual*. [online] London: Earthscan. Available from https://www-dawsonera-com.proxy.library.lincoln.ac.uk/readonline/9786000011185 [Accessed 18 November 2015].

Chapter 6

Event marketing and promotion

6.1 Introduction

In the first chapter it was outlined that one distinction between events management and project management is that of audience and, potentially, promotion – in the sense that events ultimately want an audience to spectate, participate and enjoy the event on offer and marketing and promotional techniques are often deployed to make this happen. Of course it is arguable that promotion can also be used in project management, for example to gain a new supplier or to promote an organisation. The importance of this chapter, however, is to explore how project management techniques can be used to assist event managers in marketing and promoting their events. Previously, marketing and promotional sources have commonly stemmed from the academic fields of personal relations, marketing and advertising. This chapter seeks to use project management as a medium for exploration and application to the wider areas of events management.

6.2 A mixture of everything

Marketing can be described as being in a triangular relationship with the communications mix, the marketing mix and consumer needs (Jackson, 2013). Traditionally marketing, personal relations and advertising literature have used the concept of 'mix' to explain the variety and blend of many different elements to create marketing success. This has resulted in references to a marketing mix, a communications mix and a promotions mix (Gardner and Shuman, 1987). There is a lot of overlap and similarities across all 'mixes', which ultimately link to the tools and knowledge needed to inform, promote and establish a relationship with different event stakeholders. The communication, promotions and marketing mix need to be appropriate and effective in order to inform, persuade and urge consumers and attendees to behave in a preferable way, for example, to buy a ticket. As events are 'non-standard services' (Daniel, Bogdan and Daniel, 2012, 5409) it is important to thoroughly assess and research the type of marketing and promotional strategy required for each individual event project.

6.2.1 Communications mix

Marketing communication takes into consideration customer attraction and retention, corporate branding, image and identity in a cost-effective manner (Jackson, 2013). Simply put, 'communication is the process whereby thoughts are conveyed and meaning is shared between individuals or organizations' (Masterman and Wood, 2006, 3). According to Jackson (2013, 16), communication is important across three dimensions, firstly to provide information, secondly to encourage attitude change, and lastly to persuade stakeholders to change behaviour. The direction of communication can either be one-way (monologue), in terms of information shared, or two-way (dialogue), relating to information and feedback shared with stakeholders (Jackson, 2013). Event companies need to be able to communicate with a vast array of stakeholders and audiences and this often involves using a variety of communication channels and platforms to present a 'tailored message' (Jackson, 2013, 44).

   Some organisations may have a communications strategy in place as well as a marketing strategy or a promotional strategy. If the events company takes a more integrated approach, they may simply have a marketing or marketing communications strategy for the business that amalgamates the several discrete areas. The notion of control is also very important to this in order to track and monitor the delivery method and effective execution of the strategy. A chart listing key milestones and targets would need to be presented to management, staff and key stakeholders in relation to how the strategy will be efficiently rolled out. This will be further discussed in the section relating to strategy building.

6.2.2 Project management and the marketing mix

It is clear that projects are associated with events and do need marketing objectives (Lecoeuvre-Soudain and Deshayes, 2006). P was, and still is, deemed the key letter to express marketing strategy across a multitude of texts and papers. Product, Price, Place and Promotion formed the original 4Ps, first developed by Jerome McCart (Anderson and Taylor, 1995) which provided a foundation for organisations to sell and market goods to consumers. Booms and Bitner (1981), however, believed this limited marketing mix did not account for the industry shift from manufacturing to services in the mid-twentieth century. In light of this, they popularised the addition of three additional Ps to extend the marketing mix to also encompass Participants, Physical evidence and Process. As guided by Booms and Bitner (1981), the 7Ps can be interpreted and connected to events as follows:

- Product: the item, event and/or service being sold or offered, including a consideration of branding, features and usability
- Price: the cost of the item, event and/or service to the customer; value for money and perceived quality should be considered
- Place: where is the item, event, and/or service coming from or going to? The location of the event in this instance needs to be considered
- Promotion: communication and advertising of the event message to relevant stakeholders
- Participants: those involved in the planning and hosting of the event.
- Physical evidence: the event site.

● Process: the project management of the event, including flow, strategies and procedural considerations.

The interesting element of the extended marketing mix is the strong connection the additional three Ps have to project management. In particular, the Participants and the Process elements relate to the management of the human resource and the project management of the logistics and practical side of marketing. When describing the Process, Booms and Bitner (1981, 48) explain it as 'the actual procedures, mechanisms, and flow activities by which the service is delivered'. This definition strongly incorporates the role of Promotion in the marketing mix in connection with project management. Product, Price, Place, Promotion and Physical evidence are all important elements of the project management procedure at some point but are arguably not as relevant as Process and Participants to the initial setup and implementation of the event project.

When viewing Participants through a project management lens it is clear that the marketing, promotion and event messages delivered both to event staff and event attendees must be clear, cohesive and persuasive. Persuasion and persuasive marketing urges the receiver to be convinced practically (head) and emotionally (heart) to make a decision (Jackson, 2013). The way in which internal staff, including volunteers, are trained, managed and motivated to promote and plan for key event messages is fundamental to event success. The events industry is different to most service providers in relation to the marketing mix because event organisers are heavily reliant on non-paid staff such as volunteers to implement the event. Motivations and training for these volunteers must therefore be specialised, thoughtful and engaging in order to create a distinctive and valuable event brand.

The addition of Process of Service Assembly (shortened to Process) by Booms and Bitner (1981) created a procedural glue to hold the other six Ps in line. The Process element can also be considered the project management part of the marketing mix, in terms of the structure and ordering of tasks, services and policies to enable effective marketing promotion. As in other areas of business, a Gantt chart could be used to manage and organise the marketing and promotional elements of the event. For a new event, key tasks such as brand design, implementation of marketing tools, training of marketing staff and online presence could be mapped onto a chart to create key milestones and deadline dates in a transparent and manageable way.

Table 6.1 illustrates the extended marketing mix in relation to events management.

6.3 Marketing strategy

Strategy can be summarised 'as how an organisation (or event) marshals and uses its resources to achieve its business objectives within its ever changing political, economic, sociocultural and technological environment' (Bowdin et al., 2011, 370). A marketing strategy in a tangible sense is a document produced by the event organisation which highlights the aims of the company in relation to marketing and communication of their events. This document may also cover internal and external communication streams and the way in which relationships between employees and external stakeholders will be managed and monitored. Typically, a marketing strategy must be integrated in its approach in order to reach out to the widest breadth of

Table 6.1 The extended marketing mix for events

Product	Price	Place	Promotion	Participants	Physical evidence	Process
Quality of the Event	Ticket price	Location of event	Social media	Event attendees	The event site/ venue (colour, layout, furnish- ings, technology, noise level)	Policies
Event Branding	Discount options	Accessibility of event	Websites	Event entertainers		Procedures
Capabilities of the Event	Payment terms	Distribution channels	E-newsletters	Personnel (training, motivations, incentives)		Flow of activities
Online Presence	Value for money	Distribution coverage	Blogs	Stakeholders		Organisation
	Quality/price interaction	Desirability of event location	Apps			Employee discretion
	Differentiation		Advertising			Customer involvement
	Online purchasing		Sales promotion			
	E-tickets		Personal selling			

These two Ps in particular strongly connect to project management in terms of the organisation and implementation of an event. The other Ps also feature in project management, especially Place but these are secondary to the initial event concept and set-up designed and activated by Participants and Process.

Source: adapted from Eooms and Bitner (1981, 50)

audience possible; this is referred to as integrated marking communications (IMC). Although an area not widely discussed in IMC research, managerial cognition; namely skillset, mindset and decision making (Otis and Nyilasy, 2015) should be considered across all strategy stages. An integrated approach is often preferred because the separation of a marketing, communication and promotional mix isolates itself from a joined up, holistic approach to event marketing. Festival marketers value both online and offline communication methods in an amalgamated strategy (Hudson and Hudson, 2013). A marketing management strategy is crucial in creating an organisation that will respond to technological, environmental, customer and stakeholder needs (Daniel et al., 2012). The marketing strategy, therefore, must be one that is considerate to the history of the organisation, but is also forward looking in terms of the evolution and flexibility of it. Flexibility is absolutely paramount to the success of the event because it is arguable that the rigid structures of project management do not always accommodate the fluid nature of events (Bowdin et al., 2011).

According to Masterman and Wood (2006), a marketing and communication strategy must be integrated in approach and include the following:

- situation analysis
- objective setting
- targeting
- positioning and message strategies
- method and media strategies
- communications budget
- implementation
- measurement, evaluation and control
- written communication plan.

By adopting this proposed method, another way to view the necessary components of the strategy would be through the four areas of research, strategy building, delivery and project management. The marketing strategy Venn diagram in Figure 6.2 demonstrates the equal importance of each section of the marketing strategy and illustrates that their relationship is not linear or cyclical, but in fact flexible and changeable. If viewing this proposal at its simplest level then, it would make sense to follow the chapter sections in order of research, strategy building, delivery, and finally project management to assess and evaluate the entire process. Project management sits outside the diagram because it takes on a holistic role and is something that occurs throughout the entire strategy process. The event marketer may need to often come back to the research and strategy stages to change and adopt the delivery process in relation to the continual management of the strategy. This approach therefore is viewed as an integrated and flexible way to build a marketing strategy. For the purposes of flow for this current chapter, the following sections will take a section in turn to explain and explore.

6.4 Research

In the first instance, a marketer needs to ascertain what the event and organisational objectives are and how this is in alignment with the organisation's vision and/or business strategy. Objective setting will depend on what the event organisation wants

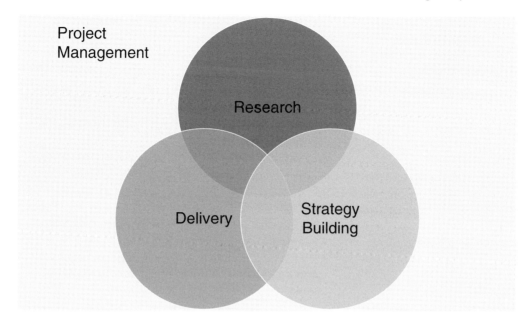

Figure 6.1 The marketing strategy Venn

Source: Developed by authors

to achieve and its current position in the market. For example, if the event is new it will be unable to compare targets and expectations with previous years and therefore will heavily rely on initial research and feasibility analysis. In contrast, if the event is established in its field then it will need to focus on bettering previous performance and ensuring it continues to progress ahead of potential and existing competitors. Understanding what each stakeholder needs and desires is key to outdoing the competition 'as this information facilitates rational decision making and helps reduce the risk of using infinite resources inefficiently' (Masterman and Wood, 2006, 18). The strategic planning stages of a marketing strategy must incorporate an analysis of the competitive, political, economical, sociocultural and technological (C-PEST) environments (Bowdin et al., 2011).

In order to further understand the use of C-PEST to assist in strategy building, take the fictional example of a company called Dynamic Sports, a non-profit organisation aimed at increasing the opportunities for women and girls to access and participate in sport. The organisation uses events to promote the business and its key aims revolve around inclusivity and equality (see Table 6.2).

An analysis of the event context is essential to the research and the eventual implementation of the marketing strategy. In addition to this the strengths, weaknesses, opportunities and threats (SWOT analysis) of the event organisation can also be examined. Strengths and weaknesses are internal to the organisation, matters such as staff engagement and training and opportunities and threats are external. The external components are widely covered by the C-PEST analysis and can be used in conjunction. Once this initial research is conducted the objectives of the marketing strategy can be formulated.

Table 6.2 An example of C-PEST during the research stage in developing a marketing strategy

Organisation name	Dynamic Sports
Competition analysis	• Community sports organisations – what age groups are they targeting? • National governing bodies – how are they targeting participants and users? • Competition here is recognition of cross-over work and understanding whether collaboration would be effective.
Political considerations	• Current government agenda – *A Living Legacy Policy* (DCMS, 2015) in relation to boosting women's sport.
Economic considerations	• Funding for non-profit organisation. • Understanding of the ways increased participation and attendance at sports events links to economic impact.
Sociocultural considerations	• An understanding of the historical roots of women's and girl's sport. • Sociocultural stereotypes around women and girls playing sport to be acknowledged and tackled with a political conscience.
Technological considerations	• Advancements in online media communications. • E-ticketing and online blogging and participant-centred techno marketing.

6.4.1 Stakeholder needs

Events can be considered as experience goods (Craig, Greene and Versaci, 2015), which means the consumer must first attend the event in order to determine its quality. This makes event marketing and promotion utterly crucial to the success of the event, because with an event there is no scope to physically *try before you buy*, and therefore brand image and reputation is everything. Further to this, events have the additional complication of being multi-faceted and reliant on many different agencies or stakeholders. It is essential that an event organiser and indeed marketer knows who their stakeholders are and how to meet their demands and needs (Masterman and Wood, 2006). When using sponsors to assist in the marketing approach, event organisers must ensure the event audience and sponsor's customer base share similar traits; in other words, 'event target markets therefore need to match up with a sponsor's target markets' (Masterman and Wood, 2006, 160).

The needs and desired outcome of the proposed event will vary considerably from stakeholder to stakeholder. The audience member stakeholder group alone may have drastically different needs and expectations within that group. Consider a music festival: one attendee may go to have fun with friends, meet new people and enjoy the atmosphere whereas another may go to see every single band possible, update their music blog with photos and provide an online commentary of the event. These two customers therefore have different needs, which the events team will need to consider when designing and delivering the event. Understanding the needs of the connected stakeholders will allow marketers to plan and distribute targeted and effective communication to each group. Other stakeholders may have more of a financial focus and want to see a return on investment; such as sponsors, business owners, venue owners and private caterers. Knowing who the event stakeholders are, what they want from the event, and how they will experience the event, both short-term and long-term is crucial to its success as well as the execution of the marketing strategy.

6.4.2 Event segments and profiles

Market research around consumers is about finding out what kind of person would be interested in what type of event. This is important for new events in the conceptual planning stages and for established events seeking to improve footfall and image. 'By nature, events are inclusive for certain groups of individuals'; an example of this is World Cup football and the associated football fans (Murthy, 2013, 35). Understanding event audiences by profile is also very useful in considering consumption behaviours (Báez and Devesa, 2014) and being able to cope with different event goers' demands.

   People are often grouped together and sometimes stereotyped in order to create more manageable segments to be researched and used in event planning. This can be understood as 'sub-dividing a market into smaller and homogenous groups' (Brida et al., 2014, 4543). These market segments can be divided by demographic (age, gender, ethnicity), geographic (location), psychographic (personality, attitude, characteristics) and behavioural (past experiences) categories (Jackson, 2013). It must be noted that this broad-brush approach to marketing and promotions is not an exact science and the complexities of human beings cannot easily be reduced to simple segments. The market segments should be used as a starting point and potential guidance to make decisions and formulate a strategy; they should not be used as an isolated marketing research tool.

   Sport England (2010) developed 19 market segments to help sports clubs and County Sports Partnerships to effectively target the appropriate people to engage in sport in their locality. The 19 segments were each given a name to be able to position that particular segment in a personal and real way. For example, 'Bens' are described as 'Competitive Male Urbanites', 18–25 years old and single. Each segment profile details potential barriers into sport as well as suggestions on appropriate marketing tones and platforms. 'Normas', the 'Later Life Ladies', prefer traditional, careful and simple marketing messages and like to receive their information via local newspapers. Although focused specifically on sport, this resource is also highly transferrable to the events industry in relation to market segments. The guidance in relation to branding, tone and marketing messages is useful across many domains and can be used effectively to promote and market events. Table 6.3 shows how Sport England's 19 market segments can be utilised within the events industry.

   Research into market segments has been conducted across many different event types. In their study on audience profiles at the Valdivia International Film Festival, Báez and Devesa (2014) discovered three discrete audience segments: the Socially Indifferent, the Film Lover and the Enthusiasts. The first group had no real interest in films but wanted to enjoy the social aspect of the event and saw cinema as entertainment rather than an art form. In contrast, the Film Lovers were hard-core, passionate film buffs who went to as many viewings as possible and relied on the quality of the

Table 6.3 Profile marketing adapted from Sport England's 19 market segments

Sport England Segment	Descriptor	Context and Motivations	Market and Promotions	Event Interests
Ben (18–25 years)	Competitive Male Urbanite	Enjoyment Socialisation	Internet/email/ mobile Dynamic, fun, informal, sociable, interactive, entertaining	More about being with friends than the actual event
Jamie (18–25 years)	Sports Team Lads	Socialisation Taking part Enjoyment	Internet/email/ mobile Experiential, cutting-edge, sociable	An event launch, new product, experience-driven
Chloe (18–25 years)	Fitness Class Friends	Enjoyment Socialisation Image conscious	Magazines/mobile Colourful Entertaining Stylish	Stylised events VIP Hospitality Glamorous
Leanne (18–25 years)	Supportive Singles	Enjoyment Socialisation	Post/text/mobile Social Value/practical Young Uncomplicated	Special event offers, value for money, practical event for friends and family
Helena (26–45 years)	Career-Focused Females	Enjoyment Fast-paced lifestyle	Magazines/ telephone/mobile Intelligent Stylish Sociable Success Aspirational	High-end event Education/ valuable Stylised Entertainment but with a purpose Glamorous and meaningful event
Tim (26–45 years)	Settling Down Males	Family orientated Professional Enjoyment	Internet/email Informative Eye catching Practical Quality Authentic	Family focused event Quality entertainment and practical for all the family
Alison (36–45 years)	Stay-at-Home Mums	Family orientated Enjoyment	Magazine/tele-phone/mobile Family fun Practical Reliable Time-saving	Family focused event with efficient processes (booking etc.) and effective facilities

Sport England Segment	Descriptor	Context and Motivations	Market and Promotions	Event Interests
Jackie (36–45 years)	Middle England Mums	Family orientated Enjoyment	Television Mass-market Down to earth Practical Mainstream Family orientated	Mainstream event that is straightforward and reliable. No gimmicks or innovative practice
Kev (36–45 years)	Pub League Team Mates	Enjoyment Socialisation	Television/text/ telephone/Internet Jargon-free Dependable Down to earth Cheap Plain	Clear, simple event to attend with friends. Cheap and cheerful approach
Paula (26–45 years)	Stretched Single Mums	Enjoyment Family orientated	Television/text/face to face Uncomplicated Kids Cheap Time saver Mass culture	A local event which has easy access and is cheap to attend. Tickets to be easy to acquire and be mainstream and functional
Phillip (46–55 years)	Comfortable Mid-Life Males	Enjoyment Socialisation Cultural	Internet/email Pragmatic Financially prudent Pragmatic Service Selective Refined	Exclusive event which offers high-end quality at a reasonable price. Thought-provoking and high customer service levels
Elaine (46–55 years)	Empty Nest Career Ladies	Enjoyment Culture Friends and family orientated	Magazine/ telephone/post Unpretentious Established Informative Intelligent Not gimmick-led	Clear and straightforward event with a value and purpose. Charity ball or a conference
Roger and Joy (56–65 years)	Early Retirement Couples	Enjoyment Culture Busy Socialising	Newspapers/face to face/post Conservative Established Informative Practical Reliable	Traditional event with strong brand recognition and quality

(Continued)

Table 6.3 (*continued*)

Sport England Segment	Descriptor	Context and Motivations	Market and Promotions	Event Interests
Brenda (46–65 years)	Older Working Women	Enjoyment Family orientated Culture	Television/local papers/face to face Hardworking Word of mouth Mass market Value for money Trustworthy	Local/regional straightforward event for friends and family. Simple event prioritising value for money
Terry (56–65 years)	Local 'Old Boys'	Enjoyment Socialisation	Television/local papers/face to face Cheap Everyday Sensible Hard-working Basic	A simple event for local friends and family which is cheap and inclusive
Norma (56–65 years)	Later Life Ladies	Enjoy lifestyle Socialisation	Television/local papers/face to face Traditional Established Careful Reassuring	A familiar event or an event in familiar surroundings for a traditional purpose.
Ralph and Phyllis (66+ years)	Comfortable Retired Couples	Enjoyment Socialising Gardening Culture	Newspapers/ magazine/post Prestigious Intellectual Classic Community Friendly	Sophisticated event, expensive with high-end customer service
Frank (66+ years)	Twilight Year Gents	Television Socialisation Enjoyment	Post/newspaper/face to face Non-technical Risk free Careful Established Modest	A straightforward event with local friends in a calm environment. Easy to access and simple communication
Elsie and Arnold (66+ years)	Retirement Home Singles	Television Socialisation Enjoyment	Post/local papers/ face to face Cautious Gentle Comforting Community	A local event with familiar friends and family in familiar surroundings. Relaxing and enjoyable in a friendly environment

Source: adapted from Sport England, 2010, http://segments.sportengland.org/

event programme. Lastly, the Enthusiasts were very satisfied with all aspects of the event and had overall high enjoyment levels. These findings could be transferrable to music festivals as well, where the motivations for attendance will impact upon event satisfaction. Event marketing can directly target these segments whether for the social dimensions, quality of programme and/or variety and calibre of content being showcased. The success of festivals in the future will be relational to the use and interpretation of segmenting festival markets (Bleši, Pivac, Stamenkovi and Besermenji, 2013). Marketing strategies must be created based on the type of audience profile an event is used to address. According to Daniel et al. (2012), an event addressing customers and other business partners should be interactive, incentivised with gifts, and intensive. In contrast, an event aimed at organisational employees should demonstrate good communication from top to bottom, offer financial incentives and be bureaucracy free (Daniel et al. 2012).

Market profiles also have an impact upon the type of processes the consumer will engage with. For example, customer occupation rather than age, gender and education was seen as the most significant indicator of whether a consumer would purchase an e-ticket rather than a physical ticket (Tanrikulu and Celilbatur, 2013). It seems individuals who work with computers and the internet regularly feel more comfortable purchasing online. This may have implications for event marketers who are targeting consumers via online only methods.

Tip box

When working out how to 'sell' event tickets (e.g. in physical form or online), think about the type of segment expected to come to your event. Will they have access to a computer, can they afford the internet and/or are they technologically minded to buy online?

6.4.3 Branding

The concept of brand is far-reaching, complex and, as Voase (2012, 78) recalls, often misunderstood: 'An authentic brand is a symbolic construct, reductionist in character, which facilitates recognition, conveys reputation and generates an instinctive response.'

It seems therefore that a brand is very powerful and of significant value to event managers and the associated success of their events. Effective brand management requires the consideration of brand positioning, marketing strategy and effective communication (Jackson, 2013). The positioning of the brand will be rooted in the type of event itself, the target audience for the event and how it wishes to be perceived in the market. For example, if the brand is needed to facilitate recognition and convey a reputation, it needs to be in keeping with the desired target event audience, something that is discussed in the research stage of this chapter. In the case of Glastonbury music festival, their branding and promotion must be in line with the ethical and green principles that underpin their event philosophy (Hong, 2015). The marketing strategy for an event can vary in size and complexity depending on the event and organisers in question. Mega-events can be used by host nations to create a brand for their nation, something that symbolises much more than a straightforward event brand: 'More recently, events have been used to present a positive image of a nation or society. In other words, not necessarily overtly to oppress people, but to give them pride in a country and, by association, its political leaders' (Jackson, 2013, 63).

As stated, the event brand links to reputation, recognition and the success of the event and its associated organisers and hosts. It is well known that branding is closely connected to image, perception and attitude (Masterman and Wood, 2006). The ability for effective communication of this brand is paramount to the integrity and professionalism of the stakeholders involved.

Social media is being used as a tool to manage and promote event branding and loyalty by organisations and individuals alike. Blaszka, Burch, Frederick, Clavio and Walsh (2012), discovered that hashtags are being used on Twitter at an increasing rate to share information, connect to branding and products, as well as provide improved customer service. Sports organisations are the focal point of their research, and brand loyalty or sports team loyalty is significant and demonstrated by fans of the team via the hashtag function. In the past decade, social media has caused a change in the way customers make decisions and engage with brands (Hudson and Hudson, 2013).

Once the brand is finalised and established it must then be seamlessly threaded through the entire marketing strategy to ensure there is consistency throughout. Some event organisations may tailor their branding to different stakeholders; for example, a venue that deals with hospitality and weddings and also business conferences may adapt the colouring and presentation of the brand to be more attractive to the image and aims of the stakeholder. Event marketers will need to ensure a new brand launch is carefully managed so that current customers and stakeholders are aware of what is happening and are updated through the entire transition period. This communications journey will be embedded in the relevant process aspects set up within the overall strategy.

6.5 Strategy building

This section concerns the actual planning and method stage of the marketing strategy. Strategy building and development connects to the Process aspect of Booms and Bitner's (1981) extended marketing mix. This section will first look at the marketing control systems of strategy building in line with project management. The use of project management feedback loop systems and understanding the role of evaluation and adaptation within a marketing strategy are also considered in this section.

6.5.1 Marketing control systems

In his textbook, *Strategic Marketing Planning and Control*, Drummond (2008) effectively highlights the connectivity between marketing strategy and project management principles and practice. He summarises the key phrases useful to project management within a marketing environment, including objective setting, planning, delegation, team building, crisis and management. In terms of objective setting, Drummond (2008) argues that the SMART concept should be followed when building a marketing strategy. In other words, objectives must be specific, measurable, action-led, resourced and time-based. For example, if a traditional events company wanted to update its communication methods and create social networking platforms they would need to follow the SMART principle.

● Specific: to set up Facebook, Twitter and Instagram accounts for the company
● Measurable: software will be used to measure the number of Likes and Follows and additional activity – Shares, Retweets, Favourites
● Action: set up the digital marketing tool and then upload content frequently
● Resourced: appropriate staff must be trained to ensure they can use and understand the technology; money is needed to purchase software analysis packages if relevant
● Time: exact timescales should be implemented, all platforms to be fully functioning and updated and managed within three months.

Furthermore, the way in which Drummond (2008) advocates using project management philosophy within marketing planning and strategising is via feedback loops. The one shown in Figure 6.2 is particularly useful for viewing and monitoring marketing control systems.

When building a marketing strategy it is important to create opportunity for revision, evaluation and continual adaptation. The marketing control systems diagram (Figure 6.2) ensures that there is a logical process in place which has the flexibility to develop, adapt and progress as the marketing strategy is implemented.

6.5.2 Event positioning and budget

How the event is positioned within the sector is crucial to its success. Event position and budget are inextricably linked and the financial resource capacity of the organisation will have an impact on the way the event is launched or redefined. According to Bowdin et al. (2011, 399), there are ten ways event positioning can be achieved and/or defined:

Figure 6.2 Drummond's marketing control systems
Source: Drummond, 2008, 277

1 Existing reputation/image
2 Charisma of management/leader
3 Focus on event programming
4 Focus on performers
5 Emphasis on the location and facilities
6 Event users
7 Price or quality
8 Purpose of event
9 Event type or event category
10 Wider attributes of the event.

An event organisation may have overlapping aspirations for its market position, and indeed stakeholders may hold different expectations as to where the event or events company should sit. The role of the marketing strategy, however, is to ensure the event organisation has a very clear vision and market position for itself, and introduces key objectives in order to meet this vision in a coherent and consistent manner.

The allocation budget of the organisation in relation to the marketing strategy will impact upon the resources to be utilised and the approach taken. Drummond (2008, 284) outlines the importance of benchmarking when setting budgeting aims and targets and he demonstrates a three-option budgeting approach. The first is *historic budgeting*, whereby the future calculations and aspirations of the organisation are based on previous years. The second is *zero-based* budgeting, which allows the organisation to wipe the slate clean and start afresh, re-evaluating the system and looking at cost versus benefits of the proposals. Thirdly, there is *activity-related budgeting*, which centres on general market statistics in order to calculate available finances. The individual situation of the events company will affect which budget approach is taken; for example, a new events company will need to take a zero-based approach initially. The strategy-building stage should be fully intertwined with the approach to budgeting and company positioning.

6.6 Delivery: Promoting events successfully

As Jackson (2013) argues, events are dual purpose in relation to promotion and personal relations (PR); they are used as a PR tool and also use PR techniques as self-promotion. This makes events very valuable and also complicated in terms of strategically managing how and when they are used. Promotion concerns information sharing and persuasion to encourage people to attend the event, work at the event and entertain at the event. Promotional advertising methods can be thought of as being both offline (face to face, newspapers, radio, and television) and digital (social media, e-newletters/brochures/magazines, blogs, websites, apps). Word of mouth (WOM), namely the exchange of information from individual to individual as an expression of personal experience, is thought to be vital in both offline and digital capacities (Fulgoni and Lipsman, 2015). Promotion and advertising must be consistent and clear throughout, as external factors such as public opinion of an event and political issues can sometimes hijack promotional campaigns. This was the case with the Pan Am and Parapan Am Games in Canada in 2015, in which there were disputes over budget and contractual agreements, a feature of the case study at the end of this chapter. It is argued that their event marketing 'narrative' lost focus:

Controversies over Pan Am executive expenses, venue costs overruns, the cost of Games infrastructure and even the question of whether we should be shelling out billions of dollars to host an athletic event, became the story. Add in the predictions of traffic chaos – and organizers' pleas for increased carpooling and outright driving avoidance – and you had a fully-fledged communications nightmare.

Burnett (2015, online)

In the events sector capturing and maintaining a positive narrative and discourse is crucial to success. This section will theorise and develop an understanding of the multi-dimensional ways in which events can be advertised and marketed successfully in relation to strategy delivery.

6.6.1 Offline marketing and promotions

Word of mouth (WOM) is a 'potent force' which has the capabilities to affect the success or failure of a product or service (Craig et al., 2015, 62), and in this case an event. Conference attendees in southeast United States were shown to provide more favourable WOM following the event if they had been satisfied with the event itself (Severt, Wang, Chen and Breiter, 2007), so event experience and post-event marketing are inextricably linked. WOM involves the person-to-person sharing of discourse by individuals about personal experiences and expectations. WOM is seen as a promotional medium that it is very difficult for event organisers to have any control over. Other offline communication methods such as telesales, leaflets, brochures, face-to-face meetings and radio/newspaper adverts can be more closely monitored. The tangible aspects of marketing and promotions such as websites, social media and adverts are more easily measured and quantified in terms of number of 'hits', 'likes', 'retweets' and so on. Measuring customer satisfaction, advertising impact and effectiveness of both the traditional WOM and e-WOM (electronic word of mouth) is much more difficult.

Study activity

Think about how you would measure WOM interactivity and marketing as part of your event evaluation? What research methods would you use and why?

6.6.2 Digital promotion and e-word of mouth (e-WOM)

Technologies are developing at a rapid rate in society and it is important that event marketers embrace, utilise and pioneer technological changes. As argued throughout this chapter, communication is the crucial factor that holds each part of the marketing mix together. Technological platforms such as websites, social media, blog sites, apps and video upload sites all affect the way in which communication between event organiser/marketer and stakeholders are taking place. Social media has seen vast growth in popularity in recent years (Hull, 2014) and it does not look to be slowing down. Digital platforms have the power to create an e-buzz (Craig et al., 2015) around products and services and therefore it is crucial that online platforms are utilised by event marketers.

Social media is a prime example of a virtual promotional platform for dialogue and is now crucial to the promotional marketing mix (Bayne and Cianfrone, 2013). Social media can be understood as virtual networking sites accessed via computers and/or electronic devices to allow for information sharing, interaction and communication. Examples of social media sites include Facebook, Twitter, Instagram, LinkedIn, Pinterest, YouTube and SnapChat, to name just a few. Social media is known as being very effective in increasing event awareness (Bayne and Cianfrone, 2013) to potential attendees. Social media, emails, blogs and forums can be thought of as digital WOM (Fulgoni and Lipsman, 2015) or e-WOM (Shalom and Yaniv, 2015), whereby people interact and share their experiences but this time online through digital networks.

The digital identity of the social media user, be that an individual or an organisation, is highly contingent on the way the user wishes to be perceived by others. 'In a sense, Twitter markets us through our tweets and, as such, shifts us more toward 'an age of advertisement', where we are not necessarily advertising products, but rather ourselves (and our self-commodification)' (Murthy, 2013, 35).

It can be argued that Twitter, in particular, is a pedestal for self-presentation for the everyday individual as well as the celebrity or business, looking to promote their latest DVD or gift idea. Event marketers, therefore, must acknowledge this shift within their marketing strategy and associated project plans. If society is driven by online presence and digital identity it therefore follows that event marketing should align to potential attendees' online identities and needs. It must also be noted that different e-WOM channels each have a varied focus and purpose, such as pleasure (Facebook, Google+, Instagram), business (LinkedIn) and shopping and lifestyle (Pinterest) (Shalom and Yaniv, 2015). Event marketers must, therefore, use the appropriate avenue to advertise and promote their event, whether it is a business conference, a food and gift show or a music festival. Twitter is also used by event entertainment acts, sport stars and musicians who can connect to the event's own digital presence. Research into golfers during a Masters event found that Twitter was used as a promotional tool linking golfers to their sponsors and funders (Hull, 2014).

In essence, promotion and marketing is about an end-product that is usually a consumer purchase or a customer buy-in, whether that is something tangible (a ticket) or intangible (a sense of community). Fulgoni and Lipsman (2015) discuss the Purchase Funnel as the process in which digital technologies connect to purchase intention. The staggered positions of the digital platforms in Figure 6.3 illustrate the consumer process of considering a purchase. In relation to events, potential attendees may first see friends (Facebook), or followers (Twitter), discuss and promote an event experience they have just had. If the potential attendee is still interested, they may then seek new platforms to further explore the particular event, in this case Pinterest. Pinterest allows for interactivity via photographs and images and promotes specific boards to summarise the different images. In this sense Pinterest will allow users to visually familiarise themselves with the associated experiences and emotions connected to the anticipated event. The top part of the Purchase Funnel, therefore, generates awareness and 'hooks' in the potential event attendee. The narrower end of the funnel sees a shift from awareness towards intent to buy. Potential attendees will then visit online sources more equipped to offer specific details and even offer reviews of specific event

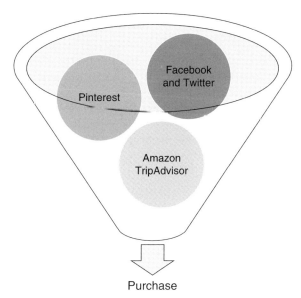

Figure 6.3 The Purchase Funnel

Source: adapted from Fulgoni and Lipsman, 2015, 19

experiences. Examples of general product and hospitality marketing are Amazon and TripAdvisor. For event-specific information local tourist websites would be a useful starting point. The output of the funnel analogy is that of purchase; the entire funnel is concerned with the conversion from awareness to purchase.

As illustrated, contemporary marketing has seen a shift away from the traditional view of the Purchase Funnel towards consumers spending more time conducting research and often entering into an open-ended relationship with the brand (Hudson and Hudson, 2013). There are several elements that event marketers must consider and utilise from the Purchase Funnel to assist in the event promotion and overall marketing. Firstly, in order to facilitate the digital WOM which occurs at the top of the funnel, the event product and services offered must be high quality and enjoyable to the stake-holders involved. WOM can be both effective and detrimental to the reputation of event organisations and therefore the event must offer a high-end service and positive experience. Through the joint promotion of event experiences and information from both the official digital sources (event website, event Twitter, event Facebook page) and event attendees an awareness level of the event will be raised. Event marketers then need to capitalise on this awareness by encouraging a conversion to intent to purchase, perhaps via direct communication on the digital platforms, and clear messages surrounding where, when, how and why to buy. Consumers may want to share their experiences with the brand or event through the relationship they have established (Hudson and Hudson, 2013), and therefore event managers must engage with this. A limitation to using e-WOM is that it is very difficult for the event goer/consumer to assess the credibility of the event organiser based on electronic messages alone (Shalom and Yaniv, 2015).

6.6.3 Technology and project management

E-marketing, and in particular e-ticketing, is a key development within the events sector (Jackson, 2013) and relates to both the Place and Process parts of the extended marketing mix. Due to evolving technology and specifically the internet, the communications environment has vastly altered in the past decade and has impacted upon how interaction and communication are facilitated (Hudson and Hudson, 2013). Even though much of the marketing materials are now intangible and online in presence, more needs to be done to facilitate tangible products through online platforms (Jackson, 2013). Event attendees and stakeholders should be provided with freely available online information, which includes access to e-brochures, virtual tours, reviews and videos which help consumers to get an understanding of the event.

It is extremely important, however, that an events organisation prioritises customer privacy and their own professionalism, because increasingly vigorous digital marketing approaches could lead to a deeper level of interrogation of customer personal information (Hudson and Hudson, 2013). Event marketers must therefore strike a balance between customer information they *need to know*, that it would be a *nice to know* and, lastly, details that there is *no need to know*. The careful management of these three concepts will ensure a trusting relationship can be developed and maintained between event company and event goer. It has been found that people who do not buy e-tickets are concerned about security and privacy details, and also feel more comfortable with a physical ticket to demonstrate the transaction is complete (Tanrikulu and Celilbatur, 2013).

6.7 Project management

It is vital that a marketing communication strategy has a planning process (Masterman and Wood, 2006) and it is this which makes it comparable to project management. As explained previously, alongside the marketing mix, project management is of key importance when viewing the two Ps of Participants (stakeholders) and Process. In a way, the process, and in connection, the project management and delivery of the marketing strategy, is the glue that holds together all the other elements. Furthermore, 'The communications strategy and tactics developed through the planning process can be translated into operational or implementation activities' (Masterman and Wood, 2006, 277).

Effective and successful implementation of marketing strategy is rooted in three areas: understanding the fundamentals of implementation, assessing the context of implementation and relating project management concepts (Drummond, 2008). The research and information-gathering stage through audience profiling, branding and stakeholder analysis can be used both to write and implement the strategy using project management tools and techniques. For example, the event marketer can use a Gantt chart to monitor and manage each area of the Venn diagram displayed in Figure 6.1. Tasks set out in relation to this area may be as follows:

- Research
  - SWOT/C-PEST analysis to ascertain the event organisation's current market position

- Competitor analysis to investigate the ways in which other event companies are using marketing and communication methods
- Customer and stakeholder needs analysis through qualitative and/or quantitative methods of research
- Consultation with internal staff and members is vital (Masterman and Wood, 2006) in relation to new ideas and challenges from previous events if appropriate
- Set event marketing objectives for the year ahead and target milestones to monitor achievements, including budgeting and resource considerations

- **Strategy building**
  - Provide a written marketing communication strategy which is evidenced by research and internal/stakeholder consultation
  - Create/adapt/revise the event branding to include a review of design, colour, logo, typography, imagery, etc.
  - Provide an integrated marketing approach which highlights connectivity to both online and offline communication methods
  - Create an event brand and mission statement that is cohesive and coherent

- **Delivery**
  - Communicate the new marketing communication strategy to internal staff members and stakeholders where appropriate
  - Have a dedicated marketing and communication events team to send out key and consistent messages to stakeholders as planned in the strategy
  - Tasks to be outlined on a Gantt chart or equivalent that link to the micro levels of the strategy, i.e. Tweets, Facebook, Instagram, e-brochures, website hits, telephone marketing, sponsorship deals, etc.

- **Project management**
  - The event organiser or organisation's manager must continue to assess and monitor the strategy delivery against the initial aims
  - The flow of activities and funds must be measured against the pre-set bench mark and marketing messages to be reviewed and evaluated
  - An on-going relationship with stakeholders must be maintained to check against the appropriateness, acceptance and favourability of marketing messages
  - Competitor analysis should be ongoing to monitor and oversee standards and relationship forming against the field.

Tip box

Each area of event management can be broken down into smaller, more manageable tasks and responsibilities using project management techniques. A marketing strategy is no different, and when faced with creating one, do your initial research using C-PEST and a SWOT analysis, and then create SMART objectives based on your initial research. Implement your strategy using project management tools such as a Gantt chart, feedback loop and stakeholder communication. Continually evaluate and monitor the progress of the strategy and do not be afraid to change things if they are not going to plan.

Control elements are extremely important within project management and the way in which processes are managed and controlled within the marketing and promotions environment is no different. It is thought that 'the basis of control is the ability to measure' (Drummond, 2008, 275) which stresses the importance of building in specific and measurable objectives and aims into the marketing strategy.

Study activity

The fictional events company, Volcano Enterprises, is launching a new marketing strategy and requires your help to build one. They currently specialise in high-end hospitality events and would like to retain their current customer base as well as attracting new customers. Currently they advertise their company and offers through client meetings and glossy publications only. You now need to do the following:

1   Conduct a C-PEST and SWOT analysis for Volcano Enterprises.
2   Based on this research, create some SMART objectives for the company.
3   Indicate how you would implement this strategy using an example Gantt chart or written presentation.

6.8 Conclusion

This chapter has highlighted the way in which the ethos of project management can be instilled across all elements of event management and design. Researching, creating and delivering an effective marketing strategy that works for the company and each stakeholder is highly significant to the future success of the organisation. By merging academic research from marketing and advertising fields with event management it is clear that that there is a lot for event managers and event marketers to learn. The changing technological landscape of events marketing should be a key feature of the marketing strategy. More detail about technology and sustainable technological practices can be found in Chapter 7. The essential areas to remember are that effective research and analysis initially will help to inform and plan strategically for a measured and specific marketing strategy.

Case study 6: Pan Am and Parapan Am Games in Toronto, Canada 2015

The Pan American Games, or Pan Am Games for short, is a multi-sport competition held in the Americas every four years. It is similar to the Olympic Games and sports include athletics, badminton, cycling, football, swimming and judo as well as many more. The Pan Am Games are followed by the Parapan Am Games, in which disabled athletes compete in disciplines such as sitting volleyball, goalball, athletics and table tennis. In 2015 the Games were hosted in Toronto, Canada. The Pan Am Games website (2015) provides the following information:

- The first Pan Am Games were held in 1951; the first Parapan Am Games came many years later in 1999.
- 6000 athletes competed in the Pan Am Games and 1600 in the Parapan Am Games in 2015, which was the largest ever Games.
- The 41 Pan American Sports Organization (PASO) members are involved in representation at the Games.
- The Games website received over 85,000 visitors and 23,000 page views each day.

Of particular interest to this case study are the marketing and advertising techniques used during the Games from a visitor perspective. Hanya Pielichaty, who attended the Games as a tourist in 2015, provides an account of her experiences in relation to the event advertising and marketing campaigns.

How did you get tickets to the Games?
Due to timings we were only in Toronto for the later stages of the competition and so ensured we got tickets for athletics at the Parapan Am Games. Tickets were easy to purchase through the Games website and e-tickets were emailed to me. The tickets cost 40CD each, which was reasonable, and once we arrived at the athletics stadium in North York our tickets were scanned on entry.

Was it easy travelling across the city to access the Games?
Yes and cheap because you could show your Games spectator ticket on the travel network to access free transport to your sports venue. Also, Games volunteers were available at key station points to direct and guide visitors to their relevant sporting fixtures.

Did the city celebrate the Games; how were they promoted?
As a tourist to Toronto, I noticed the Games were heavily advertised at transportations spots, key tourist sites and central areas. In particular, Nathan Phillips Square (see Figure 6.5) was the venue for many of the cultural events associated with the Games and a large Toronto installation set beside the water allowed for great exposure and tourist photos. The Games mascot Pachi was also a consistent and regular feature around the city, the 'coloured quills' on its back, as shown in Figure 6.4, each represented a different characteristic of the Games: green – youth; fuchsia – passion; blue collaboration; orange – determination; and purple – creativity. (Pan Am Games, 2015 online)

The Games' colours were widespread throughout the city and featured in places close to tourist attractions. The photograph in Figure 6.6 was taken outside the CN Tower and new Aquarium.

(Continued)

Case study 6 (*continued*)

Figure 6.4 Meet Pachi the mascot, Toronto, Canada

Source: © Hanya Pielichaty

Figure 6.5 Nathan Phillips Square, Toronto, Canada

Source: © Hanya Pielichaty

What marketing tools were used to engage your interest?
In Nathan Phillips Square you could use the public digital marketing machines to take your photo and get it emailed to you. These photos were linked to the Games and it helped to create interest and engagement with spectators. As well

Figure 6.6 CN Tower, Toronto, Canada

Source: © Hanya Pielichaty

(*Continued*)

Case study 6 (*continued*)

as the Games' official store, there were also Games countdown clocks on site to create excitement and anticipation for the event.

Were you aware of any marketing conflicts whilst you were there?
It was only after the Games that I learnt about the marketing criticism of the Pan Am Games because of financial and political issues relating to the competition

Figure 6.7 Digital marketing machines at Nathan Phillips Square, Toronto, Canada

Source: © Hanya Pielichaty

Figure 6.7 (*continued*)

(Burnett, 2015). As a tourist new to the country and the event, I was unaware of any wider issues of criticism. In terms of marketing the event concept, the colours and images of the Games were consistent, vibrant and omnipresent.

(*Continued*)

129

Case study 6 (*continued*)

Figure 6.8 Countdown Tower at Nathan Phillips Square, Toronto, Canada

Source: © Hanya Pielichaty

Evaluative student questions

1   Does your perspective affect your impression of event marketing, i.e. tourist/resident?
2   How important is the need for a strong and clear narrative throughout the entire marketing journey for an event?

3 Will e-marketing and technology advance or restrain the effectiveness of event marketing in the future?

Further reading

Booms, B.H. and Bitner, M.J. (1981) Marketing strategies and organization structures for service firms. In: James H. Donnelly and William R. George (eds), *Marketing of services: conference on services marketing*. Chicago: American Marketing Association, 47–51.

Fulgoni, G.M. and Lipsman, A. (2015) Digital word of mouth and its offline amplification: a holistic approach to leveraging and amplifying all forms of WOM. *Journal of Advertising Research*, 55(1) 18–21.

Murthy, D. (2013) *Twitter: social communication in the Twitter age*. Cambridge: Polity Press.

References

Anderson, L.M. and Taylor, R.L. (1995) McCarthy's 4Ps: timeworn or time-tested? *Journal of Marketing Theory and Practice*, 3(3) 1–9.

Báez, A. and Devesa, M. (2014) Segmenting and profiling attendees at a film festival. *International Journal of Event and Festival Management*, 5(2) 96–115.

Bayne, K.S. and Cianfrone, B.A. (2013) The effectiveness of social media marketing: the impact of Facebook status updates on a campus recreation event. *Recreational Sports Journal*, 37(2) 147–159.

Blaszka, M., Burch, L.M., Frederick, E.L., Clavio, G. and Walsh, P. (2012) #WorldSeries: an empirical examination of a Twitter hashtag during a major sporting event. *International Journal of Sport Communication*, 5(4) 435–453.

Bleši, I., Pivac, T., Stamenkovi, I. and Besermenji, S. (2013) Motives of visits to ethno music festivals with regard to gender and age structure of visitors. *Event Management*, 17(2) 145–154.

Booms, B.H. and Bitner, M.J. (1981) Marketing strategies and organization structures for service firms. In: James H. Donnelly and William R. George (eds), *Marketing of services: conference on services marketing*. Chicago: American Marketing Association, 47–51.

Bowdin, G., Allen, J., O'Toole, W., Harris, R. and McDonnell, I. (2011) *Events management*. 3rd edition. London: Butterworth-Heinemann.

Brida, J.G., Disegna, M. and Scuderi, R. (2014) Segmenting visitors of cultural events: the case of Christmas Market. *Expert Systems and Applications*, 41(10) 4542–4553.

Burnett, D. (2015) What you can learn from the Pan Am Games marketing disaster. *Financial Post*. Available from: http://business.financialpost.com/entrepreneur/what-you-can-learn-from-the-pan-am-games-marketing-disaster [Accessed 20 January 2016].

Craig, C.S., Greene, W.H. and Versaci, A. (2015) E-word of mouth: early predictor of audience engagement. *Journal of Advertising Research*, 55(1) 62–72.

Daniel, M., Bogdan, G. and Daniel, Z. (2012) The use of event marketing management strategies. *Social and Behavioral Sciences*, 46 5409–5413.

Department of Culture, Media and Sport (DCMS) (2015) *A living legacy: 2010–2015 sport policy and investment*. London: DCMS. Available from https://www.gov.uk/government/uploads/system/uploads/attachment_data/file/417394/1580-F_Sport_Report_ACCESSIBLE_2.pdf [Accessed 26 June 2015].

Drummond, G. (2008) *Strategic marketing: planning and control*. London: Butterworth-Heinemann.

Fulgoni, G.M. and Lipsman, A. (2015) Digital word of mouth and its offline amplifications: a holistic approach to leveraging and amplifying all forms of WOM. *Journal of Advertising Research*, 55(1) 18–21.

Gardner, M.P. and Shuman, P.J. (1987) Sponsorship: an important component of the promotions mix. *Journal of Advertising*, 16(1) 11–17.

Hong, P. (2015) Festival marketing: brands getting into the festival groove. *Momentology*. Available from: http://www.momentology.com/6968-festival-marketing-brands/ [Accessed 20 January 2016].

Hudson, S. and Hudson, R. (2013) Engaging consumers using social media: a case study of music festivals. *International Journal of Event and Festival Management*, 4(3) 206–223.

Hull, K. (2014) A hole in one (hundred forty characters): a case study examining PGA tour golfers' Twitter use during the Masters. *International Journal of Sport Communication*, 7(2) 245–260.

Jackson, N. (2013) *Promoting and marketing events: theory and practice*. Abingdon: Routledge.

Lecoeuvre-Soudain, L. and Deshayes, P. (2006) From marketing to project management. *Project Management Journal*, 37(5) 103–112.

Masterman, G. and Wood, E.H. (2006) *Innovative marketing communications: strategies for the events industry*. Oxford: Elsevier Butterworth-Heinemann.

Murthy, D. (2013) *Twitter: social communication in the Twitter age*. Cambridge: Polity Press.

Ots, M. and Nyilasy, G. (2015) Integrated marketing communications (IMC): why does it fail? *Journal of Advertising Research*, 55(2) 132–145.

Pan Am Games (2015) *About the Pan Am Games*. Available from: http://www.toronto2015.org/about-us/pan-am-games [Accessed 22 January 2016].

Severt, D., Wang, Y., Chen, P.-J. and Breiter, D. (2007) Examining the motivation, perceived performance, and behavioral intentions of convention attendees: evidence from a regional conference. *Tourism Management*, 28(2) 399–408.

Shalom, L. and Yaniv, G. (2015) How credible is e-word of mouth across digital-marketing channels? *Journal of Advertising Research*, 55(1) 95–109.

Sport England (2010) *Market segments*. Available from: http://segments.sportengland.org/querySegments.aspx# [Accessed 5 May 2015].

Tanrikulu, Z. and Celilbatur, N. (2013) Trust factors affecting e-ticket purchasing. *Social and Behavioral Sciences*, 73 115–119.

Voase, R. (2012) Recognition, reputation and response: some critical thoughts on destinations and brands. *Journal of Destination Marketing and Management*, 1(1–2) 78–83.

Chapter 7

Technology and sustainability

7.1 Introduction

Since Elkington (1997) introduced the concept of the triple bottom line (TBL) it became almost synonymous with sustainability. Measuring business performance based on economic, environmental and social aspects is a more commonly recognised business practice. Building on the concept of the triple bottom line, Getz (2005) argues that sustainable events are those events that augment the benefits of the three pillars (economic, environmental and social) and at the same time reduce the negative impacts as 'no event will have zero environmental impacts' (Bladen et al., 2012, 365). Current best practice in the events industry involves ensuring events are sustainable, and a stronger emphasis is now placed on delivering green events (Bowdin et al., 2011). Event managers have an ethical responsibility, and increasingly also a legal one, to produce events that are 'socially, culturally and environmentally responsible' (Getz, 2005, 123). Exploiting the discourse on responsible tourism, Getz (2009, 71) has adopted and adapted the general principles of responsible tourism for the events sector, and argues that events should:

- reduce negative economic, social, cultural and environmental impacts
- enhance the wellbeing of communities by creating economic prosperity through the improvement of working conditions and employment facilities
- move the decision-making process from a central to a more local level to encourage involvement
- contribute to conservation of natural and cultural heritage
- embrace diversity and provide access for all members of society
- create enjoyable experiences by enabling visitors to connect meaningfully with residents
- encourage respect between event attendees and hosts linking to local pride and confidence.

One of the main characteristics of an event manager's role is the need to make efficient decisions on a daily basis. Successful events are not the result of chance but of thorough planning and collaboration between stakeholders in a constantly changing environment.

'A constantly changing environment is one that is influenced by specific aspects affecting event design: technological advancements, sustainable and green issues,

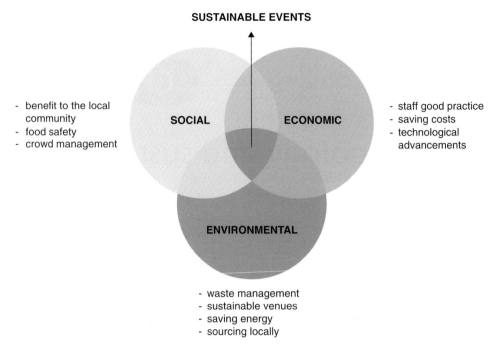

SUSTAINABLE EVENTS

- benefit to the local
  community
- food safety
- crowd management

SOCIAL

ECONOMIC

- staff good practice
- saving costs
- technological
  advancements

ENVIRONMENTAL

- waste management
- sustainable venues
- saving energy
- sourcing locally

Figure 7.1 Sustainable events

Source: developed by the authors

events as generators of profit focusing on the business side, increased security and safety and globalization' (Adema and Roehl, 2010, 206). Among service professionals, however, there is still an ingrained fear of using technology (Ali and Frew, 2013), associated with lack of knowledge of the practical applicability of the latest technological advancements in the daily routine operations of the events sector. This fear is linked to the existing disparity between generations when it comes to using technology, a gap between the generation of the digital natives and that of the digital immigrants (Prensky, 2001), which has significant implications for the future of technology in events planning and design (Adema and Roehl, 2010). This is a factor that becomes even more meaningful if event organisers are to follow Getz's (2009) standpoint that events are trendsetters in terms of leveraging wider economic and business change. Ali and Frew (2013) underline that the important aspects for the implementation of technology for sustainable events are beyond the control of events stakeholders alone, as further support is needed from governments which have the crucial role in formulating sustainable policy and planning, both at national and local levels. Furthermore, 'Events policy needs to recognise the complexity of stakeholder interests in events, and acknowledge that there are multiple motivations, needs, expectations and attitudes with respect to the development and implementation and management of events' (Dredge and Whitford, 2010, 12).

Ciuchete and Kane (in press) believe that in order to create something innovative and sustainable, entrepreneurs must have the ability to utilise existing areas of support. Support includes political and financial capital, capabilities and knowledge of the local stakeholders, and the inherent worth of the natural world for the sustainable develop-ment of spaces and regions through events. Holmes et al. (2015) suggest applying holistic thinking to planning and organising events as a means of better perceiving events' component elements and the way they fit in with the broader events context in which the experience takes place. Usually, the economic benefits prevail as this factor is the basis of survival; without financial means the event cannot be sustainable and is unlikely to take place. It is argued, however, that further tangible (e.g. increased job opportunities, injection of cash) and more intangible (e.g. improved quality of life for the local community, new infrastructure and facilities) economic benefits should be considered part of the long-term sustainable development of the host location (Holmes et al., 2015, 122).

Following the concept of the triple bottom line, the connections between sustainability and technology in an event's context are here further reviewed and discussed by analysing sustainable principles and solutions based on the three pillars discussed earlier. In addition, a set of useful tools and relevant industry examples are given and interpreted, taking into consideration the latest technological advancements that are contributing to significant sustainable practice.

7.2 Economic

Digital technologies continue to transform the world at a rapid pace. Advancements in information technology are impacting on the life, business and service delivery of the leading economies and are making society more productive. Although, 'the lives of the majority of the world's people remain largely untouched by the digital revolution' as described by the latest World Bank (2016, 6) report on digital dividends. The expansion and potential of digital technologies has increased the development of the information base, lowered the overall information costs and created information goods. Increased connectivity, however, has had limited effects in lowering information inequality. To exemplify the point, the World Bank (2016, 8) highlights that there are more contributors to Wikipedia from Hong Kong SAR and China than from all of Africa combined, although Africa has 50 times more internet users.

The growth of the mobile industry and the use of smartphones in people's personal and professional day-to-day activities has transformed the way people communicate: arguably, through a sophisticated, interactive, social system. The advancements of smartphones, data plans and application facilitate the blending of traditional means of communication with new innovative methods of information distribution, communication, interaction and entertainment (Greenwald, Hampel, Phadke and Poosala, 2011). In the early days of advertising, consumers were targeted 'on the go' by the use of radio or billboards; nowadays, with the newest digital technology available, advertisers are using customised platforms and models that not only acknowledge where consumers are, but also what they do at each moment of the day, from where they do it (e.g. home, office, car) and on what device (Martin and Todorov, 2010). Adema and Roehl (2010) believe that, in one way, events are in competition with technology because event participants are becoming more technologically savvy and their expectations of events are likely to increase. Thus, there is the constant need to increase event standards and experience in order to exceed the benefits of online virtual event attendance, also favoured by reduced attendance costs. The most novel digital platforms deviated 'from being disruptive to providing a utility, whether by introducing a new behaviour or meeting a perceived need' and thus, passing on the brand story to consumers by providing more significant and pertinent content (Martin and Todorov, 2010, 61).

Developing a beneficial lasting collaboration in the digital technology realm urges event stakeholders to think outside the box of current event experience practices towards sharing and managing data, knowledge and infrastructure (McCabe, Sharples and Foster, 2012). The event experience can be enhanced by focusing on attendees' needs and desires, which can be addressed by the latest smartphone apps (see Table 7.1). Yeoman (2013) views technology as a showcase where events participants can sample events before they happen, regardless of the shape and form the experience takes; there is always a story to share and tell.

Table 7.1 Major functions of mobile devices in events

Function	Description	Event Application
Informing	The capacity to source and access information while attending events (and travelling to/from the events)	Event information Timetables and schedules Reading QR codes Currency conversion
Contextualising	Not only the ability to communicate with other participants at events, but also having access to the internet in search for opportunities	Real-time interactive information and push notifications of context, location, status and safety
Personalising	Tailoring to targeted/customised groups of event participants according to personal interests and needs	Event planning and scheduling Facilitating networking Targeting
Socialising	Communication capabilities	Mobile phones Messaging and calling (e.g. WhatsApp, Viber, Facebook instant call) Personal blogs Social media (reviews, sharing)
Managing	Applying management tools and techniques to change behaviour after collecting data on event participants	Data mining Push notifications
Sharing	The ability to distribute up-to-date information in real time by personalising the list of recipients	Photos, videos Updates, news feed Experiences
Augmenting	Superposing the digital content with the real world and day-to-day life	Interpretation of information attained through event participation
Translating	Advanced capabilities that allow the translation of sound, text and image	Real-time translations at international events Multi-lingual applications
Purchasing	The capacity to source and book event services and products	Contractors/suppliers

Gamifying	The use of digital technology to enrich event experience by using game design elements	Gaining badges Treasure hunt games
Geofencing	The capacity of sending personalised messages to any predefined geographical area	Checking in with a geofence app Receiving deals in the geofence area
Queuing	The ability to queue virtually and then be at the front of the queue when arriving physically to the event	Connectivity to internet: laptop, smartphone, iPad
Reflecting	Capturing event experiences for the future Personal level: recreation and indulgence Professional level: networking	Photographs, videos Personal diaries, messages, posts, blogs

Source: Benckendorff, Sheldon and Fesenmaier, 2014, 158–159

In order to determine the economic impacts of an event/business, Morgan and Condliffe (2006, as cited in Bladen et al., 2012, 360) propose a methodology that assesses benefits from the construction to the operation phase by:

● defining the study area (country, state, region, city)
● identifying the industry (e.g. for events, the industry receiving direct economic impact is leisure and hospitality)
● collecting and/or estimating direct impact (e.g. employment, sales).

One practical application of this blended approach is the concept referred to as *geofencing* which is applied in events management mainly for marketing and security purposes. A geofence is a virtual perimeter around any defined geographic area (e.g. convention centre, exhibition, hotel, etc.) which delivers relevant customised location information to mobile subscribers, when entering or exiting the geofence, by mobile notifications and alerts. A fast-evolving technology, geofencing opens new opportunities for marketers and event organisers by targeting and customising the information sent and the category of attendees to whom the messages are delivered.

Tip box

Apple developed a new geofencing technology called iBeacon which sends out low-energy Bluetooth connectivity (known as Bluetooth 4.0) that can exchange information with both iOS and Android devices to create engagement opportunities at events (e.g. check in to an event by using a geofence application; information can be sent to attendees by venues, local businesses and merchants; receiving discounted prices in the geofence area). Being aware of this type of technology is useful for event organisers.

Geofencing is a dynamic and powerful marketing tool which gives investors, businesses and local event planners an increasingly innovative, more interactive, more targeted approach to engaging participants and helping them make the best decisions and purchase choices according to their individual needs.

Alongside the development of geofence technology for customised event information, event organisers are increasingly using techniques and technologies developed in the area of game design by employing them in an event context. *Gamification* is the use of game design principles and elements in a non-game context with the purpose of stirring desired user behaviours, positive experiences and motivations (Deterding, Björk, Nacke, Dixon and Lawley, 2013) in order to increase satisfaction and attendance. This concept can be applied to various businesses, including the events sector. According to Robson et al. (2015, 412), the definition of the term 'gamification' may be misleading as it does not represent the use of actual games or game theory in an organisational setting, as the name might suggest, but is instead 'the application of lessons from the gaming domain to change behaviours in non-game situation'. Day-to-day experiences, from your loyalty card being stamped when buying your morning coffee to earning Foursquare 'badges' or posting updates on Twitter, represent the application of gamification, mostly using mobile device technology (Benckendorff et al., 2014). Robson, Plangger, Kietzmann, McCarthy and Pitt, (2015) suggest that the increasing interest in gamification is the direct result of three recent developments. On the one hand, the growing development of the computer game industry led to more practical and theoretical research in game design and management which enabled the understanding of players' engagement, dynamics and emotions. Secondly, the thriving popularity of social media, web-based and mobile technologies changed the way in which 'digital natives' publish, share, play, network, buy and localise experiences (Prensky, 2001, cited in Tuten and Solomon, 2014, 2). A vast amount of valuable data on participants' feelings, opinions, behaviour and preferences is available to companies which help to produce substantial gamified employment and consumption experiences. Thirdly, companies are in a constant search to find new innovative ways to connect, influence and learn from customers/attendees and employees (Robson et al., 2015). Following on from these three points, it is important to remember that an event company's main purpose is to use gamification systems as tools for engaging customers and employees and not to lose their business focus and 'become the next great gaming company' (Ruhi, 2015, 14).

In the first instance, an event needs to be financially profitable in order to become sustainable. The advancement in technology and the rapid expansion of the internet has arguably enhanced the event experience and thus increased opportunity of participation and numbers. Events are increasingly seen as dedicated spaces where participants are either highly connected to technology and devices, or, in contrast, consciously choose to unplug and disconnect. Either way, there is something new to experience or share, and event organisers need to seize upon the emerging trends and the growing marketing potential.

7.3 Environmental

New innovative technologies have the ability to reduce the negative impact of events operations on the surrounding environment. There is a worldwide trend of making events more sustainable, and a stronger emphasis is placed on the delivery of green events (Bowdin et al., 2011). Events will need to 'go green' mainly because of increased sustainability demands placed on organisers by participants and sponsors, as well as new government regulations that are shaping the way event organisers operate. In the past, a practice such as recycling was used to position an event as a leader in the environmentally friendly movement, but nowadays this is seen as the minimal level of sustainable practice in most cases (Adema and Roehl, 2010). In order to determine the environmental impacts of an event, data should be collected using the following categories (Adapted from: Bladen et al., 2012, 365):

1 Before the event (planning process): environmental guidelines on event location
2 The event itself (construction process): the setup (facilities and infrastructure), recycling and waste management, the carbon footprint of the event
3 After the event: determine the impact of pollution made by participants through the use of facilities/accommodation/transport

There is an increasing demand from events participants to know the ecological footprint of an event, and the measures and considerations the organisers have taken in relation to minimising negative impact on the environment. Hence, an event organiser has to make informed, accurate and reliable decisions on resource allocation, waste reduction, the supply chain (ideally supplying locally) and measures to preserve the environment. Ali and Frew (2013, 4) stress the importance of the application of ICT to sustainable tourism development as the perfect tool and mechanism for professionals, discussing some of the latest technological advancements aimed at reducing negative environmental impacts. Table 7.2 illustrates the main global environmental challenges and proposes technologically enabled solutions to these challenges from an event perspective.

Nowadays, a growing number of event organisers are implementing policies to ensure that the events they plan and organise consider environmental issues as addressed in Table 7.2, especially in the context of growing pressure from governments and consumers. Innovative events are exploiting and engaging the latest technological advances to drive the event experience forward, so how do the social aspects of the experience connect to the latest technologies?

7.3 Social

The experience economy has been radically changed by the use of technology due to new discoveries and novel types of activities have emerged that can transform traditional experiences and develop avant-garde ones (Neuhofer, Buhalis and Ladkin, 2014). Yeoman (2013) strengthens the idea of increased digitalisation of leisure experiences by predicting a further increase in small, local live events due to a flourishing need for diversity and connection in local cultures as the experience economy matures into authenticity. McCabe et al. (2012) claim that due to the rapid development and availability of new technology, not all stakeholders are keeping up with the pace of emerging technologies and the benefits of their application to the visitor experience, and thus are missing valuable opportunities. To illustrate the point, take the example of a generic scenario of a 'day in the life' of a marathon runner and her accompanying family to the Experian Robin Hood Nottingham Marathon. The marathon day could be technologically instrumented by a professional research team, with the aim of showing the increase in technological display. Marathon competitors can wear technological devices (e.g. chips, GPS tracking devices) to collect race data and generate an online visualisation of

Table 7.2 Technological solutions and tools for the most pressing global challenges

Sustainable Principle	Global Challenge	Goal for Events	Technological Solutions and Tools
Zero Carbon	Climate change due to CO_2 emissions and greenhouse gases	All energy demand (buildings and infrastructure – lighting, IT) is supplied either on site from renewable sources or from an off-site source of renewable energy.	• Sustainable architecture and design solutions for conserving energy and using the natural landscape and light as much as possible. • Technological systems can be designed to power off the non-essential services when not in use and can be programmed for the duration of an event (e.g. heating, air conditioning, computers, and artificial light). *Tools*: a carbon calculator is used to determine the CO_2 emissions of the event and the result of the calculation is known as the carbon footprint of the event – in other words, the impact of the event based on the energy consumed. A low carbon footprint for the event brings long-term environmental, economic and social benefits.
Zero Waste	Unsustainable use of natural resources and disposable challenges	Reduce the exploitation of resources and avoid waste at events through conscious purchasing and supplying.	• Store documentation online and go paperless, provide facilities for online registration and check-in. • Avoid printing hand-outs and materials by using the latest events technology: apps for presenting and storing useful materials (e.g. Evernote, the digital storing container, a cross-platform support that collects all the information you select from desktop, web apps, mobile apps). • Invest in or work with contractors/suppliers that would provide recycled or reusable materials (e.g. dry-erase boards instead of flip chart paper, recycled paper). • Avoid packaging and the use of plastic. *Tools*: environment management information systems are computer based programmes that would gather, analyse and report integrated business information on environmental management such as waste tracking and waste monitoring.

Sustainable Transport	Climate change Noise and air pollution Congestion	To minimize CO2 emissions of all forms of transport at events by providing transport and infrastructure that reduces dependence on fossil fuel use.	• Select a connected location to the public transport network or one that is accessible by walking and provide all necessary information in terms of best routes and alternatives (e.g. car sharing options). • Select the latest options for transport in terms of: (1) low CO2 emissions such as electric, hybrid, hydrogen, biogas and biofuel; (2) soft CO2 emitters' transportation modes such as boat, walking, cycling. • Minimise air travel. *Tools*: Intelligent transport systems that have the ability to provide accurate information on traffic. Thus, event managers can better plan and advice in terms of transport choices and modes of transport, travelling times and congestions.
Sustainable Materials	Unbalanced resource exploitation and use of non-local products/services which reduces the profits and gains for local economies	Influence the supply chain by demanding the use of local, recycled and renewable materials up to the point where the entire chain is influenced and produces a net positive impact on the environment and local economy.	• Source locally and use materials and products that are made out of biodegradable materials or recycled content. *Tools*: computer simulations can be used to showcase the reproduction of a model where the entire supply chain adopted environmentally friendly solutions and to depict operational and long-term benefits on the environment.
Sustainable Food	Harming local ecosystems by the industrialisation of agriculture and food production	Plan and organise events that promote locally sourced, organic food in low-impact packaging, processing and disposal.	• Organising events that would offer locally sourced food, preferably organic and balanced healthy menus *Tools*: location-based services (LBS) provide participants with targeted information based on geographical location, which offers a wide range of sustainable choices (e.g. what food products to consume while participating at the event). LBS were developed alongside the development of localising a mobile phone through GPS technology (Greenwald et al., 2011).

(Continued)

Table 7.2 (*continued*)

Sustainable Principle	Global Challenge	Goal for Events	Technological Solutions and Tools
Sustainable Water	Water supplies are diminishing worldwide and the quality of water is deteriorating. Also, due to changes in climate, some regions are experiencing flooding, while others suffer from a scarcity of water	Achieve a positive impact on local water resources and supply.	• Determining the quality of tap water and using filters instead of bottled water. • Systems that would detect leaking sources of water. *Tools*: weather forecasting software is used to monitor changes in the climate and water. The information is useful for event organisers when bidding for events in order to make conscious decisions about development and risk management measures (e.g. the risk of flooding).
Natural Habitats and Wildlife	Degradation of habitats and loss of biodiversity due to unsustainable development and over-exploitation	Regenerate the environment and prevent biodiversity loss.	• Select the areas/locations for outdoor events in such a way that they have no negative impact on the local biodiversity. • Raise awareness of the degradation of local ecosystems. *Tools*: GIS (geographical information systems) are used to analyse and display large amounts of geographical data. Data from GIS can be used by events managers to evaluate proposals and decide on locations with minimal impact on the environment for planning, developing and organising events.

Culture and Heritage	Culture Heritage is being affected worldwide by two major factors: climate change due to extreme weather conditions and globalisation that leads to the loss of local identity	Protect and build on local cultural heritage and diversity. • Where possible in the events organised, integrate local culture heritage and foster regional identity. • Optional trips can be organised at the local heritage sites. *Tools:* virtual events at cultural and heritage sites for those fragile places that have exceeded their carrying capacity. An online visual and interactive event can make participants experience a heritage site without actually being physically present at the destination. In addition, augmented reality (AR) is regarded as a viable technology for cultural and heritage sites due to the development of both AR smartphone apps such as Time Traveler and smart glasses such as Past View, which represent 'a realistic and practical response to the trend of wearables' (Tscheu and Buhalis, 2016, 609).
Equity and Fair Trade	Local resources are not sufficiently maximised thus impacting on the local economic development	Ensure that the event has positive economic links with the wider local and global community. • Promote local production and/ or fair trade products at your event. • Collaborate with local organisations and charities (e.g. excess food can be donated to local charities). • Try to leave a positive environmental legacy. *Tools:* gamification – can be used to connect participants with the local community and encourage sustainable behaviours.
Health and Happiness	The concepts of wellbeing and happiness are questioned by development, increased wealth and longer life expectancy	Increase health and wellbeing of participants, employees, the local community and other stakeholders. • Time away from technology by providing dedicated spaces and resources for practising relaxation (e.g. mindfulness, yoga, stretching). • Promote healthy activities (e.g. cycling, rowing, walking). *Tools:* LBS (offering a wide range of location and activity choices) and gamification (engage participants).

Source: adapted from Ali and Frew, 2013, 66, and Jones, 2010, 235, and WWF Report on Organising a Green Event (2016, online)

the competition which can later be augmented, personalised and managed by the participation and experience of the entire family (e.g. video clip editing of the day, reviews, badges, race timings and biometric data) (McCabe et al., 2012, 39). This demonstrates the extent to which technology can be used at events.

Another good example of how technology can enhance event experience is the use of augmented reality (AR) applications which supplement reality with digital information. Augmented reality is a technology relatively new to the events sector that merges the virtual and real worlds by providing essential support in all planning processes (Garau, 2014).

Tip box

Event organisers need to be aware of the use of tools and apps for mobile devices (e.g. smartphones, tablets, wearables) which can use augmented reality to create a 'new reality' of our surrounding world; a reality that is digitally enhanced.

Yeoman (2013) exemplifies the entertaining event experience by providing the case of Headphone Music Festival organised in Tokyo 2012. This collaboration between Sony and Naked Communications was a festival aimed at promoting a new range of smartphone-compatible headphones that work by scanning the AR codes on the festival posters. The 3D-augmented reality technology called 'SmartAR' was developed by working with popular local rock groups, and videos could be accessed by simply spotting the poster and scanning the AR code. The implementation of AR represents an opportunity for increasing competiveness (Tscheu and Buhalis, 2016), but it is not widely developed and implemented in the events sector compared to other industries. In contrast, event organisers are taking full advantage of the connectivity infrastructure and the use of smartphone devices by event participants to provide business intelligence such as virtual queuing (VQ) for increased satisfaction in the event experience. Queuing at events may cause dissatisfaction and therefore virtual queuing systems have been implemented which enable event goers to secure a place in a virtual queue; they are then notified through the VQ mobile app when they need to be physically present (e.g. Qsmart). Benckendorff et al. (2014) argue that VQ systems not only reduce the actual waiting time, but can also cut down on perceived waiting time as lack of information and boredom can often make waiting times feel longer than they actually are.

The development of technology and the proliferation of wifi connectivity allow event participants to connect to devices and apps that enhance their experience, but there is a debate about the willingness to adopt available services because of certain constraints and challenges (Tanti and Buhalis, 2016). Venkatesh et al. (2003) developed a unified theory of acceptance and use of technology (UTAUT) based on four main constructs (performance expectancy, effort expectancy, social influence and facilitating conditions), which was later revised and supplemented with three new constructs (hedonic motivation, price value and habit) (Ventakesh, Thong and Xu, 2012):

● Performance expectancy (mitigated by age and gender): the degree to which a person believes that the use of technology will help him/her obtain gains in job performance (e.g. the use of a professional social network to gain insights about influential people in your area/field)

- Effort expectancy (influenced by age, gender, and experience): the degree of ease associated with the use of technology. The effort expectancy is more obvious in the early stages of using a new technology when there are certain challenges to overcome. The effort expectancy construct is formed by three aspects:
  - Perceived ease of use: the extent to which a person regards a targeted technology to be free of effort
  - Complexity: the extent to which a technology is perceived as quite complicated to understand and use
  - Ease of use: the extent to which an innovation is regarded as being complicated to use.
- Social influence (influenced by age, gender, and experience): the degree to which a person perceives the use of technology to be important for their social network (e.g. family, friends, peers – if a social network is used by work colleagues, an individual part of that group would be more likely to join). Studies show that women tend to be more sensitive to other people's opinions and thus, find social influence to be more pertinent when forming an intention to use a new technology (Venkatesh et al., 2003)
- Facilitating conditions (mitigated by age and experience): the extent to which a person considers that an organisational and technical structure is in place to support a technology (e.g. an individual would be more likely to take part in a dedicated professional social network if one colleague would help and assist with the use at the beginning)
- Hedonic motivations: the thrill, fun and enjoyment received from using technology, thus being an indicator of consumers' manner and intention to use technology (e.g. if a dedicated event professional social network is entertaining to use, participants are more likely to use it)
- Price value: has a positive impact on consumers' intent when the benefits of using the technology outrank the monetary costs (e.g. if an dedicated social network would offer clear benefits for event participants and joining and monthly membership would be offered at a promotional cost or even for free, participants would be more inclined to use it)
- Experience and habit: have two main distinct differences (1) experience is crucial in the formation of habit, but not enough; as (2) with the passing of time, experience can lead to the development of habit levels and patterns that are reliant on degree of interaction and familiarity that is refined with a target technology (e.g. if event participants use social networks and mobile apps in their daily lives on a regular basis, they would use them in an event setting, their level of habit being dependent on their daily use of a technology).

With the developments in digital technologies, today's society is a truly global network in which coordination and cooperation across nations is easily facilitated by the use of the internet as a powerful platform. Three main areas that aim at global partnerships for solving stringent economic, environmental and social problems have been identified – governance of the internet, creating a global digital market, and providing global public goods that promote sustainable development and poverty reduction (World Bank, 2016, 36).

Study activity

In small groups, discuss the three pillars of the Brazil 2016 Olympic Games Sustainability Management Plan (SMP) (see Further reading section) and answer the following questions:

1 Does the SMP address all sustainable principles covered previously in the chapter?
2 What are the technological advancements that can be employed for sustainable completion of each of the SMP's objectives?
3 Who are the parties that would benefit the most if all pillars are addressed?

7.4 Conclusion

The focus of the chapter evolved around the concept of sustainability applied in an event context and augmented by the latest developments in technology. By following the well-established notion of economic, environmental and social sustainability, the most pressing global challenges that affect the sector and the innovative technical solutions and tools that can be adapted for events have been discussed. It is important to understand the logic behind the long prioritisation of economic performance in the sector, but with the rapid development of technology and increased event expectations, the importance of the environmental and social pillars is prevailing. Event organisers need to ensure not only that their events are financially sustainable, but also that they are meeting the increased environmental, social and technological needs of their stakeholders.

Case study 7: Polar bears in Churchill, Canada (How technology can be employed for sustainable small events in a tourism context)

Dr Jeremy Pearce, University of Lincoln

Introduction

Climate change and the plight of the polar bear (*Ursus maritimus*) are often argued to be interrelated. This issue is controversial and complex and accompanied by many project challenges. This case study showcases the efforts of one cross-sector partnership between a prominent commercial enterprise operating in Churchill Canada, Frontiers North Adventures (FNA) and the premier polar bear NGO, Polar Bears International (PBI). It explores how this partnership works to use technology as a tool to educate people about polar bears and the challenges they face, particularly in the remote and often hostile conditions of the subarctic.

FNA is a family business based in Churchill, Canada. It has been operating for three decades delivering extraordinary wildlife adventure events for tourists. The business specialises in experiential travel, culture, wildlife and adventure tourism and events (FNA, 2016). The company has a strong reputation as a leading polar bear tourism provider and is known for its corporate responsibility platform and operating framework (Pearce, 2016). Questions of sustainability apply beyond ecological and environmental considerations. For FNA to discontinue its business creates sustainability questions for its owners, employees and the broader community (Stewart and Draper, 2007). The sustainability of polar bears is inextricably linked to both the FNA business and the PBI organisation as well as the local community. Herein lies one of the sustainability challenges in the context of this cross-sector partnership. PBI has a mission to 'conserve polar bears and the sea ice they depend on. [They] also work to inspire people to care about the Arctic and its connection to our global climate' (PBI, 2016b). Both FNA and PBI have an interest in happy, healthy polar bears. Without polar bears, FNA cannot promote the adventure tours and events that showcase polar bears in their natural habitat, and without polar bears PBI has no mandate to exist. The FNA/PBI partnership is strong and has existed for many years (Pearce, 2016). There are many facets to this partnership and this case study concentrates on their use of technology to enable education about polar bears and the circumpolar Arctic.

Technology and sustainability

Part of this partnership is the FNA sponsorship of PBI, which comprises a number of elements including, the supply of 'Buggy One' for PBI to use as a roving television studio on the tundra. This allows PBI to beam television footage from the subarctic tundra around the world and allow audiences from far and wide (many of whom will never have the opportunity to make the trek north) to see polar bears in their natural habitat live on camera. PBI hosts leading polar bear and polar scientists on Buggy One. This enables global communication of the latest research on polar bear conservation to be shared via a unique and engaging format.

The use of 'Buggy One' for television broadcasting is one part of the PBI Tundra Connections™ program. This program occurs in the fall and spring. The fall season entails three to four weeks of live webcasts, videoconferences and Google Hangouts from the tundra near Churchill Canada (PBI, 2014b, 1). A number of collaborations ensure the connections reach as many people as possible. The partners include: AAC network, Discovery Educator Network, TakingITGlobal, the Centre for Global Education and explore.org. These connections are not just one-way. Participants are able to send their questions to the experts on the panel on Buggy One and have them answered as part of a two-way education process (PBI, 2014b, 5).

A second program called Live Cam Outreach is another example of how PBI and FNA work together to use technology to reach a wider audience to enable

(Continued)

147

Case study 7 (*continued*)

education about polar bears and the Arctic. In the Live Cam Outreach program a number of collaborations are used by PBI to host fixed live cams that allow real-time viewing of polar bears (and beluga whales). Again, explore.org is a key partner in this program along with Parks Canada, which hosts one cam in Wapusk National Park. Churchill Northern Studies Centre hosts one cam and FNA hosts the majority of the cams at three separate locations: Lodge South, Lodge North and Buggy One.

Program impact 2014

Tundra connections

- PBI (2014b, 4–5) reached viewers from each of the 50 states of the USA and from 109 countries:

  - Seventy-five per cent of viewers are from the USA and 11 per cent are from Canada.
  - Eighty-seven per cent of registered viewers are teachers/educators.

(See also Table 7.3.)

Impact evaluation survey responses

The following information is sourced from PBI (2014b, 6):

- Of respondents 95.7 per cent stated they would recommend this program to a friend or colleague.
- Of respondents 92.9 per cent strongly agreed or agreed that they learned something brand new about climate change and/or polar bears.
- Of respondents 91.43 per cent strongly agreed or agreed that the program enhances what they are already doing to act against climate change.
- Of respondents 95.65 per cent strongly agreed or agreed that the program enhances what they are already doing to create awareness.
- Of respondents 81.16 per cent strongly agreed or agreed that they learned something brand new about how to take action.

Table 7.3 Tundra connections® viewing figures

Date	Total Views	Unique Views	Live Viewer Hours	Recorded Viewer Hours
10/1/2014	47,046	22,071	7094.1	938.2
11/1/2014	374,394	143,333	48308.69	5838.3
Totals	**421,440**	**165,404**	**55,402.79**	**6776.5**

Source: PBI, 2014a, 5

Live cam outreach

The following information is sourced from PBI (2014a, 4):

- Over 55,000 live viewer hours
- Over 421,000 total views.

Viewers by country/state

Including Canada and the US, 169 countries tuned in to watch the Polar Bear Cams (PBI, 2014a, 4):

1 USA: 288,888
2 Canada: 59,149
3 Great Britain: 13,226
4 Germany: 5745
5 Netherlands: 4555
6 Denmark: 4249.

Program impact 2015

Tundra connections

The fall 2015 program received over 400,000 views (PBI, 2016a, 6).

Viewers by country/state:

- Viewers from 54 countries, information sourced from PBI (2016a, 6)
  - United States: 73.5 per cent of all registrants tuned in from the US (just under 2014 at 75 per cent).
  - Texas, California, North Carolina, Florida, and Pennsylvania had the most viewers.
  - Canada: 9.6 per cent of all registrants came from Canada, the same as in 2014.
  - Fifty-two other countries make up the other 20 per cent of views including the UK, Australia, Germany, South Korea, and Switzerland, Luxembourg, Romania, Thailand, and Ukraine.

Impact evaluation survey responses

The following information is sourced from PBI (2016a, 10):

- Of respondents 99.1 per cent of respondents stated they would recommend this program to a friend or colleague.
- Ninety per cent of people learned something brand new about climate change or polar bears.

(Continued)

Case study 7 (*continued*)

Some quotes from participants

I think the kids really enjoyed hearing the questions that other kids from around the world had and the realization that they could do the same thing.

The difference between polar bears and brown bears and how they differ and have adapted differently . . .

The level of interaction between the participants and the quality of the moderation made the broadcast very engaging.

My group really enjoyed these broadcasts since we do not get to do field trips so these are like virtual field trips for them. This was by far the best webcast in which my students have participated. They were all engaged and learned a lot. They could relate the topics to their daily lives, which is hard to do living in remote Alaska Bush communities.

PBI (2016a, 11)

Conclusion

The programs show how effective technology is as a means for both PBI and FNA to get their message across to a broad and diverse global audience. It also

Figure 7.2 Polar bears sparring in front of Buggy One

Source: © Frontiers North Adventures

shows how technology can bridge the obstacles of time and distance to allow for remote locations to speak to one another and learn through connecting. The programs show the educational benefits for participants and the value of interacting in relation to better understanding of the plight of polar bears and the future of the Arctic.

Without the use of technology these programs would not exist and it is difficult to imagine how this type of education would otherwise take place. Given the remote and often hostile nature of the Arctic environment the inherent difficulties of ensuring both mechanical (e.g. Buggy One) and technical reliability are a constant issue that PBI and FNA need to deal with to keep the programs running. This takes dedication, ingenuity and teamwork combined with a passion for solving problems and a commitment to their collective purpose.

Thank you to Dr Jeremy Pearce for writing this case study.

Evaluative student questions

1   How important do you think the use of technological advancements is in remote areas such as the Arctic?
2   What are the benefits and drawbacks of the global live connection between participants who are sending their questions to the panel experts on Buggy One?
3   Please check the data provided in the case study and discuss the development of the Live Cam Outreach programme from 2014 to 2015. How do you see the programme developing in the future?

Further reading

Ali, A. and Frew, A.J. (2013) *Information and communications technologies for sustainable tourism*. Abingdon: Routledge.
Benckendorff, P, Sheldon, P. and Fesenmaier, D. (2014) *Tourism information technology*. 2nd edition. London: CABI Publications.
Dredge, D. and Whitford, M. (2010). Policy for sustainable and responsible festivals and events: institutionalisation of a new paradigm – a response. *Journal of Policy Research in Tourism, Leisure and Events*, 2(1) 1–13.
Rio 2016™ (2013) Sustainability Management the Rio 2016™ Olympic and Paralympic Games Report, 85-87, Available from: http://www.rio2016.com/en/transparency/documents [Accessed 24 March 2016].

References

Adema, K.L. and Roehl, W.S. (2010) Environmental scanning the future of event design. *International Journal of Hospitality Management*, 29(2) 199–207.

Ali, A. and Frew, A.J. (2013) *Information and communications technologies for sustainable tourism*. Abingdon: Routledge.

Benckendorff, P, Sheldon, P. and Fesenmaier, D. (2014) *Tourism information technology*. 2nd edition. London: CABI Publications.

Bladen, C., Kennell, J., Abson, E. and Wilde, N. (2012) *Events management: an introduction*. Abingdon: Routledge.

Bowdin, G., Allen, J., O'Toole, W., Harris, R. and McDonnell, I. (2011) *Events management*. 3rd edition. London: Butterworth-Heinemann.

Ciuchete, G. and Kane, K. (in press) Social enterprise ecosystems – a case study of the Danube Delta region of Romania. In: Sheldon, P., Daniele, R. and Pollock, A. (eds), *Social Entrepreneurship in Tourism*. New York: Springer.

Deterding, S., Björk, S. L., Nacke, L. E., Dixon, D. and Lawley, E. (2013) Designing gamification: creating gameful and playful experiences. In: *CHI '13 Extended Abstracts on Human Factors in Computing Systems*: 3263–3266. New York: ACM Press.

Dredge, D. and Whitford, M. (2010) Policy for sustainable and responsible festivals and events: institutionalisation of a new paradigm – a response. *Journal of Policy Research in Tourism, Leisure and Events*, 2(1) 1–13.

Elkington, J. 1997 *Cannibals with forks: the triple bottom line of twenty-first century business*. Oxford: Capstone.

Frontiers North Adventures (FNA) (2016) *Various website pages*. Available from: http://www.frontiersnorth.com/ [Accessed 14 January 2016].

Garau, C. (2014) From territory to smartphone: smart fruition of cultural heritage for dynamic tourism development. *Planning Practice and Research*, 29(3) 238–255.

Getz, D. (2005) *Event Management and event tourism*. New York: Cognizant Communication.

Getz, D. (2009) Policy for sustainable and responsible festivals and events: institutionalization of a new paradigm. *Journal of Policy Research in Tourism, Leisure and Events* 1(1) 61–78.

Greenwald, A., Hampel, G., Phadke, C. and Poosala, V. (2011) An economically viable solution to geofencing for mass-market applications. *Bell Labs Technical Journal*, 16(2) 21–38.

Holmes, K., Hughes, M., Mair, J. and Carlsen, J. (2015) *Events and sustainability*. Abingdon: Routledge.

Jones, M. (2010) *Sustainable event management*. London: Earthscan.

McCabe, S., Sharples, M. and Foster, C. (2012) Stakeholder engagement in the design of scenarios of technology-enhanced tourism services. *Tourism Management Perspectives*, 4(0) 36–44.

Martin, K. and Todorov, I. (2010) How will digital platforms be harnessed in 2010, and how will they change the way people interact with brands? *Journal of Interactive Advertising*, 10(2) 61–66.

Morgan, A. and Condliffe, S. (2006) Measuring the economic impacts of convention centers and event tourism: a discussion of the key issues. *Journal of Convention & Event Tourism*, 8(4) 81–100.

Neuhofer, B., Buhalis D. and Ladkin, A. (2014) A typology of technology-enhanced tourism experiences. *International Journal of Tourism Research*, 16(4) 340–350.

Pearce, J. (2016) Polar bears, climate change and cross-sector partnerships: a governance case study. *Fifth International Polar Tourism Research Network Conference*, Raufarhöfn, 29 August – 2 September, NE Iceland.

Polar Bears International (PBI) (2014a) *Live Cam Outreach Overview 2014*, Unpublished paper.

Polar Bears International (PBI) (2014b) *Tundra Connections Program Overview 2014*, Unpublished paper.

Polar Bears International (PBI) (2016a) *Tundra Connections Program Overview 2015*, Unpublished paper.

Polar Bears International (PBI) (2016b) Home page. Available from: http://www.polar-bearsinternational.org/ [Accessed 15 January 2016].

Prensky, M. (2001) Digital natives, digital immigrants. *On the Horizon*, 9(5) 1–6.

Rio 2016™ (2013) Sustainability Management of the Rio 2016™ Olympic and Paralympic Games Report, 85–87, Available from: http://www.rio2016.com/en/transparency/documents [Accessed 24 March 2016].

Robson, K., Plangger, K., Kietzmann, J.H., McCarthy, I. and Pitt, L. (2015) Is it all a game? understanding the principles of gamification, *Business Horizons* 58(4) 411–420.

Ruhi, U. (2015) Level up your strategy: towards a descriptive framework for meaningful enterprise gamification. *Technology Innovation Management Review* 5(8) 5–16.

Stewart, E.J. and Draper, D. (2007) A collaborative approach to understanding local stakeholder perceptions of tourism in Churchill, Manitoba (Canada). *Polar Geography*, 30(1–2) 7–35.

Tanti, A., and Buhalis, D. (2016) Connectivity and the consequences of being (dis) connected. In: Inversini, A. and Schegg, R. (eds), *Information and Communication Technologies in Tourism*, Proceedings of the International Conference in Bilbao, Spain. New York: Springer, 31–44.

Tscheu, F. and Buhalis, D. (2016) Augmented reality at cultural heritage sites. In: Inversini, A. and Schegg, R. (eds), *Information and Communication Technologies in Tourism*, Proceedings of the International Conference in Bilbao, Spain. New York: Springer, 607–619.

Tuten, T. and Solomon, M. (2014) *Social media marketing*. Harlow: Pearson Educational Limited.

Venkatesh, V., Morris, M.G., Davis, G.B. and Davis, F.D. (2003) User acceptance of information technology: toward a unified view. *MIS Quarterly* 27(3) 425–478.

Venkatesh, V., Thong, J.Y. and Xu, X. (2012) Consumer acceptance and use of information technology: extending the unified theory of acceptance and use of technology. *MIS Quarterly* 36(1) 157–178.

Yeoman, I. (2013) A futurist's thoughts on consumer trends shaping future festivals and events. *International Journal of Event and Festival Management*, 4(3) 249–260.

World Bank (2016) *World development report 2016: digital dividends*. http://www-wds.worldbank.org/external/default/WDSContentServer/WDSP/IB/2016/01/13/090224b08405ea05/2_0/Rendered/PDF/World0developm0000digital0dividends.pdf [Accessed on 25 March 2016].

World Wildlife Fund (WWF) (2016) *Organising a green event*. Available from: http://wwf.panda.org/how_you_can_help/live_green/at_the_office/green_events/ [Accessed 24 March 2016].

Chapter 8

Event management law and legislation

8.1 Introduction

Being aware of the legal environment which surrounds an event is of significant importance to any events company, the general public and associated stakeholders. It should be a key priority for event managers to maintain a good working knowledge of the 'ever-changing legal landscapes' (Bladen et al., 2012, 81). The legal environment is different in each country and therefore it is crucial for the event organisation to research their host's culture and legislation. This chapter will focus on the law of England and Wales as a grounding in law for event managers. For the most part, events are enjoyable, successful and valuable to the local, regional, national and potentially international stage. The effective project management of events is of key importance to keep disruption and crisis at bay, but sometimes events do go wrong and it is crucial to understand what the legal consequences and guidelines are in relation to both successful and failed events. An understanding of the legal environment is essential 'To protect your legal interests, to abide by ethical practices, to ensure the safety and security of your event stakeholders, and to protect your financial investment' (Goldblatt, 2008, 379).

Law and legislation can rarely be understood in 'black and white' terms and it can be difficult to work out how it can be applied across varied contexts. The law will always be open to interpretation, debate and challenge by legal experts, and indeed this is how law and legislation evolve. This chapter should therefore be considered with that in mind, and with the guidance to any event organiser that they should undertake their own independent legal advice. Examples contained within this chapter are generalised and simplified in order to illustrate possible consequences and issues that may arise within the events setting. Even past case results should not be seen as a guarantee that the same circumstances, if they happened again, would produce the same result.

It is said that there are three types of reason for complying with a country's legal system. Firstly, the *moral* reason: in most societies it is not acceptable for someone to organise an event and to cause harm without there being some recourse to compensation or punishment for that individual or organisation. The second reason may be less obvious, but perhaps just as much of an incentive: the *financial* reason. If an events company complies with a country's legislation, and is known to do so and provides evidence they are doing so, it is likely to be able to negotiate lower insurance premiums. Furthermore, the company will gain a positive reputation and be more likely to be able to work with quality and competent contractors/suppliers who will want to engage with the event organisation. Compliance with legislation, such as carrying out risk assessments, can also be an appropriate measure to ensure the events company has the right staffing levels and resources. Lastly, the *legal* reason: as an event organiser, failure to comply with the law and legal principles may lead to imprisonment or financial sacrifice, and therefore understanding legislation and how to ensure compliance with the relevant legal principles is extremely important. The following sections will discuss these aspects in more detail.

8.1.1 The moral reason

On moral grounds, events should be professional and responsible and where possible protect those that attend, work at and are connected to the event. An organisation has a *duty of care* to those involved in the event to take all reasonable measures to protect them from harm. 'For event managers, duty of care means taking actions that will prevent any foreseeable risks of injury to the people who are directly affected by, or involved in, the event' (Bowdin et al., 2011, 576–567).

Duty of care is a key term to recognise when learning about the legal environment and it comes under the jurisdiction of tort law, where a tort links to a duty or breach of that duty. Injuries and even fatalities that may result from an event incident may negatively impact on the individual and associated family members for ever. As an event organiser, it is important to ensure that every measure is taken to protect and create a safe and pleasant event environment. The impact of not providing a safe event site could result in a case being brought against the event organiser in court. This may have both psychological and financial impacts upon the events company in terms of the stress and concern involved in the situation and the monetary cost of defending the matter in court. In addition, the connected reputational damage to the event and event organisation will impact on the future running of the event.

In 1988, at Donington Park, England two people died at the music event Monsters of Rock. Their deaths were the result of asphyxiation when they fell into the muddy ground under the weight of a crowd crush at the front of the stage (Upton, 1995). As a result of the enquiry into this incident, the *Pop Guide* was published, the first edition of a document that came to be known as the *Purple Guide*, which gave industry guidance on the management of a safe event. This guide (at the time of writing) is in its third edition, and was re-issued by the Event Industry Forum in 2014. The Monsters of Rock event did not take place in 1989 but did re-establish itself in 1990 and is now titled Download Festival.

8.1.2 The financial reason

The financial rationale for law abidance is thought to be less obvious. It is mythical to think that it costs the event organiser more money to organise and host a safe event. If an event is well planned, and a risk assessment is used to ascertain what the issues are, this can focus where action needs to be taken. This in turn can ensure that action is not taken unnecessarily, i.e. if the risk assessment shows that the event is unlikely to attract disorder, then this can minimise the number and type of stewards needed. In identifying where action needs to be taken, the events team can identify where money needs to be spent, and at what level. It can also help to identify if a solution of lower cost is as effective as the high-cost solution.

Typically, a well-planned event, which manages risk, will be charged a lower premium for its insurance cover. Furthermore, some event insurance brokers also offer discounts to organisers who can demonstrate a high level of planning and risk management. It can be seen therefore that an investment in the planning and risk management of the event can lead to monetary savings further down the line. This monetary saving does not only apply to the whole event insurance, but also to the different parts of the event, and the different contractors/suppliers who comply with and adhere to industry standards.

8.1.3 The legal reason

In general, there are two types of law that can be said to be relevant to events, namely civil law and criminal law, both of which will be expanded upon in the next sections. Perhaps the most relevant or often seen type of civil law that the organiser is likely to encounter is generally connected to negligence (i.e. the suing of someone to claim recompense or damages for some injury or damage, alleged to be caused by the negligence of another). In most societies it is possible to purchase insurance to cover legal action being taken against the person/organisation in the civil court. The cost of this insurance will depend on what cover is required, as well as the maximum amount of claim to be covered. In contrast, criminal law is usually written legislation put in place by the country or state. If the legislation is not complied with, the most likely scenario is that the person or organisation breaking the law will be punished. This can mean a prison sentence, and it is not possible to insure against this.

Bladen et al. (2012) explain that it is necessary to understand who owns the event. This is only a small part of the legal responsibilities and obligations, however, and does not necessarily need to be resolved before a civil case can commence. In the criminal law part of this chapter, the Occupiers' Liability Act 1957 and Occupiers' Liability Act 1984 will be considered alongside their impact on events, with regard to land owners, event owners and those contracted to deliver an event.

8.2 Civil law

Civil law is generally seen as legislation that allows one member of society to take a case against another member to obtain redress. Using England and Wales as an example, one of the most common situations found in the event industry is that in order to successfully sue someone for loss or injury it is necessary to show that they were negligent. This is commonly broken down into three parts: a situation where a duty of care is owed to someone (*plaintiff/claimant*), that duty of care is breached, and as a result of that breach there is a resultant loss or injury.

A useful example of negligence is an event visitor who trips over cables trailing across the public arena and as a result of this breaks their ankle. It can be expected that as the person was a visitor to the event, the event organisation owed them a duty of care to keep them as safe as reasonably possible. It was the event organisation's trailing cable that caused the trip and in turn resulted in a broken ankle. The fact that all three aspects of negligence are covered means that the visitor may sue the event organisation for recompense for the injury, pain, loss of earnings, inconvenience, etc. The visitor will no doubt allege that the event manager or organisation was negligent, and that it was as a result of this negligence that they received their injury.

In a large number of cases the injured party will sue not only the event organiser, but also the land/venue owner and the owner of the trailing cable (e.g. the contractor/supplier who laid the cable, or the contractor/supplier who used the cable at the event). This is logical and a very common tactic employed by legal representatives. For example, if the event visitor sues the event organiser, they may well be able to defend themselves, stating that it was not their fault, but the fault of the land/venue owner or the contractor/supplier. If the visitor, therefore, sues them all, it will be difficult to defend and one of them will be the responsible party. As stated previously in this chapter, no legislation is 'black and white', and undoubtedly in this example the defendants will suggest contributory negligence. Contributory negligence means that the defendant may have contributed to their own injury; for example, this visitor may have been wearing wholly inappropriate or inadequate footwear for the event.

Study activity

During an outdoor music festival an event attendee becomes so excited hearing her favourite song that she decides to crowd surf to the front of the crowd. As the other event attendees present are not used to dealing with crowd surfers, she falls through the crowd and onto the ground, and receives an injury, dislocating her shoulder. Discuss, with reasons, whether the three ingredients of negligence: duty owed, breach of duty and a resultant injury are present in this incident. What needs to be considered when reviewing this case?

Taking into consideration the previous discussions, it is now worth considering some other simple examples to ascertain whether the *negligence test* is met. The second example is this; a man is visiting an event, and whilst in attendance witnesses another person being run over by a vehicle moving on the event site. The man suffers a heart attack after seeing the incident. Thirdly, a child is visiting an event and trips over some temporary flooring that has been installed. The child, however, is uninjured. Fourthly, a visitor to the event is walking through the event site when they are knocked over by a street performer whom the event organiser has booked to perform. The visitor damages their knee as a result of being knocked over. In all of the examples provided the involved person is a visitor to the event so it is reasonable to state that a duty of care is owed to them, therefore meeting the first point of negligence on the test.

In the second example, it is not immediately clear as to whether that duty of care is breached; the first piece of extra investigation that would be required is the need for more details into matters such as the health of the man prior to his visiting the event. In the third example, it is straightforward to conclude that the duty of care is breached, as the child has tripped over the temporary flooring. No loss or injury, however, has occurred as a result because the child is uninjured. In the fourth example, it can be concluded that the duty of care was breached as the street performer was engaged by the event organiser to perform at the event, and they have knocked over a visitor. There has also been an injury as a result of the breach of duty of care; the visitor has damaged their knee.

Example four provides an interesting case because there is the prospect of more than one event stakeholder being involved in the suing process. The event organiser, or their insurer, will no doubt be concerned to ascertain whether the street performer was working in the area they had been given permission to operate in, whether the area in use was in the state the organiser had anticipated to allow the street performer to perform, and whether the performer complied with their instructions/contract to perform. For the visitor (or their legal adviser), taking the action to gain recompense for their personal injury or their associated losses, they will want to cover all angles, and will most likely sue both the organiser and the street performer, to ensure someone is 'held responsible'. They may also consider where the most recompense can be obtained: who has more money, the organiser or the street performer? More information about the complexities of negligence and responsibility will be discussed in the end of chapter case study on *Dreamspace*.

In most, if not all, instances where the plaintiff/claimant sues an event organisation or contractor/supplier, there will be defences available to the defendant. The more difficult aspect may be for the defendant to 'prove' their defence. For example, in the case of the visitor tripping over some trailing cables and damaging their ankle, the event organisation may well state that they had covered all trailing cables with appropriate tunnelling or had dug them into the ground. They may add that they were conscious of this being a hazard at their event, and had taken steps to ensure that the cabling was safe. In order for them to 'prove' that this was the case, they are likely to need to show that this formed part of their event risk assessment and that there was regular monitoring of the cabling to ensure it was safe to walk over, and that this monitoring was recorded to show that it had indeed taken place.

Of course event organisations would be advised to have insurance in place to try to offset any damages they may receive as a result of court cases. Raj et al. (2009) explain employer's liability insurance is compulsory for all businesses with employees as per the Employer's Liability Compulsory Insurance Act 1969. Public liability insurance is different from this as it is a voluntary insurance which if bought covers claims brought to the event's organisation from the general public. Insurance is extremely important to have within the events environment (Bladen et al., 2012) and being covered this way demonstrates that the event's organisation is professional and responsible.

8.2.1 Contracts for events

Another consideration for civil law is that of contract law. According to Raj et al. (2009, 46) contracts form 'legally binding agreements'. Figure 8.1 highlights the five different aspects which come together to build an event contract.

Contracts for events arguably come in several types. The singular contract is for one-off events only. An example of this might be a charity ball. There are also contracts available for more than one event to be held at many locations; for example, a music concert forming part of a country/continent/world tour. A third type of contract situation may relate to the use of one location for many different events, perhaps a purpose-built venue which may be hired out to different organisers for different styles of event. In purpose-built venues/sites, it is common for the site/venue owner to have long-term contracts with a number of providers which they then use to carry out core contracting activities (e.g. lighting, sanitary provision, electrical provision, perhaps even traffic management).

Figure 8.1 The five aspects of constructing a contract

Source: Bowdin et al., 2011, 574

The terms and conditions of any contract must be clear and easily understood to avoid conflict and misunderstanding. It is worth noting that different companies may require a contract to be determined under a particular country's legislation (e.g. an American company operating in the United Kingdom may have their contract determined by US legislation). It must also be remembered that a contract can be both written and verbal, but it is important for an event organisation to be able to evidence any claims made with documentation, and so written contracts may be more appropriate. A breach of contract is a situation in which one of the parties involved in the contractual agreement has not delivered on the agreed terms of service outlined in the contract. This may result in legal action and a bid for compensation. Contracts, however, will include clauses that are viewed by Bladen et al. (2012, 86) as 'fixed' and add certain stipulations and caveats to which the involved parties must adhere. According to Bladen et al. (2012), examples of clauses revolve around cancellation, force majeure (unpredictable circumstances such as natural disasters and terrorism), billing, insurance and indemnification, for example protection against losses. Clauses within contracts will be a consideration when discussing contract breaches.

In the events world, clauses are often referred to as 'riders', especially when they are applied to the requirements of an artist or band. Some artists and bands use 'riders' for a different, but equally valid, purpose. Van Halen, an internationally known band popular in the 1980s had a 'rider' written into their contract which required them to have M&Ms (chocolate confectionery) in their dressing rooms and relaxation areas (Ganz, 2012). The additional part of the rider was that the brown ones should have all been removed. David Lee Roth, their lead singer explained that this gave them a simple, but quite reliable way of checking whether the venue had taken note of the band's technical specification written into the contract (Ganz, 2012). The logic was that if there were brown M&Ms in the bowl then the contract had not been read fully and carefully by the venue, and that it was therefore necessary to check all of the technical specifications for the gig. If there were no brown M&Ms provided, then it gave an indication that the contract had been read and adhered to by the venue.

8.3 Criminal law

The second type of law featured in this chapter is the criminal law. The primary difference between criminal and civil law is that it is not possible to insure against a criminal prosecution, and that the main purpose of criminal law is to punish – in the worst-case scenario, this can be a prison sentence. This chapter deals primarily with legislation relating to England and Wales, but it is extremely likely that other countries will have parallel or associated legislation. Criminal legislation breaches in England and Wales will be investigated by the agency which has been given enforcement powers. These are usually the police, the fire service, the local authority or the Health and Safety Executive. In relation to events, it may often be the case that the agencies involved carry out joint investigations.

> The Health and Safety Executive (HSE) is an executive non-departmental public body, sponsored by the Department for Work and Pensions. It is the national independent watchdog for work-related health, safety and illness. It acts in the public interest to reduce work-related death and serious injury across Great Britain's workplaces.
>
> (Department for Work and Pensions, 2015, online)

The rest of this section will highlight some of the pieces of legislation relevant to the events industry under the themes of the event workplace, injury and harm, trespassing and sports events and venues. It should be mentioned, however, that the legal environment is continuously adapting and changing, and therefore the content of this chapter does not provide an exhaustive list. All event organisers should ensure they seek the most up-to-date legislation and guidance information prior to event hosting.

8.3.1 The event workplace

The Health and Safety at Work Act 1974 relates to the health, safety and welfare of employees in an organisation. Non-employees, such as event visitors, are also covered under section 3 of this Act. Using the previous example of the visitor with the broken ankle, it could be argued that in addition to being sued by the visitor, the event organiser may also be prosecuted by the state for breach of the Health and Safety at Work Act 1974 with regards to the duty of care to non-employees. A successful prosecution under this Act can mean a prison sentence, community punishment or fine for the event organiser, commonly called the defendant in criminal court cases. As discussed none of these punishments can be insured against. The Health and Safety at Work Act provides information and legislation guiding organisations on creating and maintaining a safe place of work. Information and legislation as to how that can be achieved can be found in the Management of Health and Safety at Work Regulations 1999. Amongst others, these regulations state the requirement for a health and safety policy, and they state the requirement for risk assessments to be carried out, with the findings of those assessments to be recorded where more than five people are employed.

Tip box

Although in legislation it is not necessary to record the risk assessment findings if there are fewer than five people employed in the organisation, it is still worthwhile keeping some form of record of the findings regardless of the number of employees. Some years down the line will you be able to remember why you made a particular decision without having made any notes?

Ultimately, the purpose of the Health and Safety at Work Act is to provide protection. It replaced previous Acts of Parliament which were perceived to require updating or altering. In the same way, in the 1990s and early 2000s several high-profile (non-event-related) incidents took place, each of them with high numbers of deceased. From this came a need for legislation to deal with organisation and corporate bodies and the Corporate Manslaughter and Corporate Homicide Act 2007 was born. In England, Wales and Northern Ireland the offence is known as corporate manslaughter; in Scotland it is known as corporate homicide.

This Act is a method to prosecute corporate bodies where the death of one or more persons is alleged to have resulted from the actions of that corporate body. The offence of gross negligence manslaughter, however, a common law offence is still available to police to prosecute an individual where the allegation is that one or more persons has died as a result of that individual's gross negligence. Gross negligence relates to a serious lack of care resulting in (in this case) the death of a person.

Other legislation in place to protect the workplace is the Regulatory Reform (Fire Safety) Order 2005. This provides legislation to be complied with regarding fire safety in non-domestic buildings. This Act is most easily learned about and understood by reading the individual relevant guidance document available online from the Fire Safety Advice Centre. These guidance documents are freely available and are split into different types of buildings or their uses, such as Open Air Events and Venues, or, Small and Medium Places of Assembly. In terms of its relevance to events, this legislation requires that a fire risk assessment is carried out and that control measures are put in place. In Scotland there is the Fire (Scotland) Act 2005, which, again, is similar to the English/Welsh Act and in Northern Ireland, the Fire and Rescue Services (Northern Ireland) Order 2006 came into force in 2009.

Due to the complex nature of events management there are many different pieces of legislation important to the running of the event. In relation to employee management, the Private Security Industry Act 2001 sought to regulate the industry relating to staff who worked at the doors of nightclubs and similar venues, commonly referred to as 'bouncers'. The Act had far-reaching impact and also relates to:

- CCTV operators
- those who guard property (known as manned guarding)
- those who act as security staff on licenced premises (known as door supervisors).

The Act required that these people be given training and be registered. Exemptions to this Act are volunteers who receive no payment (whether monetarily or in kind) and in-house staff working at specified sports grounds.

Other regulations affecting event employees are the Working Time Regulations 1998 which are based upon a European Directive and guide businesses on how to staff and govern employee work hours. These regulations give direction with regard to the amount of hours any employee is allowed to work, when and how they should be given breaks in their daily, weekly and fortnightly working period. It also requires the employer to keep records of the working time of their employees, and differentiates between those employees working during the night and those working during the day. Whilst the regulations do allow exemptions in some employment sectors, the events industry is not one of those automatically exempted. Some of the roles that are associated with events, such as security roles, may be able to take advantage of some of the exceptions to the Act. There are many other acts/regulations that will be relevant to the event industry, particularly in the build-up or breakdown phase of an event. These are usually related to the work activity (e.g. the Provision and Use of Work Equipment Regulations 1998, and the Lifting Operations and Lifting Equipment Regulations 1998).

Event organisations must be aware of the Control of Noise at Work Regulations 2005 which require that the risks of being exposed to high levels of noise are assessed and managed with regard to any staff working at an event. This is particularly important within the events sector; noise and volume are issues in relation to music festivals and sports events, for example. Another piece of legislation relevant within the events sector is that of the Control of Substances Hazardous to Health Regulations 2002 (COSHH). This can deal with matters as far removed as the types of cleaning products in use to the way in which events such as 'colour runs' are operated. In 2015 the Health and Safety Executive issued guidance relating to combustible substances, which include dust clouds. This was in response to an incident in Taiwan where coloured powder used at a water park ignited and injured several hundred people (BBC, 2015).

The Equality Act 2010 replaced and amalgamated numerous disability and equality legislation, the most well-known being the Disability Discrimination Act 1995. The Equality Act aims to prevent discrimination on the grounds of disability, gender reassignment, age, pregnancy and maternity, race, marriage and civil partnership, sex, religion or belief and sexual orientation. It requires that *reasonable adjustment* be made to accommodate the protected characteristics. Considering these protected characteristics it is easy to see the relevance to the event industry; examples are making an event site inclusive and perhaps ensuring that food on site is suitable for all religions. In terms of event recruitment and human resource management, it is very important to ensure equality and inclusivity. It is important that event organisations guarantee that their event is 'accessible to all members of society' (Bladen et al., 2012, 81). Furthermore, 'Considering that over 10 million people within the UK have some sort of disability, it makes business (as well as legal) sense to ensure that events are accessible' (Bowdin et al., 2011, 578).

As discussed in this section there are many aspects of event site legislation that an event manager must consider and implement when putting on a safe and secure event.

8.3.2 Event licensing

Event licensing and the issue of permits is very pertinent to the events industry and the following situations would require attention in relation to licences, permits and/or risk assessment (sourced from Bladen et al., 2012, 85):

- alcohol consumption
- food handling
- staffing
- noise
- building regulations/standards
- fire precautions
- health and safety at work
- first aid regulations
- lifting equipment and manual handling
- occupancy levels
- music and performance
- intellectual property
- electricity at work
- environmental protection
- signs and signal regulations
- waste disposal
- street trader or temporary market trader
- street closures
- public entertainment
- Criminal Records Bureau checks (now known in UK as Disclosure and Barring Service checks).

Whilst this list refers to alcohol consumption, the Licensing Act 2003, which is in force in England and Wales, regulates the *retail sale* of alcohol, not consumption, and the use of *regulated entertainment*, both of which are central to the event industry. Regulated entertainment is defined as live or recorded music, but it can also include the playing of films or boxing and wrestling matches. Licences to sell alcohol or use regulated entertainment are issued by the local authority for the area in which the *premises* are located, and can be applied for by the land/venue owner or by the event organiser. It is important to note that the word premises does not necessarily mean a building; it means any location, so would include a farmer's field where a festival is to take place, or a marquee that has been erected for a wedding.

Any person applying for a licence under the Licensing Act will have to demonstrate in their operating schedule the way in which they are complying with all four of the licensing objectives shown below:

1 Public safety
2 The prevention of public nuisance
3 The protection of children from harm
4 The prevention of crime and disorder.

(Licensing Act 2003, s.4)

All four objectives carry equal importance, and some agencies or departments, known as Responsible Authorities, have the right to make representation to a Licensing Committee Hearing if they feel that an applicant has not given sufficient consideration to the objectives in their operating schedule. In making a *representation*, these Responsible Authorities may propose conditions that they wish to be placed upon the applicant's licence, or they may object to the granting of the licence. It must be noted that in Scotland, the Licensing Act 2005 is similar to the English/Welsh 2003 Act, but has a fifth licensing objective: that of protecting and improving public health (Licensing (Scotland) Act 2005, s.4).

Responsible Authorities who may make representation include the police service, fire authority, licensing authority, child protection service, environmental health, health and safety enforcing body, health authority, planning authority and trading standards.

Tip box

Try to ensure that there is a licence in place, or that it is likely to be granted, before paying out money for contractors/suppliers, etc. Otherwise, if the licence is not granted, the event may not be able to take place and any monies spent may not be recovered.

There is an alternative to a 'premises' licence, a Temporary Event Notice (TEN), which places limits on the size of the event, but allows for occasional smaller-scale events to take place with less bureaucracy.

In the same way that there is a need to regulate the sale of alcohol and the provision of regulated entertainment, food sales must also comply with certain standards. The Food Safety Act 1990 gives a framework to all legislation that applies. There is similar legislation to cover Northern Ireland. The legislation relating to food is most frequently seen by the public and event organisers to be that which is regulated by the Environmental Health Department of the local authority, with whom all food businesses must be registered. This registration places obligations and standards on the way in which businesses are conducted. These obligations and standards relate to the preparation, cooking, storing and selling of food or food products, and are aimed at ensuring that the public does not suffer from food poisoning or other illnesses contracted due to poor health and hygiene standards. Most recently, legislation was introduced in 2014 relating to the need for allergens to be clearly identifiable in or on food, whether pre-prepared or freshly made, or for tasters, something that is particularly relevant to the event industry. This is called the Food Information Regulations EU 1169/2011 (Food Standards Agency, 2014).

While food, alcohol and entertainment licensing may be rather obvious requirements, other aspects of events entertainment may not be. For example, the Fireworks Regulations 2004, and the Fireworks (Scotland) Regulations 2004 define four categories of firework from indoor fireworks (category 1) to professional use (category 4). These Acts also detail night timings for the use of fireworks, as well as prohibiting their possession by under-18-year-olds in public places. In Northern Ireland, the legislation is the Explosives (Fireworks) Regulations (Northern Ireland) 2002, the main difference in this legislation being the ban on possession, purchase or use of fireworks unless a Fireworks Licence has been issued by the Secretary of State. This section has addressed some of the main licensing and regulatory provisions important to event management.

8.3.3 Premises and trespassing

Many places also have legislation relating to how a premises or location may be used. Aside from the legislation on regulated entertainment, under the Licensing Act 2003, planning regulations also need to be taken into account: perhaps the site is a residential premises and cannot be used for commercial purposes, for example. Premises may have covenants within their deeds that limit the way in which they can be used, or there may have been injunctions taken out to prevent their use in certain ways. Any organiser wishing to use a location for a particular event should make sure that they carry out checks on the permitted use.

The Occupiers' Liability Act 1957 and the Occupiers' Liability Act 1984 relate to the need for an occupier to take such care as is reasonable to ensure the safety of visitors who have been invited or are permitted to be at the site/premises (1957), and to owe a level of care to trespassers (1984). The term *occupier* refers to anyone who has responsibility for a site or premises. In the event industry this can mean the land/venue owner, the person or organisation hiring the land/venue or the person or organisation that has been contracted to put on the event on behalf of the person or organisation hiring the land. It can be the case that there can be more than one *occupier*, and this follows the same line that was presented in civil litigation, where the injured party may sue many different people.

8.3.4 Sports events and venues

All of the legislation referred to within this chapter is not event-specific; it relates to many aspects of life including events. Sporting events and associated facilities and organisations are different and do have specific legislation that relates to them. The Safety of Sports Grounds Act 1975 enables a sports ground to be *designated* by the Secretary of State if it has a spectator capacity level above 5000 for football (soccer) or 10,000 for any other sport. Once a ground has been designated local authorities must issue a safety certificate for the whole ground, which must be adhered to by the ground's managers. A general safety certificate is intended to be part of the management of health and safety of a sports ground, and should contain conditions that the Local Authority (having consulted with the police, fire authority and building authority) considers necessary to ensure the reasonable safety of spectators when the ground is being used for activities detailed on the certificate. This will usually be the core use of the ground (e.g. in a football ground, the activities detailed on the general safety certificate will relate to football).

Where such as a football ground wishes to use the site for an alternative use (e.g. a popular music concert), it is most likely that this activity will not be detailed on the general safety certificate, and the ground's managers will need to apply to the local authority for a special safety certificate that will give permission for this alternative use. One of the most common differences between the general safety certificate and the special safety certificate is the capacity figure. Using a popular music concert in a football ground as an example, at a football match all spectators sit or stand surrounding the pitch on which the match takes place. When that same ground is used for a concert, it is usual to remove the capacity of some of the seating/standing accommodation for spectators but it is also most likely that the pitch will now be available for their use. In dealing with the Safety of Sports Grounds Act 1975, a sports ground is defined as a place where sports or other competitive activities take place in the open air, and where accommodation is provided for spectators; this includes artificial structures or natural structures which have been artificially modified. Where a sports ground has a roof that can be closed or opened, it will still fall under this definition so long as some sport is played with the roof open; an example of one of these grounds is the

Millennium Stadium in Cardiff, Wales. If the sports ground is an indoor arena, the Act does not apply.

Another aspect related to sporting events is that of 'regulated stands' (Fire Safety and Safety of Places of Sport Act 1987). Where a sports ground is not designated, but has covered stands which can accommodate 500 or more spectators, either seated or standing, the local authority is required to issue a safety certificate relating to the stand or stands. In Northern Ireland, the previous Acts are paralleled in the Safety of Sports Grounds (Northern Ireland) Order 2006. There are further pieces of legislation that relate to football: the requirement for all-seater grounds/appropriate standing accommodation, and the behaviour of spectators in line with the Football Spectators Act 1989 and the Football (Offences) Act 1991.

A very old Act which is still in place and relevant to temporary structures at events is the Public Health Acts Amendment Act 1890:

Safety of platforms, &c. erected or used on public occasions.

(1) Whenever large numbers of persons are likely to assemble on the occasion of any show, entertainment, public procession, open-air meeting, or other like occasion, every roof of a building, and every platform, balcony, or other structure or part thereof let or used or intended to be let or used for the purpose of affording sitting or standing accommodation for a number of persons, shall be safely constructed or secured to the satisfaction of the proper officer of the authority.
(2) Any person who uses or allows to be used in contravention of this section, any roof of a building, platform, balcony, or structure not so safely constructed or secured, or who neglects to comply with the provisions of this section in thereof, shall be liable to a penalty not exceeding level 3 on the standard scale.

(Public Health Acts Amendment Act 1890, s.37)

Whilst most legislation relating to sport deals with spectators and can be found more commonly in team sports, there is also legislation that applies to other sports, and tackles the conduct of competitors or how the event can take place. For example, the Cycle Racing on Highway Regulations 1960 explain under what conditions cycle racing can take place on the roads. This Act has been amended since 1960 to bring up to date some of the conditions that have to be adhered to, but the basic tenet still applies: cycle racing on roads and highways is lawful under certain conditions. The British government has also recently enacted legislation as the first step to allowing motor racing to take place on the highway, although this will be on closed roads. This legislation is an amendment to the Road Traffic Act 1988, and requires a further piece of legislation; this was expected in 2015 but at the time of writing had not been enacted.

Another piece of legislation that may be relevant to events where there are vehicles as part of the display, or as part of the actual event is the Motor Vehicles (Off Road Events) Regulations 1995. Normally, when an event takes place, the site on which it is held becomes a public place, and therefore all matters relating to the driving/use of vehicles under the Road Traffic Act will apply. If an event is held in accordance with its affiliated Motor Sport Association code of practice, then certain aspects of the Road Traffic Act do not need to be taken into account. This is provided that the Motor Sport Association has been given permission under the Off Road Regulations to authorise events. An example is the National Traction Engine Trust, which deals with events in which steam traction engines are displayed or used.

When considering access to an event, and how traffic can arrive or leave, it is common to consider some form of traffic management. This may consist of 'No Waiting' areas to prevent visitors parking in inappropriate locations or causing inconvenience to residents nearby, or it can consist of speed restrictions for safety or the closing of roads. Local authorities, or those responsible for managing traffic on a daily basis, have to comply with legislation to ensure that traffic is kept flowing on roads. It is clear that a road which usually copes well with a small number of cars each day/week will not cope well if that volume of traffic is increased due to an event. Those responsible for managing traffic will therefore want to work with an event organiser, and want the event organiser to work with them, to ensure that local traffic travels with the minimum of inconvenience, and that event traffic has the minimum of queuing in and out of the venue.

In order to manage both of these aspects, temporary traffic regulation orders may be applied for by the organiser, who will then take responsibility for having the traffic managed in line with these orders. The most recent legislation in place for this is the Road Traffic Regulation Act 1984 (s.16a) which allows for traffic on a road to be restricted or prohibited for the purposes of:

- facilitating the holding of a relevant event
- enabling members of the public to watch a relevant event
- reducing the disruption to traffic likely to be caused by the relevant event.

It should be noted that a *relevant event* is any sporting event, social event or entertainment held *on a road*. The other piece of legislation that is sometimes used for this purpose is the Town Police Clauses Act 1847 (s.21) which allows for orders to be made on the route of public processions and similar, and provided they take place *on a road.* This clearly leaves a large gap in the legislation; a significant number of large-scale events are held on private property or, put another way, not on the road. Recognising contemporary issues to events prevalent in the twenty-first century, many local authorities take a pragmatic view of traffic management and may grant temporary traffic regulation orders, even where the event is not held on a road. The way in which this is achieved varies between the different Highways Authorities, so it is crucial that an event organiser makes contact with their local area for guidance.

Tip box

Ensure that contact with the local Highways Authority is made at the earliest possible stage as there are usually timescales, sometimes several months, which need to be adhered to.

The number of employee fatalities of construction workers building mega-event stadia is well documented. There is legislation in place within England and Wales to govern this type of work. The Work at Height Regulations 2005 apply to all work carried out at height. Height is defined as where there is a risk of personal injury to someone if they fall. In other words, this does not mean the height above ground at which an employee is working, but the distance they have to fall and the likelihood

167

that this would cause injury. These regulations require that, where possible, working at height is avoided in the first instance. If it cannot be avoided then specialised work equipment should be used to prevent a fall, and if that is not possible then specialised equipment should be used to minimise the distance and consequence of the fall.

One of the most recent pieces of legislation to have been introduced is the Construction (Design and Management) Regulations 2015, which regulates the way in which temporary structures, such as those seen at event sites, are built and managed. These regulations are from an EU Directive, and are designed to ensure safety during the build-up and breakdown of an event, as well as during the live/public phase.

8.4 Money laundering

Money laundering is the act of using finances acquired through illegal channels within supposedly law-abiding companies or assets. The Money Laundering Regulations 2007 require 'financial, accountancy, legal and other sectors to apply risk-based customer due diligence measures' (Money Laundering Regulations, 2007, n.2157, 1). Customer due diligence can be interpreted as 'knowing your customer' (Trajovski and Nanevski, 2015, 39) in relation to identification and their business connections. This legislation has particular significance for mega-events and the way in which host nations are chosen by organising bodies. As reported in the media, at the time of writing, FIFA is undergoing investigations linked to bribery and potential corruption with regards to the hosting of World Cup events (NBC News, 2015; BBCa, 2015). Mega-events such as World Cups and Olympic and Paralympic Games can have very positive economic and financial impacts on the host nation and therefore are desirable events to host. It is however of prime importance that the accountant or event manager associated with any event organisation and delivery must be aware of how events are financed and where income stems from. Having a positive and trusting relationship with stakeholders and employees will be beneficial in ensuring events are law abiding.

Money laundering can be linked to events or event venues associated with gambling. Gambling is a regulated activity and the government originally perceived it as negative and socially unacceptable, but now there is a shift towards its economic use to create revenue (Johnson, 2006). Sporting events such as horse/dog racing, snooker and soccer, as well as casinos or even just casino nights are all associated with gambling. According to a news article, more than £83 billion of money is laundered through sports gambling per year (Conway, 2014). Both FIFA and the IOC have developed organisations to monitor betting on their events (McCarthy, 2015). Match fixing is also a threat to the integrity of sports events, including virtual e-sports (Marsh, 2015), and happens across the world (Aaron, 2015).

8.5 Consumer rights

The protection and relationship building between the events organisation and their consumer base, whether that be the event visitors, clients or sponsors, is paramount to event success and effective event project delivery. There are many different legal aspects significant to events management such as the Consumer Protection Act 1987, which states that a consumer has the legal right to claim for negligence and therefore compensation if a faulty product causes injury or damage (Keenan, 1995). The Consumer Rights Act 2015 was introduced to combat concerns over previously complicated and fragmented legislation and to respond to technological advancements in the area. This updated Act considers contracts (written and verbal) for consumer goods and digital content as well as services. When re-selling tickets for an event (perhaps as a secondary ticket seller) information about seating, value and any restrictions must be clear to the customer. Ultimately, the law is in place to protect consumer interests in relation to the consumption of goods and services (Consumer Rights Act 2015, c.15). Furthermore, the Data Protection Act 1998 gives more control to individuals in respect of their personal data and to what extent organisations can hold this information (Raj et al., 2009). The marketing communications strategy for an events company must ensure that information they hold or request from event consumers is treated in a law-abiding way.

In a similar vein to consumer rights legislation, but significantly older, is the Pedlars Act 1871. This allows anyone who has been granted a certificate by the Chief Officer of Police to trade, i.e. sell, their wares:

> The term 'pedlar' means any hawker, pedlar, petty chapman, tinker, caster of metals, or other person who, without any horse or other beast bearing or drawing burden, travels and trades on foot and goes from town to town or to other men's houses, carrying to sell or exposing for sale any goods, wares, or merchandise, or procuring orders for goods, wares, or merchandise immediately to be delivered.'
>
> (Pedlars Act 1871, s.3)

The Chief Officer of Police may issue the certificate to anyone who has resided in their area of enforcement for one month previous to the application, who is above the age of seventeen years, is a person of good character and intends to carry on the trade of a pedlar in good faith. It is likely that pedlars will be found at many open-air, free or market-type events. It is possible that a stall at a market-type event may cost several hundred pounds and be out of reach to many small businesses. A pedlar may trade, however, without the cost of a stall, so long as they comply with the legislation. For the customer, there is reassurance in the knowledge that the pedlar is of good character and has been issued a certificate by police; the pedlar must show their certificate to anyone they offer to sell their goods to. There may be conflict between an event organiser, who will want to sell stall space as means to make their event profitable, and the pedlar, who may trade free from the ties and costs of a stall.

Tip box

If your event is likely to attract 'pedlars', it is worthwhile identifying an area of your event where they may trade. This area should allow them to comply with the relevant legislation, but it should also allow you to ensure the safety of your event. Manage the expectation of your stallholders, who may feel conflicted at the appearance of someone trading similar products, and try to work with all parties.

8.6 Guidance documentation

The type and level of law and legislation, or rules, that need to be obeyed vary between countries. The enforcement of these rules also varies. Complying with legislation should be central to the planning of any event, and if planned for in detail and in collaboration with key community stakeholders, the likelihood of emergency incidents will arguably be reduced. It is very important that event organisers are aware of any legislation with which they must comply. Table 8.1 summarises important guidance and documentation connected to this aspect of event management.

8.7 Conclusion

This chapter has provided a starting point for understanding the legal frameworks surrounding event management and project management within an events setting. Law discussed in this chapter mostly derives from England and Wales and it must be stressed that other countries will have their own laws and legal environment in which to operate. It is crucial that the event organisation and events manager researches the rules and regulations appropriate to the place of event hosting. The events industry is

Table 8.1 Guides and resources available to assist event managers

The Purple Guide to Health, Safety and Welfare at Music and Other Events	Written by the Event Industry Forum, a group of representatives from all parts of the event industry. Created after the 1988 Monsters of Rock fatalities. http://www.thepurpleguide.co.uk/
The Guide to Safety at Sports Grounds ('The Green Guide')	Its first edition was attributed to the Wheatley Report following the Ibrox Stadium disaster of 1971. Whilst it is a guide, and has no statutory force, much of it comes from the Safety of Sports Grounds Act 1975 and the Fire Safety and Safety of Places of Sport Act 1987. http://www.safetyatsportsgrounds.org.uk/publications/green-guide
Temporary Demountable Structures: Guidance on Procurement, Design and Use	This guide relates to the use of temporary structures at events, i.e. those which are put up and taken down on a regular basis, such as marquees, tiered seating and stages. It gives guidance on ensuring the safety and integrity of the structure in event conditions. This guide is written by the Institute of Structural Engineers, and endorsed by the Health and Safety Executive. http://www.shop.istructe.org/temporary-demountable-structures.html
Codes of Practice	Many countries produce documents called Codes of Practice. These are not legislation that must be complied with, however, they are documents which give standard guidance to assist users in achieving their desired result.

dynamic, fluid and complicated and this involves lots of legalities. It is important to work with local authorities and key partners and services to organise and host an event. The event organisation and team have a duty of care to all of those people connected to the event to be kept safe from harm. It is important to scrutinise an event prior to delivery to assess and investigate potential, reasonable and foreseeable issues that may arise. Due to the complexities and changing nature of law and legislation, this chapter can only provide a general overview, and further research by the event organiser must be undertaken to understand the specific legal environment related to their event.

Case study 8: *Dreamspace*, UK

In July 2006 an inflatable art installation called *Dreamspace* opened to the public in Riverside Park, Chester-le-Street, County Durham. This case study presents the legal ramifications connected to an incident related to this installation. SHP Online (2009) describes *Dreamspace* as follows:

> Measuring 50 x 50 x 5 metres, *Dreamspace* was an interactive 'experience' through which visitors could walk and enjoy changes of space, light and colour, enhanced by a pre-recorded sound-track. It comprised numerous ovoid cells constructed of very thin, translucent PVC, arranged in different colour combinations. Internally, columns were formed where cells were glued together. The structure was inflated by fans, such that it was supported by air under pressure, and it retained a relatively stable shape, having been fixed to the ground by a system of ropes and pegs.

The art structure had been created by Maurice Agis, and promoted by Brouhaha International Limited, a company in which his son, Giles, was an executive director. Riverside Park was a public open space owned by Chester-le-Street District Council and *Dreamspace* was sited there at their invitation. Maurice Agis had created previous similar inflatables and there are reports relating to previous incidents. One of these occurred in Germany in 1986 when an inflatable called Colourspace broke free of its moorings and injured several people who had been inside it and fell out (Stewart, 2009). A further incident occurred in Glasgow in 1988, when Agis, hanging on to another inflatable structure as it took off, was injured (Stewart, 2009).

Approximately 3.30 pm on 23 July 2006, there were numerous people inside the inflatable at Chester-le-Street. The structure broke free of its moorings and lifted off the ground, only stopping when it snagged on a CCTV pole in the park. There were several casualties as a result of this incident, caused by falling out of the structure or being inside the structure when it fell to the ground. These included the deaths of two women who were inside the structure when the incident occurred. Reports at the time also stated that the life of a child was saved by the presence in the park of an off-duty anaesthetist.

(Continued)

Case study 8 (*continued*)

A joint investigation of this incident took place, involving Durham Police and the Health and Safety Executive, and resulted in criminal charges of gross negligence manslaughter against Maurice Agis. Maurice Agis, Brouhaha International Limited and Chester-le-Street District Council were also charged with offences under the Health and Safety at Work Act 1974. After a five-week court case in 2009, the jury was unable to reach a verdict on the charge of gross negligence manslaughter, but all parties were found guilty, or had earlier pleaded guilty, to the Health and Safety at Work offences.

The Crown Prosecution Service took the decision not to press for a retrial of Maurice Agis on the charge of gross negligence manslaughter (Leigh Day, 2009; Summers, 2009). Mrs Justice Cox ordered Maurice Agis to pay a fine of £10,000, Brouhaha International Limited to pay £4,000 and Chester-le-Street District Council £20,000. Maurice Agis's fine was later reduced on appeal and soon after he died. It was reported that he had not taken out insurance for the event.

In 2010 an inquest was held into the deaths of the two women who died at the event. The verdict of the inquest was that of accidental death (Leigh Day, 2010). A year later, in 2011, a court case was held to apportion blame, and the percentage of compensation that Chester-le-Street District Council and Brouhaha International Limited should each pay. The court concluded that Chester-le-Street District Council was 45 per cent responsible, and Brouhaha International Limited was 55 per cent responsible (Health and Safety at Work, 2011, online).

This case study illustrates what may be referred to as a 'worst-case scenario' situation; the running of an event which results in death and injury to visitors attending it. After an investigation, individuals and companies were subjected to criminal prosecution, resulting in guilty verdicts and associated punishment. The punishments in this case were monetary. An inquest followed, which dealt with the two deaths that took place during the event. Lastly, civil court cases were held to prove a case for compensation. Whilst there is no suggestion that the injuries and deaths will be forgotten in any timescale, this case study illustrates that the legal aspects of this incident took five years to complete and were complex to administer.

Evaluative student questions

1 What are the key lessons to be learnt from this case study?
2 Discuss, using the legislation in the chapter as well as further reading, what offences could have been considered by the police and HSE joint investigation.
3 Using the guidance documentation listed in the chapter, consider what could have assisted in preventing this tragedy from happening.

Further reading

Health and Safety at Work Act 1974 (c.37). London: HMSO.

Trajovski, G. and Nanevski, B. (2015) Customer due diligence: focal point of the anti-money laundering process. *Journal of Sustainable Development*, 5(12) 39–50.

Vardi, N. (2015) The men and money behind the FIFA corruption charges. *Business Source Complete*, 27 May.

References

Aaron, C. (2015) Match-fixing cases underline need for new laws. *International Centre for Sport Security Journal*, 1(4). Available from: http://icss-journal.newsdeskmedia.com/Match-fixing-cases-underline-need-for-br-new-laws [Accessed 8 July 2015].

BBC (2015) Taiwan Formosa Water Park explosion injures hundreds. 28 June. Available from: http://www.bbc.co.uk/news/world-asia-33300970 [Accessed 4 March 2016].

BBCa (2015) Fifa corruption crisis: key questions answered. Available from: http://www.bbc.co.uk/news/world-europe-32897066 [Accessed 28 March 2016].

Bladen, C., Kennell, J., Abson, E. and Wilde, N. (2012) *Events management: an introduction*. London: Routledge.

Bowdin, G., Allen, J., O'Toole, W., Harris, R. and McDonnell, I. (2011) *Events management*. 3rd edition. London: Butterworth-Heinemann.

Construction (Design and Management) Regulations 2015 (n.51). Available from: http://www.legislation.gov.uk/uksi/2015/51/contents/made [Accessed 7 March 2016].

Consumer Protection Act 1987 (c.43). London: HMSO.

Consumer Rights Act 2015 (c.15). London: HMSO. [Accessed 12 February 2016].

Control of Noise at Work Regulations 2005 (n.1643). Available from: http://www.legislation.gov.uk/uksi/2005/1643/contents/made [Accessed 4 March 2016].

Control of Substances Hazardous to Health Regulations 2002 (n.2677). Available http://www.legislation.gov.uk/uksi/2002/2677/regulation/7/made [Accessed 4 March 2016].

Conway, R. (2014) *Sports gambling: £83bn laundered through betting, new study shows*. BBC, 15 May 2014. Available from: http://www.bbc.co.uk/sport/0/27422078 [Accessed 8 July 2015].

Corporate Manslaughter and Corporate Homicide Act 2007 (c.19). London: HMSO.

Cycle Racing on Highways Regulations 1960 (n.250). Available from: http://www.legislation.gov.uk/uksi/1960/250/contents/made [Accessed 4 March 2016].

Data Protection Act 1998 (c.29). London: HMSO.

Department for Work and Pensions (2015) Health and Safety Executive. London: HMSO. Available from: https://www.gov.uk/government/organisations/health-and-safety-executive [Accessed 18 May 2015].

Disability Discrimination Act 1995 (c.50). London: HMSO.

Equality Act 2010 (c.15). London: HMSO.

Explosives (Fireworks) Regulations (Northern Ireland) 2002 (n.147). Available from: http://www.legislation.gov.uk/nisr/2002/147/regulation/8/made [Accessed 4 March 2016].

Fire and Rescue Services (Northern Ireland) Order 2006 (n.1254). London: HMSO. Available from http://www.legislation.gov.uk/nisi/2006/1254/contents [Accessed 4 March 2016].

Fire Safety and Safety of Places of Sport Act 1987 (c.27). London: HMSO.

Fire (Scotland) Act 2005 (asp.5). Edinburgh: OQPS.

Fireworks Regulations 2004 (n.1836). Available from: http://www.legislation.gov.uk/uksi/2004/1836/contents/made [Accessed 4 March 2016].

Fireworks (Scotland) Regulations 2004 (n.393). Available from: http://www.westlothian.
gov.uk/media/7113/The-Fireworks-Scotland-Regulations-2004/pdf/The_Fireworks_
(Scotland)_Regulations_2004.pdf [Accessed 4 March 2016].

Food Safety Act 1990 (c.16). London: HMSO.

Food Standards Agency (2014) *Food Information Regulations 2014: Summary guidance
for food business operators and enforcement officers in Scotland, Wales and
Northern Ireland*. Available from: https://www.food.gov.uk/sites/default/files/fir-
guidance2014.pdf [Accessed 4 March 2016].

Football (Offences) Act 1991 (c.19). London: HMSO.

Football Spectators Act 1989 (c.37). London: HMSO.

Ganz, J. (2012) The truth about Van Halen and those brown M&Ms. *The Record: Music
News from NPR*. Available from: http://www.npr.org/sections/therecord/2012/02/14/
146880432/the-truth-about-van-halen-and-those-brown-m-ms [Accessed 4 March
2016].

Goldblatt, J. (2008) *Special events: the roots and wings of celebration*. Chichester: John
Wiley & Sons.

Health and Safety at Work (2011) *High court rules on Dreamspace responsibility*.
Available from: http://www.healthandsafetyatwork.com/hsw/dreamspace-high-
court-ruling [Accessed 12 February 2016].

Health and Safety at Work Act 1974 (c.37). London: HMSO.

Johnson, J. (2006) An analysis of the obligations of gambling entities under the FATF's
2003 anti-money laundering recommendations. *Journal of Money Laundering
Control*, 9(1) 7–18.

Keenan, D. (1995) *English Law*. 11th edition. London: Pitman Publishing.

Leigh Day (2009) *Dreamspace sentence passed*. Available from: https://www.leighday.
co.uk/News/Archive/2009/March-2009/Dreamspace-sentence-passed [Accessed 12
February 2016].

Leigh Day (2010) *Accidental death ruling in Dreamspace inquest*. Available from: https://
www.leighday.co.uk/News/2010/May-2010/Accidental-death-ruling-in-Dreamspace-
inquest [Accessed 12 February 2016].

Licensing Act 2003 (c.17). London: HMSO.

Licensing (Scotland) Act 2005 (asp.16). Edinburgh: OQPS.

Lifting Operations and Lifting Equipment Regulations 1998 (n.2307). London: HMSO.
Available from http://www.legislation.gov.uk/uksi/1998/2307/made/data.pdf [Accessed
4 March 2016].

McCarthy, D. (2015) Looking for better fraud. *International Centre for Sport Security
Journal*, 1(4). Available from: http://icss-journal.newsdeskmedia.com/Looking-for-
betting-fraud [Accessed 8 July 2015].

Management of Health and Safety at Work Regulations 1999 (n.3242). Available
http://www.legislation.gov.uk/uksi/1999/3242/contents/made [Accessed 4 March
2016].

Marsh, J. (2015) The rise of E-sports: vulnerabilities and opportunities. *International
Centre for Sport Security Journal*, 3(1). Available from: http://icss-journal.newsdesk-
media.com/the-rise-of-e-sports-vulnerabilities-and-opportunities [Accessed 8 July
2015].

Money Laundering Regulations 2007 (n.2157). Available from: http://www.legislation.
gov.uk/uksi/2007/2157/memorandum/contents [Accessed 8 July 2015].

Motor Vehicles (Off Road Events) Regulations 1995 (n.1371). Available from: http://
www.legislation.gov.uk/uksi/1995/1371/contents/made [Accessed 7 March 2016].

NBC News (2015) *U.S. indicts 16 more soccer execs in FIFA corruption probe*. Available from: http://www.nbcnews.com/storyline/fifa-corruption-scandal/u-s-indicts-16-more-soccer-execs-fifa-corruption-probe-n473821 [Accessed 28 March 2016].

Occupiers' Liability Act 1957 (c.31). London: HMSO.

Occupiers' Liability Act 1984 (c.3). London: HMSO.

Pedlar's Act 1871 (c.96). London: HMSO.

Private Security Industry Act 2001 (c.12). London: HMSO.

Provision and Use of Work Equipment Regulations 1998 (n.2306). London: HMSO. Available from: http://www.legislation.gov.uk/uksi/1998/2306/contents/made [Accessed 4 March 2016].

Public Health Acts Amendment Act 1890 (c.59). London: HMSO.

Raj, R., Walters, P., and Rashid, T. (2009) *Events management: an integrated and practical approach*. London: Sage.

Regulatory Reform (Fire Safety) Order 2005 (n.1541). London: HMSO. Available from http://www.legislation.gov.uk/uksi/2005/1541/contents/made [Accessed 4 March 2016].

Road Traffic Act 1988 (c.52). London: HMSO.

Road Traffic Regulation Act 1984 (c.27). London: HMSO.

Safety of Sports Grounds Act 1975 (c.52). London: HMSO.

Safety of Sports Grounds (Northern Ireland) Order 2006 (n.313). Available from: http://www.legislation.gov.uk/nisi/2006/313/contents [Accessed 4 March 2016].

SHP Online (2009) *Creative abandon*. Available from: http://www.shponline.co.uk/creative-abandon/?cid=searchresult [Accessed 7 March 2016].

Stewart, C. (2009) Near disaster of artist's early work. *BBC TV Newcastle*, 6 March. Available from: http://news.bbc.co.uk/1/mobile/england/wear/7907686.stm [Accessed 12 February 2016].

Summers, M. (2009) Dreamspace: the tragic moment. *Northern Echo*, 29 January. Available from: http://www.thenorthernecho.co.uk/news/4084453.Dreamspace__the_tragic_moment/

Town Police Clauses Act 1847 (c.89). London: HMSO.

Trajovski, G. and Nanevski, B. (2015) Customer due diligence: focal point of the anti-money laundering process. *Journal of Sustainable Development*, 5(12) 39–50.

Upton, M. (1995) *Incident at Donington Monsters of Rock, 1988*. [seminar] Mass Crowd Events, Easingwold, 8 December.

Vardi, N. (2015) The men and money behind the FIFA Corruption Charges. *Business Source Complete*, 27 May 2015.

Work at Height Regulations 2005 (n.735). Available from: http://www.legislation.gov.uk/uksi/2005/735/contents/made [Accessed 7 March 2016].

Working Time Regulations 1998 (n.1833). London: HMSO. Available from http://www.legislation.gov.uk/uksi/1998/1833/contents/made [Accessed 4 March 2016].

Chapter 9

Cost and financial planning

9.1 Introduction

Any professional project that is planned for and implemented must first have the financial backing and support required to successfully meet objectives. Managing event projects is no different in principle, though the financial sums involved in hosting and staging global/major events can be breathtaking. The London 2012 Olympic and Paralympic Games is reported to be the most expensive UK event in recent history (Giulianotti, Armstrong, Hales and Hobbs, 2015), and with so much at stake it is essential to ensure financial planning is effective, detailed and appropriate. The purpose of this chapter is to consider and explore the financial pitfalls potentially involved in event planning from a practical perspective. There are other very good texts available to assist with the mechanics and technicalities linked to financial planning and communication; these are recommended in the further reading section.

Financial planning for an event is crucial to its success. It is very easy for an event organiser to find themselves or their company or charity in financial difficulty as a result of a lack of financial planning. In order to hold a successful event, it is necessary to have the same depth of financial planning in place as expected for a business start-up or expansion plan. A lack of strategic planning arguably contributed to the downfall of the World Student Games in 1991 hosted in Sheffield (Bramwell, 1997). This event cost the city £658 million and is due to be fully paid off in 2024 (BBC, 2011) after misjudgements were made in relation to infrastructure development, event demand and marketing. It is important in the events sector that stakeholders receive a return on investment (ROI) for their outlays. According to Bowdin et al. (2011, 298), 'ROI is the measure of the financial return for the investment in the event. The ROI will be different for each of the stakeholders.' Initial investment will only occur if the original event proposal and plan appear inviting to event stakeholders and sponsors. As mentioned by Maylor (2010, 189), 'the rejection or deferral of a project proposal may have nothing to do with its intrinsic merit. The decision will be based on the availability or otherwise of the necessary cash.' Financial viability is a crucial aspect of dutiful financial planning and, if managed meaningfully, can help to foresee and therefore cope with potential event challenges.

9.2 Financial viability

As part of the financial planning process, a feasibility study should be implemented by the events team or organiser in order to assess whether an event is financially viable to go ahead. This is further discussed in section 9.3. Viability can be understood as researching whether an event is capable of working; this can be in terms of finances, staffing, venue, marketing, profile and expertise. This chapter will focus purely on financial viability and the importance of securing funds to ensure event success. The seasoned event organiser should be aware of the pitfalls involved in creating a new event, and will understand that it may take some years before the event reaches a 'breakeven' point. The experienced event organiser will therefore have a long-term strategy and be very savvy about their contracts, contractors/suppliers and equipment or artist/event provision. Perhaps due to this level of knowledge, the seasoned event organiser is likely to be involved in organising large-scale or high-profile events, which take place in well-established venues and locations and have the ability to attract the top performers and contractors/suppliers. Experienced event managers should be aware of the critical success elements associated with event achievement. There are 12 critical success factors linked to financing events according to Schnitzer (2014, 130–131) as adapted here:

1 The dynamics of budgets: be aware of the fluidity of the environment in which events are set.
2 Contingency planning: have backup finances in case unforeseen risks and issues occur.
3 'Big bucket' costs are not quantifiable: this involves managing funder expectations, especially those of public and political stakeholders.
4 Unpredictability of results of sports events: host nation success or failure can have wider impacts.
5 Principles of good governance: be transparent and clear with communicating financial issues.
6 Planning liquidity: manage the increased costs immediately before and after the event effectively.
7 Written agreements: having these in place reduces complications and discrepancies.
8 Empowerment: providing team members with financial ownership can assist in boosting motivation and commitment levels.
9 Setting priorities: these must be communicated efficiently across all team members so it is clear which areas of event planning and implementation need enforcing before others.
10 Value-in-kind sponsorships: these sponsors are valuable to the overall impression and success of the event and bring to the event resources that may have been off budget.
11 Knowledge: it is important to have team members with knowledge and experience of financial planning and management to effectively execute plans and budget requirements.
12 Right people: having confident and experienced staff teams in charge of budgets and financial decisions is valuable.

These critical success factors are not always reflected in the events world due to the experience, expertise and agenda of different event organisers. For example, a community event organiser may be new to the world of events; they may perhaps be motivated by good intentions but could equally be naïve in terms of knowing or understanding the requirements of putting on an event, in both the legal and practical sense. It must be remembered that these organisers and their committees potentially provide the backbone of a local events scene and are most likely trying to achieve a positive outcome for a community or charity. In this instance, it is even more pertinent that they should be supported in putting on a safe and successful event by local support groups. Inexperienced event organisers may be naïve not just in terms of their lack of prior experience but also in terms of recognising whether their event is or is not viable. It is important to have realistic financial goals which may involve a long-term return on investment or donation to their associated event charity. Charity fundraising events 'may be run to raise awareness for the cause, often without the objective of maximising funds raised' (Webber, 2004, 133). Needing clear financial targets is a common trait amongst business ventures in many other sectors; it is not solely reserved for the events industry. Inexperienced event organisers may be unaware of the amount of work involved in organising an event. This relates to the actual work of planning what the event will be, where and when it will take place, who needs to be involved and how to achieve the end result.

This type of organiser can also be inexperienced about the amount of money required 'up front' to create an event. This is forgivable because if they have not been involved in arranging or organising an event before, it is extremely difficult to know the different aspects needed, and how much they cost. Very often the new organiser only finds out that they need a particular service or contractor/supplier when another part of the event prompts the question because it links into their contracted work (e.g. the staging company asking for details of the lighting being used on stage so they can ensure the correct loading calculations, or the artist whose contract directs a specific set of sound requirements). Cutting costs, contractors/suppliers, ticket sales and feasibility will now be considered in the discussion about event viability.

9.2.1 Budgeting

Budgeting within the events sector can be complex and demanding due to the pressures on stakeholder working and potential unforeseen costs, as will be explained later in this chapter. Budgeting does not take place in isolation but should be fully integrated with the overall business or event plan, and is an ongoing process (Wilson, 2013). As extrapolated from Bowdin et al. (2011, 302), the budget process involves five elements (see Figure 9.1).

The initial step taken in the budgetary process is to scope out the current economic and financial climate both internally and externally to the event company. This stage forms part of the feasibility study, which is crucial within event planning and discussed later in this chapter. Budget guidelines should be found in the event documentation and linked to the stakeholder's aims and objectives for the event project. Estimated expenditure costs involve careful and meticulous research, and it is always best practice to find several quotes for the same service to get an understanding of market value. The preparation and evaluation of draft budgets involves, in simple terms, the review of both income and expenditure. Example incomings and outgoings can be viewed in Table 9.1.

The more complex and large the event, the more lengthy and complex the budgeting process will be. There have been many examples of poor and under-estimated

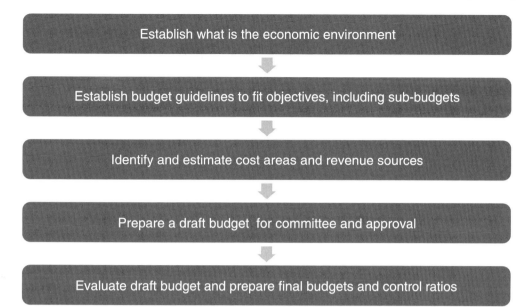

Figure 9.1 Budget process

Source: Bowdin et al., 2011, 302

Table 9.1 A demonstration of potential income and expenditure linked to events

Event Income	Event Expenditure
Ticket sales	Insurance
Fundraising	Venue hire
Grants/loans	Event equipment
Sponsorship	Catering
Merchandise	Marketing
Donations	Staff
Private funding	Transport
Broadcasting	Media coverage[1]

[1] Some commercial media outlets charge for their broadcasting or services

budgeting in mega-events which have led to financial challenges and indeed political and economic problems. In their study on mega-event budgeting, Solberg and Preuss (2015) discovered that the 2010 South Africa World Cup appeared to be 15.5 times more expensive than initially budgeted for, and the 2011 FIS World Skiing Championship in Oslo 17.5 times more expensive. These oversights were due to changes in the initial event objectives' post-bid win, which meant that event expectations changed and therefore cost implications changed with them.

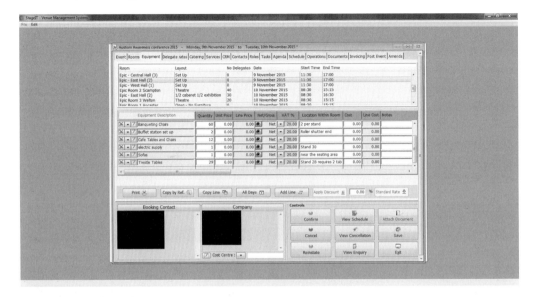

Figure 9.2 Budgeting and costing demonstration for equipment using StageIt software

Budgeting oversights can be avoided if realistic initial estimates and forecasting are planned for prior to the event implementation stages. There are many methods and resources that can assist with this and computer software programmes can help with budgeting and financial planning for events. Figure 9.2 illustrates an example event case from the StageIt programme which works out the equipment and associated costs for an event before transferring the information to an invoice for the connected company.

Other methods of displaying financial information include profit and loss statements, financial forecasting and balance sheets. An events manager does not necessarily have to be a qualified accountant, but it is crucial to have an understanding of the rules and principles that guide financial planning, and to collate this in the appropriate documentation (Wilson, 2013). Furthermore, it is always useful to have a team member who is experienced with accounting and finances as part of the organisation to manage and monitor this aspect of event management.

9.2.2 Cutting costs

It is frequently the case, however, that event organisations do not have the luxury of loans or an on-site accountant to assist in the financial planning and budgeting of an event, and therefore financial issues can occur. A common misconception held by new or inexperienced event organisers is that downscaling or downsizing an event will lead to decreased costs of equal proportion. Regrettably, this is not usually true: event costs will perhaps be lowered but not in proportion to the downscale. One of the best ways to demonstrate this is to consider what changes may be made to an event to downsize its scale and then focus on the potential financial implications of this.

One of the first ideas connected to downsizing an event is to consider shortening the event opening hours. This means that the same numbers of staff are required, but for a shorter period of time. That would seem to result in a decrease in costs associated with staffing. There may, however, be an unforeseen or unexpected and unwanted result of shortening the opening hours. Visitors may be condensed into a shorter period of time, so the event may be more crowded, meaning that staff numbers have to be reinforced for safety, and thus costs may increase. This may have other cost increase factors, such as a larger medical provision or more toilets. Both of these matters need to be considered and the number and type required must be proportionate to the number of visitors to the event at any one time. If this number has now increased, because the opening hours have been shortened, then this apparent easy option may become more costly.

Another option would be to limit the visitors who may attend the event at any one time. In terms of reducing costs, this would be considered a means to decrease the number of staff needed to ensure visitor safety, as there are now fewer attendees. This does not necessarily mean that fewer people would attempt to visit the event. Unless advance ticketing has been in place, which may not be suitable to some types of events, the possible result of this is large visitor queues waiting to enter the event. These queues need to be managed, attendees need to be provided with information and it is likely that those queuing will have welfare needs to be met. Welfare needs of the visitors queuing will depend on the size of the queue, the time they have been queuing, weather conditions and the circumstances of their queuing. Welfare needs may range from the provision of stewards to provide information and to ensure orderly queuing, to the provision of toilets outside the event, and/or the provision of drinking water or cover against any adverse or extreme heat, cold or windy weather. So, again, the attempt to reduce costs may have unwanted and unexpected cost increases.

A consideration that event organisers may take into account in an attempt to reduce costs is to downscale the event by removing certain parts of the event offering. This will save on the costs of whatever aspect of the event has been removed. If this was live music, then it may mean a stage is not required, or aspects of the sound or lighting system have been reduced or become unnecessary. The downscaling of the event, however, may have the unintended consequence of ticket holders asking for a refund. If the event no longer appears to look, feel and be the same event as was advertised due to the downscaling, then there will be dissatisfaction. Another unintended consequence may be that the event is less attractive, and ticket sales will drop as fewer people want to attend. Concessions such as the food provision or other stalls who would sell merchandise relating to the live acts may also request a refund, as the event no longer fits into their sales profile. Alternatively, stalls may ask for a smaller trading pitch or a discounted pitch as the event has changed in profile and style. So the aim of reducing costs has been achieved, but along with this there will be a reduction in income from ticket sales and traders attendance.

Another aspect of the event world which is an unknown to new organisers is the specifics of what equipment works best and where. Equipment hiring and installation may have cost implications which may not have been researched. An example of this is the different types of barrier that can be used in the events industry. Which one to use in which circumstance is important, usually learned from experience, or from other event organisers or contractors/suppliers; it is not something that is easily found in a book or online. Whilst some barriers are made for specific situations (e.g. the pit barriers used at the front of a crowd), they come with an associated level of cost that will differ from other more common barriers. Lightweight pedestrian barriers cost significantly less than the correct pit barriers and, generally speaking, can be more easily erected. Pit barriers, however, will need to be erected by someone with specialist knowledge to ensure that they work in the intended manner. This means that not only do pit barriers cost more; they also have the human cost of erecting them attached. There may also be a cost incurred in transportation of the specialist barrier, which is probably not present when more general-purpose barriers are used. Effective financial planning will ensure that event organisers find out about these 'hidden' costs in the planning and feasibility stages and not during the event implementation.

9.2.3 Contractors/suppliers

Understanding the various contractors/suppliers needed to run a successful event is extremely important and inextricably linked to financial effectiveness. This section will continue to review the potential issues a new or inexperienced event organiser may come across when dealing with event contracts. Very often this is where the new event organiser begins to understand that the different aspects to an event do not come as one complete package, but are more akin to a series of interlinked contracts. This is often found at a music event, where the new organiser is not familiar with the way in which stage and production are managed and may not realise that when they booked the stage structure, this did not necessarily include the stage lighting, and almost certainly did not include the sound system required.

Other issues may occur with site type or staging a 'green field' event, where the new organiser may not have realised that their event will attract extra traffic to the area, and that the management of this traffic will be their responsibility. The event organiser will need to realise that traffic management rules are set by legislation, and therefore professional companies or competent individuals are required to carry out this work and will charge a fee. Some event organisers may believe that they will be able to achieve some of the necessary work through 'calling in favours' from their friends. Significant costs can incur when event organisers use practitioners or equipment that do not meet up-to-date legislation and standards, and therefore it is always better to ask for professional assistance than informal help from friends.

The cost implications are linked to the limited time available before the event when many contractors/suppliers, especially the competent ones, are already booked up and not available. In addition, the cost of employing a contractor/supplier at short notice may be higher than if the contractor/supplier had been engaged several months prior to the event. Due to this short notice the cost may not be able to be spread in instalments, which may have been an option if the contractor had been secured earlier in the event planning process.

Many event organisers may not have any money in a budget to hold an event, but still have the aspiration to host one. Even if the event is being put together using services provided free of charge, there may well be monetary aspects that will not have been foreseen. These may be crucial aspects such as insurance for the event or they may be 'soft-touch' matters such as providing food or drink for contractors/suppliers or invited VIPs who are giving their time or services for free. Whilst these may be aspects that are not always considered or remembered, they can form a large part of the smooth running of an event. Treating people considerately who are giving their time or supporting the running of the event for free can have a positive effect on the fluid running of the event.

It should be noted that established contractors/suppliers are aware of the difficulties that event organisers may face with regard to ticket sales. Many of them will have previous experience of not being paid after a failed event. This may cause them to exercise caution, and when working with an event organiser who is new to them, or new to the industry, they may be more reluctant to offer easy payment methods. Perhaps worse than the cautious contractor/supplier is the 'cowboy' contractor/supplier; this type of stakeholder may take advantage of the new, naïve or inexperienced event organiser. They may recognise that the event is financially unstable or that the organiser does not have the necessary experience and use this to their advantage. Examples of this may be the quoting of higher than usual prices for an activity, implying there is a shortage of particular contracting expertise at the time required, advising a larger amount of a product be supplied than is actually needed, or saying they require full payment significantly ahead of the event or else they will withdraw.

Study activity

During a seminar session, work in pairs to conduct a piece of role-play. One of you should take the part of the inexperienced event manager and the other that of the 'cowboy' contractor/supplier. The inexperienced event manager believes the contractor/supplier is quoting too high a price for their services and at an unreasonable cost; these terms must be negotiated with the contractor/supplier. In pairs negotiate this discussion from your own standpoint, add in your own details, and form an appropriate line of defence and argument.

9.2.4 Ticket sales

The sale of tickets for an event can be perceived as the most obvious and straightforward way to fund an event:

> Any profit is based on getting the price correct. Constructing the pricing strategy is a complex process which involves balancing competing factors, such as when the event is to be held, the nature of the target audience, the costs of the event and the positioning of the event.
>
> (Jackson, 2013, 82–83)

Inexperienced event organisers may plan to use ticket sales to pay their event bills after the event has taken place. It may be assumed that the event will sell enough tickets to pay all of the bills and associated charges connected to the event. This approach inevitably brings challenges and problems. Many contractors/suppliers require a reasonable deposit to secure their attendance, and may require the remainder of the contracted amount before the event takes place, or within a period of time after the event, usually a short one. If ticket sales are being used as the only source of income, unless tickets are selling well in advance of the event, it may not be possible to pay the deposit to secure the contract. If the event does not achieve the level of ticket sales necessary, the organisers will not have sufficient money to pay the bills after the event.

This situation can worsen if insufficient ticket sales mean the event has to be cancelled, and ticket money has to be refunded. If this has been used to pay the contractor/supplier's deposit, where does the money come from to refund the tickets? Alternatively, if ticket money has been kept aside and is refunded, then how is the contractor/supplier's bill to be paid? Even if events are cancelled, it is usual for there to be a sliding scale of payments to the contractor/supplier, depending on the amount of notice given in cancelling the event. This is to recompense the contractor/supplier for the loss of the contract, and is not unique to the events sector. It is worth considering the reputational damage to the organiser and/or the sponsors and/or the associated charity if the event is cancelled and ticket holders are not refunded their money or contractors/suppliers cannot be paid. This can snowball into legal complications and court cases too.

Ticket prices are usually calculated by new or inexperienced organisers by adding up all known costs and then dividing it by the numbers they wish/hope to attend. It is necessary, however, to consider other factors when calculating the price of a ticket. Ticket prices often need to represent value for money for those attending. This may conflict with the need to reflect the costs of putting on the event. Experienced event organisers are aware that they may not make a profit, or break even, for the first year (or more) and put plans in place to ensure they can continue trading, or running their enterprise.

Tip box

Ticket prices should not be calculated based on the cost of all of the foreseen expenditure divided by the estimated attendee numbers. Events often involve unforeseen costs and estimations may not always be accurate, so add in a contingency budget.

Events can be unpredictable in terms of ticket sales and the costs involved; however, one way in which financial planning can be maximised is to incentivise the buying of tickets. A common example of this is the 'early bird' ticket. This translates to a discount for anyone who purchases a ticket early. More information about ticket prices and strategies can be found in the Bestival case study at the end of this chapter. Many events offer a staggered early bird ticket, which gives the best discount in price for those who purchase as soon as tickets become available. A lesser discount would then be applied over a period of time as the event draws closer, and the full-price ticket may be the only one purchasable from a set time limit before the event. This discount is often in the form of money off the price of the ticket, but it can also include other advantages such as a better view, a better quality seat, or an additional gift. Additional gifts will usually take the form of free T-shirts, signed photographs of the artist, etc. They are items that the organiser, or promoter who is working in conjunction with the organiser, can access at low or no cost to themselves, but that are of sufficient interest to the ticket holder to attract them to buy a ticket at an earlier time. Often this will be advertised as 'a new release' of tickets, which provides a valuable publicity platform as well as allowing the organiser to make continual assessments before each release. If the event does need to be modified or downsized, then it can be done in a planned manner, rather than as a reactive decision.

9.3 Feasibility study for financial management

This section is a guide to conducting a feasibility study for an event in terms of finances and costs, which will help to understand the financial viability for the event to run. The first questions that should be asked when organising an event include:

- Is the location/site/venue suitable?
- Is there sufficient interest in the event?
- Is there sufficient time to prepare to put on this event?
- How much will it cost?
- What costs require to be paid for 'up front'?

Of course, depending on the reason for putting on the event, some of these questions and their answers will be less relevant than others. One way of obtaining the answers to the above questions is to carry out a feasibility study.

Tip box

A feasibility study should be conducted prior to the event implementation stages to assess the practical and financial challenges that will arise in event planning and management.

9.3.1 Venue suitability

A feasibility study to identify the site suitability will need to be undertaken. This will need to cover matters such as:

- What is the style of the site; is it the right style to fit in with the look and feel of the event?
- What infrastructure will need to be built/placed on site?
- What is the accessibility of the site – can the infrastructure get onto site, or are there weight, height or width restrictions which will compromise the ability to move infrastructure efficiently?
- How is it expected that visitors will arrive and leave the event? This will depend on the type of event, as well as who it is to appeal to and where it is to be advertised. A vehicle exhibition event will see the majority of exhibitors and a lot of visitors arrive using the type of vehicle that is on display, as they will want to show off their own version. In this case, it is most likely that only a small number will attend by public transport or on foot.
- What routes and methods are available to access the event? If the event is being held at a regional or national arena, then it is extremely likely that investment has taken place in the surrounding area to ensure that transport links are good and

that there is minimal negative impact on any local businesses or residents. There may also be permanent signage and transport methods already in place, which can be used by the organiser. If the event is being held in a local area, there are less likely to be the necessary event transport links, so there may be a need to provide transportation for the event, or to consider how visitors' arrival and exit can cause the least impact on residents. If the event is to be put on for the benefit of the local community and targeted at the local community then transportation may not be an area of concern.

- Using two people per square metre as a guideline figure, what is the safe site capacity? Bearing in mind that the space taken up by the infrastructure is not available for visitors to use, is the safe capacity of the site sufficient to make the event viable?
- What is the purpose of the event? Is it to highlight a purpose, raise funds for a charity, is it a commercial enterprise or is it for community engagement? All of these will have different priorities and may influence the site suitability. As an example, if the event is one of community engagement, then the location or venue is very likely to have to be in the heart of the community it is aimed at. In this instance, whilst it will still be necessary to ask the other suitability questions, these may be of less importance than the location, and compromises may have to be made.

9.3.2 Event interest

This is another aspect of the feasibility study, and whilst some of the previous questions will be relevant, there are other significantly different ones to be asked:

- Who is the event aimed at? It is important to identify who would be attracted to attend the event, as this can focus marketing in the correct areas, and avoid wasting money advertising to a mismatched clientele.
- How wide is the market scope for this type of event? Again, if this event is to attract a particularly specialist type of visitor, then it is necessary to identify if there is sufficient interest from those people who could attend this location.
- How will the event be advertised? This relates back to identifying clearly who the event is aimed at, so as to avoid wasted spend on marketing and advertising. It is also worth identifying what types of media are used by visitors to this event. If the appeal of this event is to an older demographic, then, generally, consideration should be given to marketing in periodicals and magazines, whereas if visitors are expected to come from a younger demographic, then social media such as Facebook, Twitter, Snapchat, etc. are more likely to achieve a better result.
- What is the cost of the event to a visitor, and can the visitor afford to attend? This links to the price of the ticket, but also links back to the site feasibility in terms of accessibility or transportation. There will need to be consideration of other costs for the visitor, such as the costs of food and drink if purchased on site, and whether they have an alternative option of bringing in their own food and drink. If they are not allowed to bring in their own food and drink, how is this to be prevented or managed?
- What market research has been done previously? Whilst there may be a cost involved, it is always worth carrying out some form of research into the proposed event. There will be many professional and commercial companies who will carry this out for an organiser but, depending on the type and size of the event being

considered, it may be possible to do this for less cost. If the event is to be for the local community it does not make financial sense to employ a nationally respected and high-profile commercial company to carry out the research. It is more likely that the answers can be gained from the local parish or district authority news-letter, or by putting leaflets or flyers in the local newspaper. Not only will this market research identify marketing strategies, costings and other event-related aspects, it will also help to identify if there is support from the local community for the proposed event to take place.

- Are there other events of this sort taking place, either in this area or regionally, nationally or internationally? It is important to identify other events of this type and consider whether this event can be cost-effective. If the events industry is satur-ated with this particular type of event, can the event currently under consideration be made sufficiently different to attract visitors?

9.3.3 Time

The planning and preparation for an event can take many weeks or months, depending on the size, scope and style of the event. It makes sense, therefore, that if planning begins too close to the event date, then parts of the event planning will not be carried out to a sufficient level. It is appropriate, therefore, to consider questions relating to timescales when conducting a feasibility study:

- Is there sufficient time to comply with legal requirements? In England and Wales it is necessary to apply for, and be granted, a Premises Licence in order to sell alcohol or play live music for the public. This licence takes a certain amount of time to be granted, and therefore if planning begins too late, the event being planned will not be allowed to sell alcohol or play live music. Refer to more information about licensing in Chapter 8.
- What tasks need to be done, are there sufficient people involved in the event plan-ning to share the jobs out, and have contracts been awarded? On many occasions events are put on by volunteers, or small committees; both of these are typified as people who give their time for free, and usually in addition to their daily lives. This limits the amount of time they have available to carry out research or planning of an event, even if their intentions are well meant.
- Are the attractions/acts/activities available for this event? Or have they already taken bookings elsewhere?
- If the original attractions/acts/activities are not available, are acceptable alternat-ives available?

9.3.4 Costings

Costs for an event will vary widely, and it is crucial that background work is done to identify what the costs may relate to. Having identified what the costs may relate to, it is also necessary to assess what the level of costs may be:

- Costs such as renting the event site, licence requirements as well as the costs of infrastructure will need to be identified at a very early stage.
- How much funding can the organisers obtain or raise? There may well be a differ-ence between the costs of the event and the funding amount available. If this is the

case, a crucial question is whether the shortfall can be bridged, and if so, how reliable is this further funding, and how easy is it to access it and what is the timescale for this? If this funding gap cannot be bridged then it may be necessary for the organisers to accept that their event is not financially viable, and that it should not go ahead. Event costs will undoubtedly influence how much is charged to concessions and activities that wish to rent a pitch at the event.

- There is also a limit to how much concessions or activities will pay for an event; there will be a 'market price'. This price will vary according to the type of event, the area in which it takes place, the time of year, how many other similar events there are taking place and the numbers of people expected to attend the event.
- In most events the concessions/traders carry out this activity as their day-to-day business and will have a business plan of which events fit their profile, and also the costs they can accommodate to trade. This means that they may be more experienced than the community organiser, and are therefore very likely to require clear and unambiguous information about their potential profit.

9.3.5 Up-front costs

Costs that may be said to be paid 'up front' are those which have to be paid at an earlier stage in order for the event to take place. These are usually costs such as the licence, the rent of the site or core infrastructure, which will include toilets, signage, generators and marquees/stages, etc.:

- These costs may also be ones which cannot be recovered if the event does not take place; however, this may depend on how much notice of event cancellation there is.
- Costs that may be said to be paid after the event has taken place usually relate to services, such as stewarding, first aid and other staffing costs.

Study activity

Conduct your own brief feasibility study for an event you are currently planning or volunteering at. Think about the aspects mentioned in this section such as time, costings, interest and venue.

9.4 Insurance

There are many varieties of insurance to be considered by an event organiser, although most are not a legal requirement. Just because insurance is not required by legislation, it does not mean that it should be dismissed and not given due consideration. The two insurances required by legislation are Road Traffic Act insurance and Employer's Liability Insurance. More information about this can be found in Chapter 8. Employer's Liability Insurance is required in the United Kingdom by anyone who employs staff, and may well be something that an event organiser is not aware of. Most event organisers

Table 9.2 An example from Anytime Show presented to demonstrate the way insurance cover may be utilised

---

Anytown Show is an event which takes place over two days and would expect to pay costs of £50,000 and achieve an income of £100,000. It has taken out cancellation insurance. Extreme weather In the form of heavy rain is forecast and during the build-up to the event and it becomes apparent that this rainfall has waterlogged the ground, making it difficult for infrastructure to access the site. Organisers also anticipate that the waterlogged ground will be hard for visitors to walk on and may result in visitors, contractors or staff sustaining injuries.

Organisers therefore reach a conclusion that they must seriously consider cancelling the event, and contact their insurance company.

Their cover with the insurance company is such that the costs would be paid for them, as well as some level of income. This payment of income will ensure the event has finances to take place in future years.

Using this hypothetical event as an example, it can be seen that paying the costs alone will cost the insurance company £50,000.

The insurance company send out an assessor who ascertains that the use of straw, wood chippings, sand or other drying medium onto the ground would make the site usable and safe. The cost of this drying medium will be £10,000.

In financial terms alone, it makes sense for the insurance company to pay for the drying medium to be laid on site: a payout of £10,000 instead of £50,000.

For the event organiser, their event is able to go ahead, thus safeguarding their potential income and their relationship with contractors/suppliers, concessions and traders (as they will still be able to carry out their business). The reputation of the event and organiser remains intact; it may even be enhanced due to the effort that the public perceive has been put in for the entertainment to continue.

---

would not consider that they would need insurance for vehicles on their site in the same way as they do to drive a motor vehicle on a road. The law relating to the driving of motor vehicles does also apply to vehicles on event sites, and must be taken into account by event organisers. Public Liability insurance is not a legal requirement, but it is in the interests of an event organiser to consider this aspect. This insurance can safeguard an organiser against claims from visitors who have received an injury at their event. One of the most useful types of insurance for an organiser to consider is that relating to cancellation of the event, often referred to as 'cancellation insurance'. Whilst its name implies that it gives cover to an organiser if an event has to be cancelled, it may also give cover to ensure that an event can continue; an example of this is given in Table 9.2.

9.5 Conclusion

Having a knowledge and competency in and around financial planning and management is advantageous within the business sector, and indeed the events industry.

Financial planning concerns the practical assessment of potential income and potential outgoings whilst understanding the internal and external pressures facing the event hosting. Creating and managing budgets is important for event success and will ensure that transparent and pragmatic approaches to the financing of the event are taken. Financial viability is the first area to consider when completing a feasibility study for the event. An event cannot run without financial backing and/or sensible financial forecasting.

When considering global events it is questionable why governments continue to bid for hosting mega-events which do not clearly indicate positive economic benefits (Mitchell and Stewart, 2015). For as long as events have been taking place people have continued to enjoy the experiences they acquire from attending them, profit or no profit. The events sector is so vast, encompassing charity, community, corporate, sporting, music and educational events to differing scales and budgets, that it is clear that financial profits are not always the main outcome for some event visions.

Case study 9: Bestival, UK

Bestival is an independent festival which takes place on the first or second weekend of every September at Robin Hill Country Park, Isle of Wight. The organisers describe it as an 'award winning 4 day boutique music festival' (Bestival, 2016a, online). Robin Hill Country Park is a green park which is ordinarily open to the public for relaxation and leisure activity.

> If I were to describe Bestival in a short sharp decree, I would say it's like being at one of your best mate's house parties. You know, the friend that's much cooler than they realise they are, effortlessly ahead of the game and making everyone feel alive and happy. That, for me, is the atmosphere of Bestival. And that atmosphere is without a doubt down to Rob Da Bank, his wife Josie and the team behind Bestival.
>
> (Bowman, 2015, 202)

The first event took place in 2004 and had a capacity of 5000 people; however, the numbers attending quickly grew as it gained in popularity. Today it has a licence under the Licensing Act 2003 for 60,000 people, although planning is geared towards a capacity of 55,000.

The festival opens its gates on Thursday for campers and runs a limited number of activities and entertainment on that day. Once the three-day event fully commences, there are eight stages which feature a wide variety of musical genres, along with art installations, and diverse attractions such as the Women's Institute tea tent and, in 2014, the world's largest glitter ball. Fancy dress is also encouraged and each year there is a different theme. The stages have differing names, including 'The Big Top', which speaks for itself and 'The Port', which is set on a ship.

Like many large music festivals, Bestival provides a variety of ticket purchasing options to accommodate a diverse demographic of potential festival attendees (Ticketline, 2016). From the 'early bird' prices to the concessionary tickets, such as teen, child and student, and continuing on to the campervan, caravan/tent costs, the website offers many options to appeal to the widest of audiences and pockets. The weekly payment plan allows their event attendee to secure a ticket without first having saved for the total cost of the ticket price. The festival can market this financial incentive with the tagline 'get your Bestival ticket for just £9 per week' (Bestival, 2016c). This is arguably a very valuable pricing strategy for both the organiser and consumer; it provides flexibility to the attendee and reassurance of attendance for the organiser. Another aspect of Bestival which may broaden its appeal to a wider audience is its connections with charities such as the Isle of Wight Youth Trust and Energy Revolution (Bestival, 2016b).

The success of Bestival as an event has arguably allowed for the development of other connected events, such as Camp Bestival, a family style festival in Dorset, Common People; an event taking place at two locations, one day after the other, and even Bestival Toronto, which takes place in Toronto, Canada (Bestival, 2016c). These other events connected to the Bestival name show how the popularity of an event may translate into financial success, which allows for expansion into other different styles of festival that appeal to different demographic audiences. This type of expansion relates to the financial management and viability of the event initially and will have cost implications.

The authors spoke with Judy Jackson of MRL Safety Limited, a company employed at the event. Judy is the Managing Director and a founder of the company. She has day-to-day accountability for managing the companies which form MRL Limited. The company is employed by the Bestival organisers to identify the risks relating to the event and agree risk management measures. They also write the safety documentation which is used by the organisers to communicate and inform their contractors/suppliers and artists and performers of what will be expected of them whilst on site. The event management company write the event operating plan which has evolved since the first festival took place, and all previous lessons learnt and good practice is included in the following year's documentation. This also allows them to concentrate on the newer attractions and activities.

During the live or public phase of the event, MRL Safety provides the staff for on-site safety roles and also manages event control. The company has the authority to make decisions on behalf of the organisers and has a long-standing working relationship with them and the event's other contractors/suppliers: a clear decision-making tree of responsibility exists. The event control includes many of the SAG members so most of those involved are familiar with both the event and the management plans. Event control also benefits from CCTV cameras.

One of the obvious challenges is that the event is based on the Isle of Wight and therefore the entire event infrastructure must be either sourced from the island (preferred option where feasible) or taken across the Solent by ferry. If the equipment has to be transported by ferry, then there are factors such as weather delays in sailings to be considered, as well as ensuring there is sufficient space or ticket availability on the required ferry journey. Whilst organisers of any event safeguard their actual finance details closely, it can be expected that transport challenges of this nature have implications for the cost of an event, and every

(Continued)

Case study 9 (*continued*)

effort has to be made to ensure these challenges do not outweigh the positive aspects or the financial viability of putting on the event. The vast majority of those attending also rely on the ferries to enable them to get to the site.

Like most outdoor events held in the UK, another main risk to this event is bad weather and the resultant mud. Contingencies include provision of extra trackway, straw and gravel. The site design also includes drainage systems to help cope with excessive rain. Costs relating to these aspects have to be planned for, as the likelihood of needing to use the contingencies is ever present.

Judy informed the authors that the build for the event usually commences nearly three weeks before it opens to the public. For the safety of the workers building the festival infrastructure, as well as for the safety of visitors to the park, areas of the park have to be closed off to the public. To ensure that the public cannot gain access a fence is built around the working area. This is the means used to ensure the organisers comply with section 3 of the Health and Safety at Work Act 1974: the requirement to ensure, so far as is reasonably practicable, the safety of persons not employed by them who may be affected by the work activity.

The event finishes on a Sunday evening, and therefore visitors have two realistic options for getting back home: they can leave the event early to ensure they catch their booked ferry, or they can travel home on the Monday. Recognising the dilemma, and wanting to ensure the best experience for the visitors, the event organisers' breakdown schedule allows for visitors to leave on Monday. The knock-on effect of this is that contractors will be carrying out the breakdown on the Monday and will not be able to leave the event until Tuesday. For a contractor this means an extra day's work at the site and extra accommodation costs for their staff, which they will hope to recoup from the organisers.

Having now seen some of the details of a large-scale musical festival, it is worth considering an estimation of some of the costs involved in putting on such an event. Financial details about an event are safeguarded closely by the organisers. Event organisers keep this information protected in order to manage their own internal processes privately, and to keep the data away from potential competition. The authors have developed Table 9.3 to highlight typical costs associated with generic music festivals within the UK. For an international event it will be necessary to consider the costings relating to that country; it is unlikely to be more cost-effective to take a UK base company's staff overseas.

From the small selection of costs shown in Table 9.3, it is easy to see how the new or naïve event organiser may underestimate the cost of putting on an event. One of the reasons that seasoned organisers of established and successful events use ticketing incentives, such as those shown and commented upon earlier is to offset the costs of pre-planning, contracting entertainment and hiring services and equipment during the months leading up to the actual event.

Thank you to Judy Jackson for sharing your experiences with the authors to formulate this case study.

Table 9.3 An example of costings associated with live music festivals similar to Bestival

Event Aspect	Cost Details
Stages	The costs vary from as low as £3000 for a stage which 'folds' out of a lorry to tens of thousands of pounds for purpose-built themed structures.
Stewarding	Safety stewards attract the 'living wage', currently at £7.20 an hour over the age of 25 yrs; whilst Security Industry Authority licensed stewards attract £10–£12 per hour. This means the cost to an organiser per hour will be higher, as it will include the hidden costs of administration, taxation and National Insurance/superannuation. The number and type of stewards required at an event should be identified using risk assessment methods. It is easy to see therefore how accurate assessment can save money, a point made in Chapter 8 about the financial reasons to comply with legislation such as the need for risk assessment.
Medical Provision	The cost to an organiser for a first aider for an event is around £9–12 per hour; however, the paramedic cost to an organiser is around £45 per hour. If your event requires an ambulance which is expected to be crewed by a paramedic and an ambulance technician, then the cost for this package is around £84 per hour. Not only is it possible to see how accurate assessment can identify the type of resource required, it is also possible to see why some organisers find it hard to provide appropriate resources, and therefore seek to 'cut corners'.
Fire Stewards	This will vary according to the requirements of the event and competency of the steward; however, the starting cost to an organiser is approximately £15 per hour.
Toilets	Within the *Purple Guide* (EIF, 2014, online) it is advised that the number of toilets required should be divided into male/female needs. Specifically for an event which involves camping, the requirements are advised as one toilet per 75 females and one toilet per 150 males, plus one urinal per 250 males The Purple Guide (EIF, 2014, online). Obviously the more toilets hired, the better the deal to be struck, and there are a vast range of types of toilet as well as the level of luxury offered. It is also worth remembering that the cost of the toilet does not include the servicing/cleaning of them. Another cost which is not included in the hire is the transportation cost, and this can sometimes be greater than that of the toilets themselves.

(Continued)

Case study 9 (*continued*)

Event Aspect	Cost Details
Traffic Management Equipment or Staff	Community Safety Accredited Stewards can cost around £30 or more per hour, the cost of signage and cones can often form part of the deal to apply for the traffic regulation orders.
Radios	These are usually hired as a package including the radios and an appropriate number of chargers for the number of radios hired. Earpieces and spare batteries are often not included and so are separate costs, as are any additional infrastructure such as aerials or equipment to boost the radio transmission signal. Again, the more radios hired, the better the deal that could be obtained. Increasing the level of technical specification of the radio will also increase its cost.
Fencing	The cost of fencing differs according to the types of fencing needed. Heras fencing, (the type with the 'block' feet often found on building sites), and pedestrian barriers, approximately 60cm to 1m in height and with the protruding feet, can cost as little as £1 per metre for a week's hire. 'Ready hoard' or 'steelshield', (approximately 2m in height and obscured so that they cannot be seen through), are approximately £5 per metre per week. Pit barriers, (perhaps the most famous brand being 'Mojo'), cost at least £20 per metre and will require knowledgeable staff to put them together. All of the above fencing costs exclude the cost of transporting them from the hire location to the event venue.

Evaluative student questions

1 List the positive and negative impacts of hosting an event on a small island, and discuss, with reasons, whether the organisers should consider the impact on the mainland.
2 Bestival use an external organisation, MRL Safety Limited, to manage the risk and event safety side of the event. What are the positives and potential challenges of outsourcing this to others?
3 In relation to ticketing strategies, consider the positive and negative aspects of the options referred to in this case study, giving reasons.

Further reading

Maylor, H. (2010) *Project management.* 4th edition. Harlow: Pearson. Chapter 8.

Schnitzer, M. (2014) Financing events. In: Beech, J., Kaiser, S. and Kaspar, R. (eds), *The business of events management*. London: Pearson, 113–135.

Wilson, R. (2013) Event finance. In: Bladen, C., Kennell, J., Abson, E. and Wilde, N. (eds), *Events management: an introduction*. Abingdon: Routledge, 136–161.

References

BBC (2011) *Sheffield's World Student Games £658m debt 'disaster'*. Available from: http://www.bbc.co.uk/news/uk-england-south-yorkshire-14134973 [Accessed 9 December 2015].

Bestival (2016a) *About*. Available from: http://www.bestival.net/about [Accessed 11 April 2016].

Bestival (2016b) *Bestival 2016 tickets*. Available from: http://www.bestival.net/tickets [Accessed 11 April 2016].

Bestival (2016c) *Homepage*. Available from: http://www.bestival.net/ [Accessed 11 April 2016].

Bowdin, G., Allen, J., O'Toole, W., Harris, R. and McDonnell, I. (2011) *Events management*. 3rd edition. London: Butterworth-Heinemann.

Bowman, E. (2015) *Edith Bowman's great British music festivals*. London: Blink Publishing.

Bramwell, B. (1997) Strategic planning before and after a mega-event. *Tourism Management*, 18(3) 167–176.

Events Industry Forum (EIF) (2014) *The Purple Guide*. Available from: http://www.thepurpleguide.co.uk/ [Accessed 1 April 2016].

Giulianotti, R., Armstrong, G., Hales, G. and Hobbs, D. (2015) Sport mega-events and public opposition: a sociological study of the London 2012 Olympics. *Journal of Sport and Social Issues*, 39(2) 99–119.

Health and Safety at Work Act 1974 (c.37). London: HMSO.

Jackson, N. (2013) *Promoting and marketing events*. London: Routlege.

Licensing Act 2003 (c.17). London: HMSO.

Maylor, H. (2010) *Project management*. 4th edition. Essex: Prentice Hall.

Mitchell, H. and Stewart, M.F. (2015) Why should you pay to host a party? An economic analysis of hosting sports mega-events. *Applied Economics*, 47(15) 1550–1561.

Schnitzer, M. (2014) Financing events. In: Beech, J., Kaiser, S. and Kaspar, R. (eds), *The business of events management*. London: Pearson, 113–135.

Solberg, H.A. and Preuss, H. (2015) Major sports events: the challenge of budgeting for the venues. *Event Management*, 19(3) 349–363.

Ticketline (2016) *Bestival tickets*. Available from: http://www.ticketline.co.uk/bestival-ticketsour [Accessed 11 April 2016].

Webber, D. (2004) Understanding charity fundraising events. *International Journal of Nonprofit and Voluntary Sector Marketing*, 9(2) 122–134.

Wilson, R. (2013) Event finance. In: Bladen, C., Kennell, J., Abson, E. and Wilde, N. *Events management: an introduction*. Abingdon: Routledge, 136–161.

Chapter 10

Plan analysis and risk

The first step in the risk management process is to acknowledge the reality of risk. Denial is a common tactic that substitutes deliberate ignorance for thoughtful planning.

(Charles Tremper, cited in Vellani 2007, 110)

10.1 Introduction

According to Frosdick (1999, cited in Toohey and Taylor, 2008), what we understand of risk in modern times, originates back to the seventeenth century and the study of probabilities associated with gambling. This was fused into economics another two centuries later, and evolving in more pessimistic connotations, mainly corroborated by the perception of hazards in the twentieth century. Nowadays, the perceived increased threat of terrorism places risk management high on the agenda for event planning and has resulted in increased security and safety measures. It also influences the way people perceive their daily lives and their future, as risk management and perceived risk have adopted a more political character (Toohey and Taylor, 2008).

In their private lives, people manage all sorts of risks and take measures to reduce the likelihood or consequences of unwelcome events, for example by securing car insurance, regularly servicing their car or stopping and looking before crossing a busy road. Event organisers also have to manage risks because events are particularly prone to risk. Getz (2012, 302) defines risk management as 'the process of anticipating, preventing or minimizing potential costs, losses or problems for the event, organization, partners and guests'. Bowdin et al. (2011) further highlight that risk management is an integral part of event project management and that it also bifurcates across other areas of knowledge and management. Risks must be identified and anticipated and the risk management plan must be an essential element of the overall strategic events plan. Risk is defined in different areas of activity and discipline, including events, where it can be described as 'an uncertain event or condition that, if it occurs, has a positive or negative effect on an event's objective' (Silvers, 2013, 22).

10.2 The risk management process

It is good practice for the risk management process to cover the way in which a project is managed, from the initial concept to its delivery. The risk management strategy should be customised for each individual event and should outline the way in which risk management will be framed within the overall project management plan. Risk management therefore can be seen as a continuous process of identifying potential risks at events and quantifying the risks with regard to the likelihood of occurrence and the possible impact they could have on the event. The risk management procedure follows five sequential steps: identify, assess, plan, implement and lastly communicate, review and update (Office of Government Commerce, 2009; HSE, 2014). These steps will be further explored in this section.

10.2.1 Identify hazards

In this stage as much information as possible is gathered on the event to determine the possible risks and triggers and to devise the risk management strategy for the event. The risk strategy should be considered from an early stage in order to analyse and prioritise the risk response. It is recommended that it should be drafted in the initiation phase of the event, when the project plan sets its initial goals and objectives, activities, processes and people involved in the forthcoming event/s (Silvers, 2013). The main goal of this first step is to pinpoint risks and opportunities that would potentially affect the event's objectives, and OGC (2009, 81) recommends a number of techniques:

- *Review lessons:* one of the most practical ways to diminish uncertainty in an event is to assess previous similar events and thus determine the threats and opportunities that could affect your own event.
- *Risk checklists*: internal inventories of previous events and the risks identified should not be overlooked by the organising team. Risk checklists could be consulted from previous similar events organised by the company or by similar events identified in the region/country.
- *Risk prompt lists*: in region/country/wider area in which the event is organised, there are specialised bodies (e.g. HSE in the UK) that make publicly available lists with risks clustered into categories and types. In this way, new sources of risk can be identified and placed in a wider context.
- *Brainstorming*: group work (if you are fortunate enough to be working as part of a team) is stimulated by gathering members from all the event sub-teams to identify and cluster risks. The discussion facilitator has the role of stimulating discussion and avoiding criticism in order to get an opinion from each individual contributing.
- *Risk breakdown structure (RBS)*: represents the hierarchical composition of the event to identify potential sources of risk. There are several ways to break down risks, and for bigger events it might be useful to do the exercise several times and create several lists. For example, the risks for an event can be broken down into: Technical, External (new policies and regulations, weather conditions and stewarding) and Organisational (finance, staffing, marketing and project delays).

Using these techniques all risks that could occur during an event are identified by gathering the team and brainstorming. This activity workshop should happen several times during the phases of an event, include representatives from all departments (e.g.

project leaders, marketing, human resource, finance, accountancy, etc.) and be facilitated by an experienced member of staff who is able to use several of the identification techniques mentioned.

10.2.2 Assess

After identification, risk characteristics will have to be assessed in order to determine if the risks are worth further analysis. Once the team has decided that a certain risk needs pursuing and a connected response is needed, then it needs to be established if the risk event information will be conducted through quantitative or qualitative means (Ahmed et al., 2007). The qualitative risk analysis provides information on the *probability* and *impact* of each risk, while the quantitative analysis is about assigning numerical values to probability and impact in order to set and prioritise the risk response.

Risk probability or likelihood is the chance of a risky event occurring; risk impact (or severity) is the outcome generated. Experts in risk management first evaluate the probability and then the impact of its consequences. Events are confronted with different types of risk that can require specific control measures which need to be considered in more detail. These control measures, however, do not necessarily need to be assessed separately but can be included in the overall risk assessment; refer to the Health and Safety Executive website for more information.

When completing the risk assessment and reviewing or assessing hazards it is advisable to consider the questions clustered into categories. For example, when organising an outdoor music event, some of the themes that could emerge include: crowd safety, fire safety, hazardous substances, security, vulnerable people and disability, first aid, etc. HSE (2014a, 26) provides a checklist of possible questions to be asked (see Table 10.1).

Table 10.1 Risk assessment checklist

- Is the number of people attending controlled or predictable?
- Is the music event going to target a certain age group (depending on the artists performing)?
- Is the crowd formed of individuals, families or large groups?
- Is the concert likely to generate strong feelings/emotions?
- How will performers affect the behaviour of the crowd?
- Will the media be present? Could this affect crowd safety in any way?
- Is the crowd likely to be gender dominant (e.g. mostly female)?
- Are young adults, vulnerable people or people with disabilities particularly catered for?
- What is the duration of the concert?
- Any other major event happening in the area at the same time?
- Is it likely that some attendees would have been consuming alcohol/drugs?
- Will alcohol be available?
- Are gate crashes likely?
- Is aggressive behaviour likely?

Source: HSE, 2014a, 26

According to Prince2 (OGC, 2009, 82) there are several techniques that can be used to estimate risks:

- *Probability trees*: graphical representations used to forecast possible outcomes to a set of circumstances in a qualitative way.
- *Pareto analysis*: a technique used by management to classify risks in the order of priority in which they should be addressed. Thus, efforts can be directed towards the risks that would have the highest impact of project objectives.
- *Probability impact grid*: a technique that ranks threats and opportunities in a qualitative way by scaling values. It can be used to provide an estimation of risk impact and ranking so that management can effectively direct its time and resources.

Managerial experience and the context in which the event is set are decisive factors in the identification and assessment of particular event risks (Ritchie and Reid, 2012). It is advisable to gather knowledge from previous or similar events, to simulate scenarios and seek advice from advisory groups (e.g. SAG).

10.2.3 Plan

This is the planning stage of the management responses to the risks and opportunities that have been identified. In the case of a risk occurring, the project team needs to be prepared, and this step aims at maximising opportunities and reducing threats. According to Greenwell et al. (2014), without the necessary planning, most events can have unreasonable levels of risk; risk management strategies need to be implemented in order to decrease the risk(s) to acceptable levels. The *risk management matrix* in Figure 10.1, adapted from Greenwell et al. (2014), outlines the levels of risks and provides a framework for establishing the impact of the potential risks.

	PROBABILITY			
IMPACT	A	B	C	D
1	5	5	4	3
2	5	4	3	2
3	4	3	2	1
4	3	2	1	1

Figure 10.1 Planning with the matrix

Source: Adapted from Greenwell et al., 2014, 154

10.2.3.1 Probability

A. Very high (frequent): likely to occur immediately or in a short period of time – will greatly impact on the project cost, schedule and/or performance
B. High (likely): quite likely to occur in time – will impact with a lower high intensity project cost, schedule and/or performance
C. Medium (occasional): may occur in time – will slightly impact on schedule, performance or cost
D. Low: unlikely to occur – will have relatively little impact on cost, schedule or performance.

10.2.3.2 Impact

1 Catastrophic: may result in death
2 Critical: may cause severe injury, major property damage, significant financial loss, and/or result in negative publicity for the organization and/or institution
3 Marginal: may cause minor injury, illness, property damage, financial loss and/or could result in negative publicity for the organisation and/or institution
4 Negligible: hazard presents a minimal threat to safety, health and wellbeing of participants.

To exemplify, the risk matrix shown in Figure 10.2 demonstrates that the level of risks at events fluctuates according to the type of event organised and the type of activities that will be in place, as described by Shone and Parry (2013, 228):

	PROBABILITY			
IMPACT	A	B	C	D
1		Motor Rally Event		
2	Adventure		Street Festivals	
3		Public Shows		Conferences
4			Dinners	

Figure 10.2 Assessing risk at events

Source: Ciuchete, 2012

- Low risk levels: usually, these are indoor events that do not involve risky activities. The organisers and staff members are experienced and well within their range of expertise. Examples: conferences, charity events, dinners, etc.
- Medium risk levels: these might be either indoor or outdoor events that have one or more of the following specifications: a certain level of risk involved, an event that is outside the usual expertise area of organisers, unusual locations/event venues. Usually, medium risk events involve large numbers of people attending large-scale occasions like street festivals, sport competitions or concerts.
- High risk levels: these events involve large numbers of people attending events that have evident dangers attached. Examples: adventure sport competitions, racing events.

According to Prideaux, Laws, and Faulkner (2003), ranking risks according to probability and impact provides data that can be used as the basis for forecasting and developing possible event scenarios. Assessing and classifying risks using the matrix enables event managers to adopt and recommend the most appropriate risk management strategies according to the level of importance in the risk process, and plan accordingly to ensure the safety and security of participants.

10.2.3.3 Risk response (dealing with the risk)

As mentioned, the planning stage involves a set of responses to risks and opportunities, and it is essential to balance the cost of response implementation against impact and probability. Silvers (2013, 42) argues that 'for every risk identified, a decision must be made about how to respond'. Recommended steps are to review what was learnt from organising previous events, to identify solutions and to implement these measures until the risk becomes manageable. Silver (2013, 43–44) refers to some of the terms below:

- *Avoidance*: this is the best solution a project manager can take in the case of risk response – if the risk is avoided, it cannot affect the event/project. Although, 'it is not realistic to avoid all risks as events would simply not take place' (Silvers, 2013, 43). Risks would be identified starting at the planning stage of an event; the project manager together with their team would brainstorm and create the Risk Brainstorming Session to categorise risks. At this session it is important to include representatives from all teams involved in the event as the risk management plan needs a holistic approach.
- *Transference*: in some cases, risks can be transferred to other parties (e.g. subcontractors), which is typically managed through contractual arrangements. The contract clauses should stipulate all the contractual duties before, during and after the event and should be individualised for different subcontractors and liabilities.
- *Mitigation/reduction*: Ritchie and Reid (2012, 164) draw parallels between mitigation and 'risk treatment measures' because they decrease the impact of a risk by lowering the possibility of that risk happening and minimising the severity of its consequences if it does happen. For example, at many events, children and young adults might be separated from their parents. Event organisers must minimise the risk by implementing a plan before the event for all staff to follow.

- *Retention/acceptance*: when none of the previous options will work (avoid, transfer or mitigate) a risk will have to be accepted. Acceptance does not mean ignoring the risk; it is about knowing that alternatives have been considered and that the risks will still be monitored. As Silvers (2013, 43) states, 'sufficient resources to overcome a risk should it occur must be allocated, as must sufficient funds be allocated to pay for losses should they occur'.

10.2.3.4 Risk assessment

Risk assessments are documents that are created by the event organiser to record and assess the risks related to the event. In England and Wales, current guidelines state that if an organisation employs five or more people, it is a requirement that a record is taken of the risk assessment and any key findings. Even if the organisation has fewer than five employees, it is still required to undertake a suitable and sufficient assessment of the foreseeable risks to health and safety of employees and others, including the audience. This assessment must be completed by a competent person. Some event organisers choose to subcontract the production of a risk assessment to an outside contractor, but that does not remove responsibility from the core organisation and it is still important that they should be fully informed and understand the process.

There may also be a temptation to copy other event risk assessments, as some risks are common to all events. This practice should never be encouraged as the event organiser has to take responsibility for their own risk assessment and management, and needs to understand the bigger picture and how risk is built in to wider safety planning for the event. Event organisers ignore this process at their peril. Following the Hillsborough Stadium Disaster, Lord Justice Taylor argued that:

> It is not enough to aim only at the minimum measures necessary for safety. That has been, at best, the approach in the past and too often not even that standard has been achieved. What is required is the vision and imagination to achieve a new ethos.
>
> (Still, 2013, 23)

Although this statement relates specifically to football, it is relevant to every event where minimum measures and costs are allowed to influence event safety.

Still (2013, 73) states that risks that go unnoticed are called 'problems lying in wait'. These are problems that have not been considered or dealt with appropriately; risks that people knew about, or should have known about. He goes on to state that failure to identify risks that prove to be the underlying causes of major incidents may be defined as negligent. If these risks are not recognised during the planning stages of the event, and the event then proceeds and the risks are realised, there may be questions of negligence raised in relation to the risk assessment, and the relative parties could be held accountable.

A risk assessment should be a detailed examination of the whole event undertaken by someone familiar with all of its aspects to examine what could reasonably happen or cause harm or damage, the extent of that harm or damage, the likelihood of it occurring, and the control measures necessary to reduce or eliminate those risks identified. The *Purple Guide to Health, Safety and Welfare at Music and Other Events* 2014 states that:

A hazard is something with the potential to cause harm, for the hazard to have effect, there has to be a hazard event, a risk is both the likelihood of that hazardous event occurring and the seriousness of its impact.

(EIF, 2014, online)

Whilst there are common hazards present at all events, the management of the risks created by these hazards will be unique to each individual event. Safety management will therefore be about managing the risks and not the hazards, and implementing control measures to try to bring the risks down to acceptable levels.

There are many templates and guidance documents available to event organisers to assist them in preparing a risk assessment. It is down to individuals to choose which method they feel comfortable with and what is most appropriate for their event. By way of an example, both a template and guidance for its completion can be found on the Lincolnshire Event Safety Partnership (LESP) website (LESP, 2012). The LESP risk assessment template is sourced from IOSH, although the guidance is authored by LESP. In addition, useful examples on how to devise a risk assessment have been produced by the Health and Safety Executive (HSE, 2014, 1–4), which recommends a five-step approach to risk assessment: (1) identify the hazards; (2) decide who may be harmed and how; (3) evaluate the risks and decide on precautions; (4) record the findings and implement; and (5) review the assessment and update. An event risk assessment must acknowledge the venue and location issues, event content and visitor profiles. It is important to consider all three of these aspects, and everything else in the risk assessment will be related to this context.

10.2.4 Implementation

At this stage, the event project manager needs to make sure that planned risk responses are correctly implemented and monitored. Depending on the size and scope of the event, the project manager needs to select named roles from the project team who would have project risk responsibilities. A common mistake to be avoided is the allocation of too many risk-related responsibilities to one role. Keeping thorough documentation throughout the event (from initiation to shut-down stage) helps to minimise the risks and disputes. Detailed project documentation should be complete, clear/easy to follow by any team member and reviewed constantly during the project.

10.2.5 Communicate, review and update

The stage of communication, review and update should be a continuous process that takes place during all phases of the event both internally (project team) and externally (stakeholders). Silvers (2013) recommends that in addition to the current written communication procedures (reports, documentations, performance, orders), meetings and team workshops offer a valuable opportunity for brainstorming and collecting ideas from the entire event team.

10.3 Types of risk

There are many different types of general risk relevant to the events setting and industry, including:

- *Project risks:* the organisation/event project's objectives that are at risk – will include a series of project tasks (e.g. covering time, quality, cost)
- *Business risks*: affect the organisation/event in a positive (profit) or negative (loss) way
- *Strategic risks*: affect the organisation/event in the long term (e.g. financial, political, environmental, etc.)
- *Financial risks*: refer to the financial liability of a business (e.g. exchange rates, cash flow)
- *Operational risks*: all the risks that are associated with running an event (e.g. lighting and electrical devices have to work in all allocated rooms when organising a conference)
- *Technological risks*: presents the risks of technological failure (e.g. if the sound system does not work at a concert, the show will have to stop until the problem is fixed)
- *Environmental risks*: when an organisation/event is affected by the environment in which it operates (e.g. extreme weather conditions such as snow, hurricanes)
- *Political risks*: can happen at different levels and depending on the situation. They can affect the organisation/event's objectives or can even lead to the cancellation of an event (e.g. violent street demonstrations)
- *Reputational risks*: when the reputation of an organisation/event is affected (e.g. negative publicity).

The management of risk is an ongoing activity that takes place throughout the life of an event and should never be based on chance. According to Kemp (2009), the most common risk in events is not the hazard itself, but the lack of preparation in dealing with it. Taking a certain level of risk in events is inevitable, as events are treated as projects and projects are facilitating change, and change brings uncertainty and consequently risks (OGC, 2009). Training initiatives and risk management education, however, are imperative to minimise risks and ensure safety and security at events (Kemp, 2009). Beside the more general types of risk mentioned, event organisers have also to deal with specific event risks around health and safety, hazardous substances, electrical installations and pyrotechnics, venue design and management, catering provision, fire safety, alcohol and drugs, crowd management and transport management (Shone and Parry, 2013; HSE, 2014a). This chapter focuses on risk, risk management and risk assessment, which are separate to threat and threat assessment. For purposes of clarification, threat assessment is the assessment of risk relating to terrorism, the security of VIPs or high-profile visitors such as members of a royal family, or the security of sensitive or secure venues such as military bases holding public events. It is beyond the scope of this chapter to include threat assessment, but it is important to be aware of what it entails and how it relates to risk.

10.4 Health, safety and security

Prevention and safety control plans are an important part of any event risk strategy (Bowdin et al., 2011). In an article discussing the concerns of health and safety among international tourists, Peattie, Clarke and Peattie, (2005) notice the confusion and overlap of the three terms health, safety and security. The same woolliness be observed when applied to an event context. For clarity the following de can be used:

- *Security*: the possibility of individuals being harmed as a result of the premeditated action of others at an event (e.g. mugging, assault, rape, murder)
- *Safety*: the possibility of attendees/organisers being injured accidentally at an event (e.g. traffic accidents, weather conditions, injuries relating to adventure or high-risk events)
- *Health*: the potential development of diseases, health casualities or harm as a result of participating at an event (e.g. food poisoning at an event where food is available).

Health and safety regulations are constantly changing and it is important for an event organiser to keep up to date with the latest regulations in the region/country/continent where the event is taking place. The map in Figure 10.3 identifies health and safety regulations in different parts of the world.

10.4.1 Control of hazardous substances

Specific health and safety regulations should be observed and followed if the event is likely to involve the use of dangerous substances (e.g. the storage and use of ignitable materials) as this could present high risks to the crowd. The event organiser should make sure that the venue and structures have been checked by the relevant competent body, that there is no restriction to access routes and that the equipment installed is maintained according to latest regulations and standards.

10.4.2 Electrical installations, fireworks and pyrotechnics

There is arguably a difference between outdoor firework displays and pyrotechnics – fireworks are generally used for entertainment purposes at a variety of different festivals and celebrations, while pyrotechnics are used to enhance a stage, a scene or to draw the audience's attention to a particular element. The most common problem with pyrotechnics is the lack of pre-planning; frequently the decision to make use of them in a show is made quite late on. The most important issue here is that pyrotechnics present high risks because once they have been ignited they are almost impossible to extinguish (HSE, 2014b). It should be noted that the fire services are likely to refer to all kinds of material used in this way as 'pyrotechnics' in their identification.

10.5 Venue design and management

The first aspect that is usually taken into account when selecting a venue for an event is its suitability for the event's needs and audience preferences. The main principle for selection should be the site's design, which would ideally encompass all health, safety and emergency procedures (Bladen et al., 2012). With the rapid increase in events locations/venues entering the marketplace, Hassanien and Dale (2011, 111) present

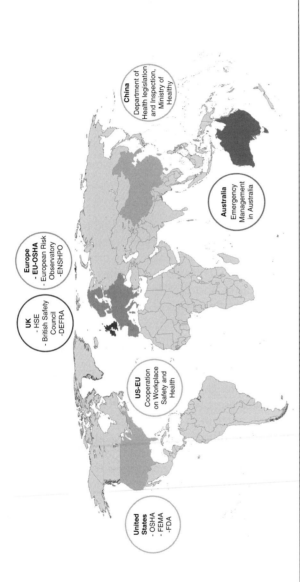

United Kingdom

HSE - Health and Safety Executive: http://www.hse.gov.uk/index.htm

British Safety Council: https://www.britsafe.org

DEFRA - Department for Environment Food & Rural Affairs:
https://www.gov.uk/government/organisations/department-for-environment-food-rural-affairs

Europe

EU-OSHA - The European Agency for Safety and Health at Work (EU-OSHA):
https://osha.europa.eu/en/legislation

European Risk Observatory: to identify new and emerging risks in occupational safety and health

ENSHPO - European Network of Safety & Health Professional Organisations:
http://www.enshpo.eu/home

US - EU

Cooperation on Workplace Safety and Health: http://www.useuosh.org/

United States

OSHA - Occupational Safety and Health Administration: https://www.osha.gov

FEMA - Fire-fighter Health & Safety (FEMA):
http://www.usfa.fema.gov/fireservice/firefighter_health_safety/

FDA - Us Food and Drug Administration: http://www.fda.gov/

China

Department of Health legislation and Inspection, Ministry of Healthy:
http://english.sina.com

Australia

Emergency Management in Australia: http://www.en.gov.au

Figure 10.3 Health and safety regulations around the globe

Source: adapted from Bladen et al., 2012, 196

a typology of event venues that encompasses the different range of sub-sectors within each main sector, including hotels, visitor attractions, conference centres, universities, etc. The authors' selection criteria is a template for the entire industry (see Table 10.2).

From the wide array of venues listed, the event organiser will select the appropriate location in terms of type, scale and scope to suit the event's capacity, capability and marketing needs. Any venue, however, has strengths, shortages, opportunities and

Table 10.2 Typology of events venues

Theme	Benchmark Principle
Strategic	• Core business activity: primary (Excel London) or secondary (Disneyland Paris – runs events alongside its main entertainment business) • Ownership: public, private or charitable trust • Management: independent, franchised, multi-national • Competitive strategy: cost leadership, differentiation, focus, etc. • Industry context: hospitality, tourism, leisure, sport, educational or religious • Product life cycle: birth, growth, maturity and decline
Market	• Buyer type: individual, corporate, association and government • Market place/space: local, regional, national and international. It is not unusual for event venues to sign their geographical presence in their title (e.g. San Diego Convention Centre) • Benefits sought: business, entertainment, training, marketing, study, etc.
Physical	• Age: historic (e.g. Edinburgh Castle, London Dungeon), classic (e.g. Chatsworth House, Derbyshire, UK) or modern (the Shard, London) • Location: city or town centre, rural or remote • Size of the venue: large, medium sized or small • Site: natural or purpose built • Space: indoor, outdoor or a combination (e.g. Biennale di Venezia, Italy)
Service	• Provision of services: in-house, outsourced or contracted • Class, grade or service quality • Facilities and services provided: full service, self-catering or residential or non-residential venues • Licensed and unlicensed
Activity	• Type: conferences, exhibition, congress and/or conventions, etc. • Duration: short or long (can last for several days like the Cannes Film Festival in France) • Admission: fee-paying or free entry

Source: adapted from Hassanien and Dale 2011, 111

risks, and this is when the risk manager's role becomes imperative as they will need to establish the feasibility for the production of the event, assess all hazards and make sure risks are mitigated (Silvers, 2013).

Study activity

In pairs, discuss the differences between security, safety and health and draw upon your own event experiences to do so.

10.5.1 Catering provision

Food poisoning can occur as a result of consuming food or drink contaminated with harmful bacteria or chemical toxins. There are two main types of bacterial food poisoning according to Safefood (2016, online):

- Contamination caused by consumption of bacteria: the result of food being stored in conditions that support the growth of bacteria
- Contamination caused by the consumption of toxins: toxins are chemicals produced in the food before consumption and sickness symptoms appear very soon after eating it.

In the UK, the HSE provides guidance on food safety management for event organisers in order to help them review existing arrangements, provides training for staff members and oversees activities related to handling food. HSE (2014c) guidance helps event organisers and health and safety inspectors to follow the mandatory law and regulations. By following the basic rules of food safety, risk managers can prevent food contamination rather than deal with food poisoning after it has happened, as little can be done in retrospect.

Tip box

A set of four simple rules should be followed in order to prevent food contamination according to Safefood (2016, online):

1 *Clean*: even it seems like the obvious advice, always wash hands before handling or eating food.
2 *Cook*: exposing food to high temperatures through cooking helps destroy any harmful bacteria that might be present.
3 *Chill*: food kept in the refrigerator at a temperature of 5°C or below prevents bacteria from growing.
4 *Separate*: to prevent cross-contamination, there should be separate sinks and containers for fruit and vegetables, meat and fish (e.g. make sure that vegetables do not come into contact with raw meat).

As an example, in 2013 approximately 400 people out of 12,000 attendees at a food festival in Newcastle, UK experienced and reported symptoms of diarrhoea and vomiting. After a thorough investigation, health experts reported that the poisoning came from uncooked curry leaves used in chutney. The three-day street spice festival suffered serious damage to its reputation because of this negligence (BBC, 2013). This example stresses the importance of taking simple precautions to guarantee hygiene and food safety and prevent outbreaks of food poisoning.

10.5.2 Fire safety

An event organiser has a duty of care to put on a fire-safe event, firstly, by creating and setting all necessary conditions for participants to exercise their personal responsibility to the fullest and secondly, by providing for their general safety and security. The golden rule is that the attendee/individual needs to be primarily responsible for their own security and actions, as opposed becoming deindividuated and failing to take personal responsibility (Berlonghi, 1995; Wilks and Moore, 2004). Starting from these two principles, with the help and advice of specialised bodies/fire safety marshals, event managers can devise appropriate fire safety plans for particular types of event. Bladen et al. (2012, 208–209) recommend some general fire safety principles for event organisers to follow:

1   Individuals at an event can walk unattended; special arrangements need only be provided for those unable to walk unaccompanied or disabled visitors.
2   Fire exits should be clearly marked and easily recognisable and accessible at any point for any of the participants.
3   Alternative exit routes should be provided and clearly signed as people usually tend to try to get out the same way they entered – additional visual assistance signage such as lights and sounds can be installed to mark exits.
4   Emergency evacuation training must be provided to all staff and stewards.

It should be noted that according to the law of England and Wales there are some specific requirements that supersede these general principles. More information about legislation affecting the events sector is given in Chapter 8. Preparation, careful planning and evacuation procedures are crucial. In a comprehensive report about safety and security risks in the Asia Pacific region, Wilks and Moore (2004, 62) have developed a checklist for fire safety at indoor premises which has been adapted here:

● Devise a fire escape plan: evacuate as quickly as possible by knowing how to get out of the premises – this information should be visible and recognisable to all attendees/participants.
● Secure the fire plan by clearly providing the fire escape routes: this is of especially high importance in events taking place in convention centres or multi-storey buildings.
● Ensure that the devised escape plan has a previously assigned meeting place and that all staff know where this is.
● Calculate escape routes through fire exits using maximum number of individuals in the premises.
● Conduct regular fire drills to ensure that the plan is followed by all staff/stewards.

- Equip key areas with fire alarms to provide early warning of fire.
- Make sure that fire escapes are visible and easily accessible.
- Ensure that escape routes can be opened from both inside and outside.

In order to successfully plan for fire safety risks, the event organisers should seek the advice of the specialised services and authorities such as the emergency services (fire and rescue), the health authority, local authorities and any existing venue managers, stewarding and security contractors/suppliers.

10.5.3 Alcohol and drug management

Alcohol and drugs are complex to manage and can present risks at a wide range of events, particularly at events targeting a young demographic. Research into the Australian event market by Harris et al. (2014) identifies eight broad generic factors that have the potential to inflict harm on participants and the type of behaviour (e.g. aggressive, violent, antisocial) that might occur at a given event/venue where alcohol and/or drugs are available. The research provides several universally applicable methods clustered under five categories that enable the reduction or even the elimination of negative impacts (Harris, Edwards and Homel, 2014; see Table 10.3).

10.6 Crowd management and control

Not being prepared and not having a planned operational strategy of crowd management and crowd control can lead to serious losses of life, health, property and money (Berlonghi, 1995). There is the assumption that an individual becomes anonymous in a crowd by losing their self identity and instead takes on the behaviour of the crowd (Cronin and Reicher, 2006). Silvers (2013) advises that broadening hard and soft systems will shape individual behaviour within the crowd and thus enable the crowd to be managed effectively. It is believed that no two crowds are the same; however, event organisers need to have an understanding of crowd behaviour and movement in unforeseen circumstances (Bladen et al., 2012). Cronin and Reicher (2006) believe that individuals in a crowd are not capable of resisting the antisocial behaviour they may become part of, because they have lost their individual identity and the 'changing self-understanding of the crowd cannot be understood without taking account of the group dynamics' (Drury and Reicher, 1999, 399). From an event organiser's perspective, developing a good knowledge of audience behaviour and of group/crowd intelligence will ease the work, as the organiser and their team will be more aware of the patterns and characteristics of different risk scenarios that could ultimately result in disasters (Kemp, 2009). This is why a widely accepted method of risk planning is formed through the employment of scenarios as the grounds for predicting the impact across a spectrum of disruptions (Prideaux et al., 2003). According to Fruin (1984, as cited in Silvers 2013, 297), understanding crowd flow principles of time, space, information and energy is crucial to the understanding of crowd movements and prevention of risks and hazards:

- *Time*: schedule and peak event periods in which capacity can be exceeeded, movement speeds, arrival and departure demand rates

Table 10.3 Event and venue alcohol and drug management practices

Entry Controls

- Restrict entry point by monitoring
- Searches at entry points to remove drugs/alcohol (e.g. bag searches)
- Fencing: protects the introduction after the event has started
- Use of ID scanners (avoiding individuals with prior recorded incidents or individuals who are underage)
- Signage at all entrances to specify codes of conduct and regulations (e.g. age restrictions)
- Establish event/venue limit capacity (e.g. limit ticket sales to avoid overcrowding)

Alcohol Service Controls

- Restrictions on types of alcohol available at location (e.g. spirits, double shots), size of containers and time restrictions (including eliminating drink promotions or discounted prices)
- Selling alcohol in open containers to avoid 'stockpiling'
- Limits on the number of drinks purchased by an individual at a time
- Checking of IDs to avoid selling to underrated individuals
- Restrict areas where alcohol can be consumed

Attendee/Patron Management

- Surveillance systems (CCTV)
- Crowd controllers, police, stewarding to identify and/or exclude drugs
- Medical service on site (e.g. St John Ambulance)
- Catering with food/free water in order to avoid dehydration
- Setting up area for drop-off/pick-up and free shuttle to avoid related road accidents
- Promoting responsible drinking messages and campaigns

Site/Venue Layout and Design

- Avoiding congestion and frustration of queuing by equipping the site with sufficient food outlets, bars and toilets
- Making sure that queues are clearly separated and there are designated areas for catering/toilets or other services
- Previously arranged 'chill out' areas where attendees can avoid congestion and noise
- Creation of alcohol-free areas
- Developing a thorough transport management plan
- Appropriate site management (e.g. maintain a clean environment, provide adequate lighting)

Regulatory and Enforcement Practices

- Restricted hours for alcohol trading
- Compliance of regulatory requirements
- Adherence to licensing conditions
- Establishment of hierarchical penalties based on the number of regulatory invasions
- Providing internal records to authorities (e.g. police) to establish the 'patron harm risk'
- High-visibility clothing for security/stewarding/police to facilitate identification

(Continued)

Table 10.3 (*continued*)

- Using a grading scale for security/stewarding to easily recognise those who are trained and more experienced in areas of risks (placing them in key points)
- Creating a comprehensive risk assessment of the venue/event in order to maintain a good ratio between crowd controllers and attendees/patrons
- Creating written guides and offering advice by the authorised bodies (police, healthcare) to attendees/patrons

Source: adapted from Harris et al., 2014, 466–467

- *Space*: area design and capacity, per person space allocation and number/size of emergency exits/evacuation areas
- *Information*: information such as sound, sights and perception at which the crowd reacts and, most importantly, good communication between all involved parties
- *Energy*: the psychological, physiological power and pressure of the crowd (pushing, pressing forward, leaning, pushing against a barrier/ wall).

Berlonghi (1995) clarifies that there is an operational difference between the terms 'crowd management' and 'crowd control', even if, at times, the two terms may be used interchangeably in the events industry. According to the Emergency Planning College (2009, 13), crowd management is the 'facilitation of crowd activities', whereas crowd control is 'the actions taken to control the crowd once behaviours become undesirable'. It must be noted that effective planning and management to prevent the crowd control stage from occurring is preferable. Furthermore, they advise that 'crowd safety concerns are equal in priority to security concerns'.

Russell (1995) argues that young single male adults are attracted by the prospect of witnessing violence at sports games, and attend hockey matches solely for this reason. In addition, small numbers are more than willing to engage in some forms of crowd disturbance, a phenomenon that is traditionally noticed among football crowds. This argument is further emphasised by Stott, Adang, Livingstone and Schreiber, (2008), who claim that crowd disorder at football games is provoked by the convergence of fans that have a predisposition towards violent behaviour. Football games are useful event settings to study crowd dynamics.

Berlonghi (1995, 245) identifies crowd catalysts that need to be taken into consideration at an event in order to effectively manage the crowd so that it does not need to be controlled:

- *Operational factors*: lack of parking, no-shows of artists, cancellations, sold-out events
- *Event activities*: special effects (smoke, lasers, fireworks), loud noises, play backs
- *Performer's actions*: racial, sexual, violent gestures or comments
- *Spectator factors*: consuming alcohol, rushing for seating, overnight waiting, crowd cheering, crowd activities (the wave, playing with inflated balls), throwing objects
- *Security aspects*: use of excessive or unreasonable force, altercations with spectators, abuse of authority, arguments with crowd members

- *Social factors*: racial tension, nationalism, gang activities, rioting
- *Weather factors*: rain, heat, humidity, lack of ventilation
- *Natural disasters*: earthquakes, tornadoes, tsunamis, avalanches, mud flows, floods
- *Man-made disasters*: fires, toxic chemicals, explosions, structural failures.

For example, Notting Hill Carnival in London 'attracts over 1 million visitors and is widely regarded as posing a major threat to public safety' (Batty, Desyllas and Duxbury, 2003, 1573) due to crowding issues at the parade itself, near the fixed sound systems and at the subway stations used by visitors to the carnival. Batty et al. (2003) propose an experimental crowd model that enables the estimation of movement at the festival from various events that are happening within the Carnival, showing how crowds develop and generate issues of public safety. The Notting Hill festival has changed dramatically over the past 46 years. Its first edition back in 1964 attracted immigrants from the old Commonwealth, but nowadays it is an international hub of celebration, attracting visitors from around the world. The festival is still supported and organised by the ethnic communities, but the area in which it is held has changed dramatically over this time. Arguably, there are tensions between the residents who organise the festival and the local authorities, and there is an urgent need to address crowd management by suggesting alternative routes and different locations of sound systems for each day of the festival (Batty et al., 2003).

10.7 Transport management

Planned special events are created for a purpose, and what was once connected to community initiatives has become the domain of entrepreneurs and professional organisers (Getz and Page, 2016). With scheduled times and locations, planned special events impact on the transport of the areas in which the event is organised due to increased travel demands, limited parking facilities and reduced roadway capacity. This is the reason why the impact of the event is hugely dependent on operation characteristics such as the number of participants, location, venue, road capacity, times of arrival and departure (Sarasua, Malisetty and Chowdhury, 2011). Transport management should be a concern of event organisers and should by no means be left to chance. After conducting a study in Clemson, South Carolina on home American football games, Sarasua et al. (2011) concluded that in small towns, as opposed to large cities, planned special events have a much bigger impact on transport because the infrastructure is not designed to deal with the high volume of traffic and large numbers of participants arriving at specific times. An example that illustrates the evolution of events in small towns and the implications of transport management for the event organiser is La Tomatine – a tomato-based food fight which takes place each August in the Spanish city of Buñol near Valencia. The festival originated in 1945; no one quite knows how it started with several theories being circulated. The number of participants has increased year by year; in 2002 the event was recognized as as Festivity of International Tourist Interest. Tickets to the festival have been capped as Buñol's population of 9,000 inhabitants expanded to 50,000 event attendees during the festival. Despite the tumult and frenzy of the day, Buñol Town Council (Spanish Fiestas, 2015 online) set out only a few rules and regulations to be followed by participants on the day:

- Do not bring bottles or hard/sharp objects as you may cause an accident or injury to other participants.
- Do not tear/throw your own or others' T-shirts.
- Tomatoes should be squashed before throwing them as the hit will be less painful.
- Keep a safe distance from trucks/lorries.
- Stop throwing tomatoes when you hear the second warning firework.
- Security staff directions must be followed at all times.

Buñol's infrastructure was not designed to deal with large numbers of participants, but as a result of the popularity of the event the Town Council has adapted logistically.

Study activity

You have been asked by the Buñol Ayuntamiento (Town Council) to devise a risk management strategy for La Tomatina Festival. Using the template provided in Table 10.4 and after researching Spanish safety regulations, assess the risks involved at the site in planning the festival.

Table 10.4 How to devise a risk management strategy

1. Purpose: the strategy will describe the steps in which risk management standards and techniques will be embedded in the event's project activities.

2. Format and Presentation: can take different formats and be an integral part of different stages of an events' life:

- a standalone risk management document
- a section of the documentation at different stages of the event
- entry in a project management tool.

3. Composition:

Introduction: states the purpose, objectives, scope and identifies the person in charge of the strategy.

Risk management procedure: comprised of the five steps discussed in this chapter (identify, assess, plan, implement and communicate/review/update). The first four steps are in a sequential order with the final one, communicate, running throughout the life of the event, as all the other steps need to be communicated at all times.

Tools and techniques: incorporates all the management systems and tools to be used.

Records: the necessity of keeping a risk register that should contain information on all identified risks related to the event.

Reporting: encompasses all the reports produced throughout the life of the event, stating their purpose, time scales and recipients.

Timing: indicates the starting time of risk management activities.

Roles and responsibilities: specifies the roles and responsibilities for risk management activities.

Proximity: what is the probability of risks and opportunities occurring? And what would be the impact of each risk/opportunity on the project's objectives in case it does happen? Planning with the risk matrix would help establish the probability and impact of each risk.

Risk categories: possible risks/opportunities should be clustered into categories after the identification phase. These risks can derive from a risk breakdown structure relating, for example, to event business risks. The formal risk framework will help in establishing risk owners and developing risk responses.

Risk response categories: depend on the previous clustering of risks and on whether a risk is a perceived threat or opportunity.

Early-warning indicators: indicators that track critical steps of the project selected in accordance with the project's objectives.

Risk budget: the overall event budget should allocate a sum of money to the risk budget. In order to set the risk budget, each risk needs to be analysed for impact costs, response costs and likelihood. It is recommended that the risk budget is used for the duration of the event/project.

4. Quality Criteria:

- Tasks and responsibilities are clear to all parties involved: event organiser, suppliers, staff members and client(s).
- The risk management procedure is documented in a clear/up-to-date manner and clearly understood and applied by all parties.
- Risk reporting requirements are defined and understood.

Source: adapted from Prince2 Project Management (OGC, 2009, 259–261)

10.8 Conclusion

This chapter has focused on the analysis and management of risk in relation to the event environment. Five phases of event management have introduced and guided the information: identify, assess, plan, implement and, lastly, communicate, review and update. A risk management strategy and associated risk assessment form part of the suite of documentation required for the event management plan. Foreseeable risks and problems can be planned for ahead of time, and strategies should be put in place ready to implement if needed. A great deal can be learnt from previous event disasters and incidents to ensure that the event industry continues to advance and improve its responsibilities to risk management and stakeholder safety. It should be noted that this chapter has focused on risk and risk assessment rather than the specifics of threat assessment, which is a separate, albeit connected, entity.

Case study 10: Las Fallas, Valencia, Spain

An interview with Mr José Martínez Tormo, manager of Junta Central Fallera, the committee which coordinates and organises the official programme of events of the Fallas Festival.

Las Fallas is a traditional Valencian celebration taking place each year on 15–19 March. The festival originated in the eighteenth century, the main theory of its history stating that it all started when carpenters used to hang up pieces of hardwood called 'parot' in the winter to support their candles to provide light to work by. At the outbreak of spring, with the days getting longer, the wood was no longer used so it would be burned to celebrate the new season. The traditions evolved over time and by dressing and personifying the 'parots' with local personalities that were easily identifiable it became an annual festival of sharp satire. Nowadays, the massive satirical sculptures often represent Spanish and international celebrities/politicians and are made of cardboard and wax. Each neighbourhood in the city has a special committee (the *casal faller*) in charge of their own *fallera* sculpture that will be burned on the last night of the March festivity. The last night of the Fallas Festival is known as *La Cremà* (the Burning) and represents the culmination of the entire event as Valencia becomes a burning city. The

Figure 10.4 Virgin Mary sculpture in Las Fallas, Valencia, Spain

Source: © Georgiana Els

tradition requires that the most impressive *falla* be burned last. Visitors are surprised by the burning *falles* ('torches'), constant explosions and locals who become 'pyromaniacs' for one evening.

Of particular interest in this case study is the organisational approach taken by the local authorities in terms of plan analysis and risks. The manager of Junta Central Fallera, the committee that coordinates and organises the official programme of events of the Fallas Festival, provided answers regarding the elaborate organisation of Fallas.

Mr José Martínez Tormo, could you tell us a few things about your background in events management and about the organisation of the Fallas Festival (FF)?
I am a professional arts and cultural manager with more than 15 years' experience in the events industry. I have worked in the public sector, NGOs and also on Fallas committees as a volunteer and organising the events for the FF in districts.

The organisation of FF does not only involve Junta Central Fallera (JCF) but also each commission of all the city's neighbourhoods. Each local commission has its own governing board and organises the festival in its district. JCF coordinates the events across all the districts and organises the festival in its final official programme. For this purpose, JCF involves the action of 190 volunteers who work all year long to organise the festival that takes place in March. The volunteers are

Figure 10.5 Las Fallas Festival, Valencia, Spain
Source: © Georgiana Els

(Continued)

Case study 10 (*continued*)

assigned to working groups and have various responsibilities for the planning of each event.

What are the key points in the organisation of FF throughout the year from a project management perspective?

FF is celebrated in March each year, but activities start to be organised in May of the previous year and continue up to the next event in March. The period in which the organisation of the event becomes most intense is between October and March because this is the time of the year when the festival's main events are planned. FF is planned by volunteers with years of practice and experience, following long embedded traditions and habits. The volunteers work in groups using work breakdown structures for the planning of the event.

Do you consider the FF to be 'risky festival'? On a scale from 1 (low risk) to 5 (high risk) where would you place it and why?

FF is a 'risky festival' (4) because is based on fire and pyrotechnics; however, security is essential in every event and its security measures are regulated and controlled by policemen and firemen. It is also a 'risky festival' because hundreds of people gather for the event, and as I have said, security is essential in the festival. The biggest risk that could occur during the festival is connected to the mass pyrotechnic shows and crowd management, more than an everyday event.

Fire is one of the biggest nightmares for an event organiser, but Fallas is the celebration of fire and its main purpose revolves around burning structures. How is it managed internally?

The risk is managed in collaboration with the professionals (firemen, pyrotechnicians, medical units, etc.) and with strict well-developed risk planning by professionals, as well as the existing knowledge of managing these kinds of events. Every structure to be burnt is analysed individually to evaluate the necessary level of intervention of the protection units.

There are three levels of fireworks user:

1 The pyrotechnics professionals, that have all the relevant authorisations and certifications of the government for manufacturing, handling and firing fireworks
2 The certified users who have passed an exam that enables them to use some specific fireworks only in the festival context, and during a determined period of time
3 The general public, who are only allowed to use licensed fireworks according to pre-determined age scales.

When talking about 'health, safety and security' what topics are encompassed under FF and its organisation?

Figure 10.6 A burning structure, Las Fallas, Valencia, Spain
Source: © Georgiana Els

Health, safety and security in FF encompass topics related to street food, beverages, traditional food, use of fireworks, crowd behaviour and traffic regulation.

A common practice during public celebrations in Spain is to initiate 'botellons'
(drinking alcohol in public). Is this a common practice during the FF?
Drinking alcohol in public is indeed a common practice in festivities, but it is intended to be officially organised only in certain contexts such as night-time public street concerts. However, there are a few instances, such as fireworks displays, in which moderate alcohol drinking is also common. During FF alcohol can only be purchased in pubs and at the night street concert events. However, low-grade alcoholic drinks (such as beer) are available at a number of crowd events.

Does FF have a risk management analysis/plan attached to it?
Every event that uses fire and/or pyrotechnics needs to have a safety plan designed and elaborated with the involvement and cooperation of the police and fire department, which later needs to be authorised by the government. This is a compulsory measure and without having it in place the event would not happen.

(Continued)

Case study 10 (*continued*)

What are the policies and regulations that need to be followed when organising an event in the region of Valencia (La Comunidad Valenciana)?
There are a lot of regulations that need to be followed, especially the local ones that are related to the use of fireworks and pyrotechnics, food safety, the management of crowds and the legal organisation of the event.

How do you measure the success and impact of the FF event?
It depends on the type of event, but generally success is measured by public opinion, lack of incidents/accidents, quality of execution and the number of people attending. There isn't an updated study of the impact of FF, but internal evidence demonstrates important economic impact on business budgets and tourists arrivals.

What advice do you have for students on events management degrees? Could you give a tip for those who are soon to enter the industry?
To study the social and geographic context very well before acting. It is important to analyse every aspect of the festival (people, tradition, laws, space, duration, etc.) before applying any change or innovation, especially in those festivals (such as FF) that rely heavily on volunteerism.

Thank you to Mr José Martinez Tormo for sharing your experiences with the authors to formulate this case study.

Evaluative student questions

1 What are the key focal points in the organisation of the Fallas Festival throughout the year?
2 Do you think that the crowd attending is likely to generate strong feelings/emotions?
3 In your opinion, what are the main risks associated with the Fallas Festival? Be prepared to give evidence for your argument.

Further reading

Batty, M., Desyllas, J. and Duxbury, E. (2003) Safety in numbers? Modelling crowds and designing control for the Notting Hill Carnival. *Urban Studies*, 40(8) 1573–1590.

Lincolnshire Event Safety Partnership (LESP) (2012) *Event organisers' handbook*. Lincoln: Lincolnshire County Council. Available on the Lincolnshire Event Safety Partnership website: http://www.lincolnshire.gov.uk/lincolnshire-prepared/Lincolnshire-Event-Safety-Partnership [Accessed 16 June 2016].

Silvers, J.R. (2008) *Risk management for meetings and events*. Oxford: Butterworth-Heinemann.

References

Ahmed, A., Kayis, B. and Amornsawadwatana, S. (2007). A review of techniques for risk management in projects. *Benchmarking: An International Journal*, 14(1) 22–36.

Batty, M., Desyllas, J. and Duxbury, E. (2003) Safety in numbers? Modelling crowds and designing control for the Notting Hill Carnival. *Urban Studies*, 40(8) 1573–1590.

BBC (2013) *Street Spice food poisoning blamed on curry leaves* [press release 19 June] Available from: http://www.bbc.co.uk/news/uk-england-tyne-22969662 [Accessed 30 March 2016].

Berlonghi, A.E. (1995) Understanding and planning for different spectator crowds. *Safety Science*, 18(4) 239–247.

Bladen, C., Kennell, J., Abson, E. and Wilde, N. (2012) *Events management: an introduction*. Abingdon: Routledge.

Bowdin, G., Allen, J., O'Toole, W., Harris, R. and McDonnell, I. (2011) *Events management*. 3rd edition. London: Butterworth-Heinemann.

Ciuchete, G. (2012) *Volunteer Your Time* [industry talk] University of Salford, 24 April.

Cronin, P. and Reicher, S. (2006) A study of the factors that influence how senior officers police crowd events: on SIDE outside the laboratory. *British Journal of Social Psychology*, 45(1) 175–196.

Drury, J. and Reicher, S. (1999) The intergroup dynamics of collective empowerment: substantiating the social identity model of crowd behaviour. *Group Processes and Intergroup Relations*, 2(4) 381–402.

Emergency Planning College (2009) *Understanding crowd behaviours: guidance and lessons identified*. York: Cabinet Office.

Events Industry Forum (EIF) (2014) *The Purple Guide*. Available from: http://www.thepurpleguide.co.uk/ [Accessed 1 April 2016].

Ferdinand, N. and Kitchin, N. (2012) *Events management: an international approach*. London: Sage.

Frosdick, S. (1999). Beyond football hooliganism. In: Frosdick, S. and Walley, L. (eds) *Sport and safety management.* Oxford: Butterworth Heinemann, 3–10.

Getz, D. (2012). *Events Studies: theory, research and policy for planned events*. Oxon: Routledge.

Getz, D. and Page, S.J. (2016) Progress and prospects for event tourism research. *Tourism Management,* 52 593–631.

Greenwell T. C., Danzey-Bussell L. A. and Shonk D. J. (2014) *Managing sport events*. Champaign, IL: Human Kinetics.

Harris, R., Edwards, D. and Homel, P. (2014) Managing alcohol and drugs in event and venue settings: the Australian case. *Event Management*, 18(4) 457–470.

Hassanien, A. and Dale, C. (2011) Toward a typology of events venues. *International Journal of Event and Festival Management*, 2(2) 106–116.

HSE (2014) *Risk assessment: a brief guide to controlling risks in the workplace*. Available from: http://www.hse.gov.uk/pubns/indg163.pdf [Accessed 18 February 2016].

HSE (2014a) *Managing crowds safely: a guide for organisers at events and venues*. Available from: http://www.hse.gov.uk/pubns/priced/hsg154.pdf [Accessed 18 February 2016].

HSE (2014b) *Explosives Regulations 2014: safety provisions*. Available from: http://www.hse.gov.uk/pubns/priced/l150.pdf [Accessed 18 February 2016].

HSE (2014c) *The event safety guide (second edition): a guide to health, safety and welfare at music and similar events.* Available from: http://www.qub.ac.uk/safety-reps/sr_webpages/safety_downloads/event_safety_guide.pdf [Accessed 31 March].

Kemp, C. (2009) Event tourism: a strategic methodology for emergency management. *Journal of Business Continuity & Emergency Planning,* 3(3) 227–240.

Lincolnshire Event Safety Partnership (LESP) (2012) Available from: https://www.lincolnshire.gov.uk/lincolnshire-prepared/Lincolnshire-Event-Safety-Partnership [Accessed 19 September 2016].

Office of Government Commerce (OGC) (2009) *Managing Successful Projects with PRINCE2.* London: The Stationery Office.

Peattie, S., Clarke, P. and Peattie, K. (2005) Risk and responsibility in tourism: promoting sun-safety. *Tourism Management,* 26(3) 399–408.

Prideaux, B., Laws, E. and Faulkner, B. (2003) Events in Indonesia: exploring the limits to formal tourism trends forecasting methods in complex crisis situations. *Tourism Management,* 24(4) 475–487.

Ritchie, B.W. and Reid, S. (2012) Risk Management. In: Ferdinand, N. and Kitchin, P.J. (eds) *Events Management: an international approach.* London: Sage, 153–172.

Russell, G.W. (1995) Personalities in the crowd: those who would escalate a sports riot. *Aggressive Behaviour,* 21(2) 91–100.

Safefood (2016) *Food Poisoning.* Available from: http://www.safefood.eu/Food-Safety/Food-Poisoning.aspx [Accessed 31 March 2016].

Sarasua, W.A., Malisetty, P. and Chowdhury, M. (2011) Using a GIS-based, Hitchcock algorithm to optimize parking allocations for special events. *Applied GIS,* 7(2) 1–13.

Shone, A., and Parry, B. (2013) *Successful event management.* 3rd edition. London: Thomson.

Silvers, J.R. (2013) *Risk management for meetings and events.* 2nd edition. Oxford: Butterworth-Heinemann.

Spanish Fiestas (2015) *La Tomatina Festival* [online]. Available from: http://www.spanish-fiestas.com/festivals/la-tomatina/ [Accessed 31 March 2016].

Still, G.K. (2013) *Introduction to crowd science.* Boca Raton, FL: CRC Press.

Stott, C., Adang, O., Livingstone, A. and Schreiber, M. (2008) Tackling football hooliganism: a quantitative study of public order, policing and crowd psychology. *Psychology, Public Policy and Law,* 14(2) 115–141.

Toohey, K. and Taylor, T. (2008) Mega events, fear, and risk: terrorism at the Olympic Games. *Journal of Sport Management,* 22(4) 451–469.

Vellani, K. (2007) Strategic security management: a risk assessment guide for decision makers. Oxford: Butterworth-Heinemann.

Wilks, J. and Moore, S. (2004) *Tourism risk management for the Asia Pacific Region: an authoritative guide for managing crises and disasters.* Published for the APEC International Centre for Sustainable Tourism (AICST). Available from: http://www.crctourism.com.au/wms/upload/resources/bookshop/Wilks_TourismRiskMgt-FINAL.pdf [Accessed 7 July 2015].

Chapter 11

Problem solving and decision making

11.1 Introduction

It is difficult to imagine any event could ever take place without there being some sort of unexpected problem or decision making that was required at some stage by the event organiser and their team. The events sector is particularly susceptible to both complexity and uncertainty (O'Toole, 2011, 123), which calls for appropriate and professional risk management and planning. There is a connection between events and risk for a wide variety of reasons; examples might include the event taking place on a green field site or at a unique venue, management of crowds in unfamiliar surroundings, new staff and volunteers, movement of equipment and machinery, temporary demountable structures, working at height, and even the weather. All should be considered and assessed, and control measures should be instigated, training delivered and management systems put in place to mitigate or eliminate risk. Problem solving and decision making focus on how risks and event challenges can be prevented, managed and, if possible, solved.

An event organiser may have been involved in months and months of careful planning to make sure everything runs smoothly at the event. They should be in regular contact with contractors/suppliers and have booked the entertainment and be monitoring ticket sales. In such times of routine it is difficult to think about potential challenges. Even the most experienced event planners have to deal with problems that arise during an event, but there are ways to plan for such issues in advance and organisers should never become complacent, even if the event has taken place annually over many years. If there were to be any sort of incident at the event, it is not acceptable as part of a defence to assume that behaviours and decisions made in the past will not need updating or changing. Furthermore, 'accidents do not *just* happen, there is always a cause' (Still, 2013, 73), but the importance of 'uncertainty management' is also a consideration for event managers (Ellert, Schafmeister, Wawrzinek and Gassner, 2015, 60). Foreseeable risks should be planned for accordingly but the savvy event manager must be confident enough to make decisions and alleviate problems that occur unexpectedly due to the complexity, changeability and uncertainty of the industry.

It is not possible to organise an event without there being some risk, but it is possible to plan events that are safe both for those working there and for those attending. The event organiser is responsible for preventing all reasonably foreseeable incidents and has a moral, ethical and legal responsibility to do so. This can be achieved by taking time out to consider the foreseeable risks and problems that might occur at all stages of the event and to put risk management strategies in place to try and mitigate those risks. This is a legal requirement under the Management of Health and Safety at Work Regulations 1999; for further information refer to Chapters 8 and 10. It is important to think of event risk as future incidents, or even problems, that may occur (Bowdin et al., 2011). For the purposes of this chapter the event cycle (rather than the project cycle from Chapter 1) will be split into five different phases to allow exploration of processes and procedures that will assist with the problem-solving and decision-making method. These five phases are planning, build-up, the event, and breakdown and debrief, which align with those outlined in the *Purple Guide*. The chapter ends with some examples of problem-solving and decision-making strategies.

11.2 Phase one: Planning

This is arguably the most important phase of the event cycle. Any prospective event organiser should have an abundance of information and guidance available to them to assist in the preparations for the event, and it is incumbent on the individual to ensure that the level and detail is proportionate to the event and the risks identified. Some events, such as sports events, are often connected to planning failure due to the link with live sport and the inability to interrupt the flow of the game/activity once it has begun (Kiaffas and Afthinos, 2013). A good event organiser is required to have an understanding of many different aspects of the business, such as publicity, marketing, licensing, health and safety and contracting to name but a few. They should also take time to look at the relevant legislation and guidance and ensure that they are familiar with them before commencing writing their event documents. This can save time in the long run.

It is always beneficial to develop good working relationships and clear lines of communication with staff, contractors/suppliers, sponsors, local authorities and the emergency services throughout all phases of the event process.

> The temporary nature of the event management environment combined with rapidly changing staff numbers often from completely different work and social cultures gives the communication process a priority not found in other industries.
>
> (O'Toole, 2011, 213)

In order to appropriately plan for and manage risk in a way that promotes effective problem solving and decision making, clear organisational communication is a must. Not all problems will relate to health and safety, although this does account for a large proportion; they may also involve, for example, financial, logistical, legal, procurement or human resources. Taking time to maintain and develop these relationships is effort well spent and can make problem solving and decision making that bit easier.

Tip box

It is important to spend time maintaining and developing relationships with colleagues and stakeholders as this can make problem solving and decision making much easier. It is always better to know the face at the other end of a telephone line rather than just a name.

It is often noted that the best way to solve a problem is to prevent it from happening in the first place. A comprehensive approach that involves full consultation with all interested parties during the pre-event planning stage can go a long way towards preventing problems occurring at an event. For example, detailed and thorough risk assessments and event management plans that have been properly tested and validated, with full cooperation with the SAG, can go a long way towards identifying any potential flaws or problems. This in turn may save a great deal of time and money and provide a clear audit trail of the organiser's actions should the need arise.

> If we review the list of incidents and accidents from around the world, we see an underlying theme that is common to several major incidents, pointing towards deficient planning and approval before events and unsatisfactory management during events.
>
> (Still, 2013, 70)

This preparation cannot guarantee that the event will be problem free as there will always be something that will arise that had not been thought of which will require the organiser to make dynamic decisions and rethink operations. The most important thing is to learn from these challenges and take any lessons learnt forward to future events.

For the purposes of this chapter, this process will be explained through the eyes of a new event organiser who has had an idea for an event and has discussed the broad concept with key stakeholders and potential sponsors and has completed a feasibility study as described in Chapters 1 and 9. If this feasibility study has concluded that the event is viable, then the decision to proceed can be made and the prospective organiser can start putting together the event team. There are no set structures for this team and there are many different examples that can be followed; refer to Chapter 4. It is important that key staff within the team are identified and that their roles and responsibilities are included in the event plan. A clear chain of command should also be included; this becomes important when problems occur and decisions need to be made. Everyone working on the event needs to be aware of this should they need to report a problem or require a decision to be made.

There are a variety of key roles that will need to be included in the structure of an event team. The larger or more complex the event, the larger the team, all members of which will be required to tackle problems and make decisions relating to the event across all of its phases. These will sometimes need to be made in the absence of the event organiser, so it is vital that there is some delegated responsibility afforded to these staff as it will not be possible for the organiser to be everywhere at the same time. There is much debate about which comes first, the risk assessment or the event management plan. Some people believe that the event management plan should be completed first and that the content should then be risk assessed and included as an appendix to the plan. The other method is to comprehensively risk assess the event and then write the event management document based on the risk assessment. Whichever method is adopted, both of these documents require completion by a suitable and competent person, and should be agreed and signed off before the event; this will greatly assist the problem-solving and decision-making process. There are some risks that remain active even after control measures have been implemented; they require careful consideration and management and procedures should be documented in relation to the strategies and monitoring used in dealing with them.

11.2.1 Event management plan

The event organiser will be required to complete an event management plan, especially if the event is a licensable one. They may choose to outsource this task but should still be actively involved and maintain an in-depth knowledge and understanding of the document. The UK Health and Safety Executive provides specific guidelines and information for what should be included and identified in an event safety plan: 'scale, type and scope of the event, type and size of the audience, location, duration of the event, time of day and year the event will be held' (HSE, 2015, online). The HSE states that it is these areas of event management that will assist the organiser in planning the appropriate resources and facilities to create an effective event management plan.

Some event organisers do not devote the appropriate amount of time and effort to this task and do not recognise the importance of a comprehensive event management plan. There have been cases where plans have been produced which have been copied verbatim from other documents. If the event is an annual one, last year's plan may have been taken back off the shelf, dusted off and a new date added. Worse still are the plans that have been taken directly from someone else's event with just a new title added. All of these practices may still take place, but they are not recommended and can come back to haunt the event organiser should something go wrong at the event or if there needs to be some sort of enquiry following an emergency.

A first event is always the most difficult to plan for. There are a variety of reasons for this. They include unfamiliarity of procedures and legislation and it may also be the first time that the organiser has had to complete this type of documentation. There is currently no industry recognised standard for event organisers, and therefore people with all levels of experience can and do get involved. It is therefore always advisable to plan for the worst. This has a number of advantages. For example, the organiser may not know how many people will ultimately attend the event but knowing the site capacity will help in calculating medical cover and the provision of toilets, and allow the organiser to build in contingencies and estimate both safe operating capacity and breakeven point. It is always easier to scale down rather than have to scale up, sometimes at short notice.

Tip box

It is always advisable to plan for the worst when putting on an event. This will aid contingency planning and help to provide a holistic view that focuses on potential areas to problem solve and manage.

What constitutes a good event management plan is the subject of much debate. The important thing to remember is that the relevant people and organisations have seen it and have had a chance to comment and make amendments in their areas of specific expertise. Refer to information about the SAG in Chapter 4. A good event management plan is a 'living document' that evolves with the event and takes account of the lessons learnt along the way. It should always consider potential problems and how they will be managed but should also remain flexible and adaptable to sudden changes and the unexpected, should unanticipated situations arise. It is better to ensure that the document remains as user friendly as possible; it is no good having a plan the length of a doctoral thesis if no one has read it or can quickly find what they are looking for, especially if there is a stressful or pressured incident. Only include the most relevant information in the main body of the plan; everything else can be attached as appendices so that people are most familiar with the information most relevant to their roles and responsibilities.

Table 11.1 lists elements that could form the basis of the event management plan. There are some areas that may not be applicable to every event and there may be additional areas that will need to be considered. The most important thing is that the document has addressed the foreseeable risks and documented them along with procedures and structures to manage them. The case study at the end of this chapter about a walking conference in the Himalayan mountains, Nepal provides an interesting viewpoint concerning *factors specific to the particular event*. Earthquakes, narrow mountain paths and participant safety were of extreme importance for the Nepalese walking conference, but these considerations may not feature as prominently in other event plans.

Table 11.1 The elements which formulate an event management plan

The Basic Elements of an Event Management Plan

Date, event timings, version number and shelf life[1]	Contacts section	Emergency procedures
A full description of the event and activities/ entertainment	Security/stewarding arrangements	Fire safety
Audience profile including attendance and capacity figures	Toilets/waste management procedures	First aid provision
Venue or site design (maps or site plans)	Licensing	Welfare arrangements
Venue/site access, circulation and egress details	External consultation/ SAG liaison	Risk assessments (including fire)
Roles and responsibilities of key staff & contractors/ suppliers	Internal & external communications arrangements	Catering provision
Health & safety policy	Contingency arrangements	Power, water, electricity & lighting provision
Command structure	Emergency evacuation procedures	Traffic management
Details of insurance	Crowd management	Extreme weather arrangements (hot, wet & cold)
Temporary demountable structures	Cancellation policy	Factors specific to particular event

[1] Shelf life refers to the particular event to which the plan relates, or for how long the plan is relevant/when it should be reviewed.

The plan will only be useful if all of the staff and key contractors/suppliers have been fully consulted and trained in the roles and responsibilities outlined within it. The plan will also require validation through some type of training event or exercise.

11.2.2 Safety advisory groups

The Safety Advisory Group (SAG) can assist the event organiser and their team with problem solving and decision making. Individual members of the SAG have specific competencies and skills along with experience from previous events that will all be of benefit. The *UK good practice guide to working in Safety Advisory Groups* (Griffiths et al., 2015) gives some useful examples of the terms of reference (p. 11) and policies (p. 17) that could be agreed at the initial SAG meeting. These make reference to the support and assistance that they can offer event organisers. It should always be remembered that the most successful SAGs see the event planning process as a partnership and steer away from the historical 'them and us' attitude which sometimes used to exist between the SAG and the event organiser. It is recognised that the event is important to the local economy but that it is equally important that it take place in a safe manner for both those attending and those working there. Refer to Chapter 4 for more information about SAGs.

11.3 Phase two: Build-up

The site of an event can vary dramatically; it may be anything from a small venue for just a few people to a huge festival site. The more complex the site or the larger the event, the more people, contractors/suppliers and equipment will be operating and moving around the site. The smooth running of this process is crucial. The build-up phase (sometimes referred to as the load-in time) of any event has the potential to encounter problems. It is therefore critical that a robust site health and safety policy has been established, and that there are safe systems of work in place.

The build-up phase is the time when the necessary infrastructure is brought in, unloaded, built and set up. There may be limiting factors that can influence this phase such as availability of equipment or hire costs. In most cases the larger equipment arrives first: stages, fencing or other temporary demountable structures, for example. Next to arrive are usually the sound and lighting equipment, and finally last-minute site decorations. It is worth noting that:

> Supervision of the arrival and set-up of the equipment can be crucial for minimising problems during the event. The contractor who delivers and assembles the equipment often is not the operator of the equipment. This can mean that once set up, it is impossible to change it without recalling the contractor.
>
> (Bowdin et al., 2011, 513)

The build-up and breakdown of events are the two phases in which arguably the most fatal and serious injuries arise (e.g. workers falling during construction work or as a result of the collapse of the structure, lifting operations or mobile plant). It may be that in the case of a tour, crews have visited many different venues and built and dismantled structures many times so that complacency may have set in. There may also be local crew on the site who may be unfamiliar with the equipment. In the case of international tours, crews sometimes have different standards of equipment and working practices. Tiredness and fatigue can also play a part. All of these issues require monitoring and careful management to reduce the risks.

The weather can also be an influencing factor. If it is especially hot, workers may remove some of their safety equipment whilst working on the site, increasing the risk of an accident. There will be an event schedule that will include the build-up; if this is running behind, corners may be cut. In wet weather equipment becomes slippery and the ground can become muddy, making it more difficult to work. Difficulties with equipment construction and site safety can be exacerbated during severe and/or changeable weather conditions. The planning phase can greatly assist with heading off many of these issues. Careful research and selection of contractors/suppliers and sub-contractors together with comprehensive contracting can ensure the quality of both the equipment and services at the event. It is good practice to do the background checks and contact other event organisers that have previously used the prospective contractors to check out their experiences of using them before awarding them contracts.

Be sure to consider contingency arrangements for the loss of critical contractors/suppliers or where to source additional or replacement key equipment at short notice in case the event organisation is let down. It is good practice to make sure key contractors/suppliers have some sort of business continuity arrangements in place if they are disappointed by one of their contractors/suppliers; this will ensure that the event will still receive what has been promised and contracted. This is particularly relevant during the summer months when there are more events taking place and equipment and services are in more demand. For example, during the London 2012 Olympic Games, portable toilets, crowd barriers and security and stewarding were in high demand. In some cases, other events had to be cancelled due to the lack of availability of these services and equipment, but had they been booked and contracted earlier, the events may have still been able to take place.

Local authorities can also assist with this, as local environmental health departments will be able to give the event organiser information pertaining to local food vendors and hygiene, and building control officers may be able to assist with temporary demountable structure guidance on site. This is another good reason for close liaison with the SAG. There should be an on-site health and safety policy detailing clear instructions on contractor/supplier and sub-contractor expectations whist working on the event, which should be built into the contracts before being awarded. This can be really useful if the service falls short of expectations and can help with any disagreements. Always check or get some other suitably competent person to check paperwork, such as contractors' methods of working, risk and fire risk assessments, to ensure that the relevant standards are being met. Any reputable company will have these readily available and will expect to have to provide them for inspection, although in some cases the event organiser may have to ask to see them.

Tip box

Always check or get some other suitably competent person to check paperwork such as contractor's methods of working, risk and fire risk assessments to ensure that they meet the relevant standards.

The appointment of an event safety officer is crucial as this is the person who should oversee all aspects of health and safety in all phases of the event. Some event organisers make the mistake of giving themselves this role in addition to being the event organiser; there is a clear conflict of interest here, as the event organiser will have multiple tasks to deal with throughout the event, in addition to safety matters. The event safety officer should work and advise the event organiser on safety matters and be given some delegated responsibility for routine problem solving and decision making on the organiser's behalf, including the decision to stop the event if necessary. The event safety officer is a standalone role and should not be mixed with any other responsibilities as sometimes happens at events.

There is currently no industry-recognised base level qualification in England to become an event (not sports) safety officer although there are many qualifications and courses available to gain competency, and many companies can provide them. Someone who has been involved with the event for years is not necessarily an ideal candidate for the role. It is important to do research, ask others about where they have worked previously and check individual qualifications and experience before deciding on awarding this role for an event.

11.4 Phase three: The event

The planning phase is now complete and the site is built ready to open to the audience or customers. This is the moment of transition into the operational phase of the event, and all of these processes need to be well documented and understood by all those involved. It should be noted that 'you can still mess up an event if you do not understand the event plan' (Still, 2013, 195). Some event organisers believe that the SAG should still be consulted if there are minor problems or incidents during this phase. It is worth clarifying here that their role belongs in the planning and build-up phases; once the event is operational, their role has ended and the event control takes over. Nevertheless SAG visits to the site both during the build-up and operational phases should be encouraged, as it can assist with last-minute problem solving and aid future planning and site familiarity.

For smaller-scale events the event control unit will most likely consist of the event team including the event organiser, the safety officer and other critical contractors/suppliers such as security/stewarding supervisors. This team will manage the event, have clear roles and responsibilities and an established chain of command that has been properly documented in the event management plan and communicated to all those working on the event site. 'The unit acts as a one-stop shop so that any external event can minimise the unnecessary communication by dealing with one team' (O'Toole, 2011, 55). This team will manage all minor incidents at the event up to the point at which the scale or severity of the incident necessitates attendance by the emergency services or other agencies. In the case of large-scale events such as music festivals or large sporting events, for example, the decision will have been taken during the planning phase that a multi-agency control room including representation from the emergency services, local authority emergency planners and any other relevant agencies will be established. This will be based on the event risks and their consequences, as well as the benefits of these agencies being on site to respond and coordinate quickly if a major incident occurs.

This team should have attended any training sessions held by the event organiser, such as the table-top exercise to validate the event management plan, and will be familiar with the site and its operations. Again there will be a clear understanding of roles and responsibilities. Minor incidents will still be managed by the event organiser and their team, and it is important to remember that if it becomes necessary to stop or cancel the event, it will be the event organiser's decision, or that of their representative, e.g. the safety officer, to do so.

In the case of a major incident, command and control primacy will be assumed by the emergency services, usually the police or the fire and rescue service. This decision will have taken place after discussion between these agencies and the event organiser. It should be carefully documented in any log together with dates and times. The event organiser, their staff and resources will then assist with any response working under the direction of the emergency services. More information on emergency management legislation can be found in the Civil Contingencies Act 2004. There are several factors that can lead to an incident at an event. The event management plans will have been agreed during the planning phase but emergencies can develop quickly and will require some dynamic decision making or problem solving as sometimes they can only be partially planned for. It is therefore critical that both the plan and the event team remain flexible and adaptable to such situations if they occur.

11.4.1 Event attendees and event design

It should be remembered that no event will ever take place without there being challenges or problems that require some sort of dynamic decision making. This is normal and to be expected. Careful monitoring, good communications and teamwork can mean the difference between those situations remaining minor or turning into something more serious. The following examples explain some factors that may influence the crowd or audience at an event and that may require careful monitoring and management.

During the event, it should be expected that the medical provider will need to treat casualties for a number of different reasons; these can range from slips and trips to more serious conditions such as respiratory problems. It is therefore important to check that the medical provider contracted for the event has suitable equipment and competent staff to deal with the range of injuries that may occur. Whilst these situations will be medical emergencies for the patient, in most cases they will not require wider emergency support from the local NHS resources (in the case of the UK). In the case of a larger event, the event organiser may have contracted the medical supplier to write the event medical plan, which should be written in a way to limit the impact on local medical services. To put this into context, a major music festival site will have an audience ranging from around 30,000 to 150,000 people. This number of people represents the population of a small to medium-sized market town. On any day in these towns, people suffer heart attacks, strokes and any other number of other injuries requiring medical intervention. The event site will be no different and event organisers should expect this.

Events also experience people attending with pre-existing conditions that require treatment. Experience by one ambulance service has shown that these cases can make up as much as 30 per cent of those treated at the event.[1] These injuries range from respiratory and heart problems to slips, trips and falls suffered before attending the event site; in one case, a patient required a change of dressing for an injury treated previously by the A&E department of the local hospital stating that it was quicker than waiting there for treatment. In most cases these routine injuries may not need to be included in the official event casualty figures. Other factors can also influence type and number of casualties at the event. For example, some events will require medical providers to treat people for the effects of excessive drug or alcohol abuse (this is particularly the case at dance events) so it is therefore advisable to contract a provider that has had previous experience of this type of event and knows what will be required of their staff. The weather may also affect casualty figures. If it is particularly hot, casualties will include an increase in respiratory and hay fever sufferers. If the weather is extremely cold, there may be an increase in those reporting chest problems or hypothermia.

'We know more about crowds now than we did 25 years ago, but we may never know *everything* about crowds' (Still, 2013, 3). The event venue or site may look impressive and the event organiser may be confident that every eventuality has been planned for, but once attendees arrive, things can change very quickly. Always try to anticipate the unexpected. There are many factors that can influence the way in which a crowd or audience behaves. Individuals will all react differently to both normal and emergency situations, but one individual's reaction can have a knock-on effect on others. Their decision-making processes may be different if they are attending the event on their own, in a group, with family or as a carer. Good crowd management should therefore be both proactive and reactive. If poor traffic management plans are in place and people have been sitting in their cars for long periods of time or the local public transport systems close to the event site are inadequate, this is the first impression visitors will get of the event and the crowd or audience will arrive unhappy and be generally less compliant. These factors are really important: if it takes a long time to get in or out of the venue, it could make the difference between them attending any future events there.

Site design can also play a part and venue and site layout are critical to event success (O'Toole, 2011). Careful consideration of how crowds will access, egress and circulate around the venue or site can influence the way they may react. For example, a site with plenty of good, clear, unconflicting signage, lighting in appropriate areas, ample toilets and catering units is much easier to navigate and manage than one which has an inappropriate number of these facilities/services. Signage and lighting will become particularly important should it become necessary to evacuate the site. If left to their own devices, most people will naturally try to leave the same way they came in, even if this is where an incident has occurred. This has been evidenced in many past incidents involving crowds and has even added to death and serious injury statistics. An example was the Station Nightclub Fire, Rhode Island, 2003 (National Fire Protection Association, 2015). The event organisers must make sure that evacuation routes and signage are positioned high up so that people can see them from a distance and that emergency lighting systems are part of the emergency power planning.

People attending events usually want high-quality entertainment, and to be able to get something to eat and drink and go to the toilet without having to queue for long periods. With this in mind, site design becomes very important as by locating all these services in one place, the event organiser can encounter or create cross-queuing, where people find themselves queuing for different things in the same place. It is important to spread these services evenly over the site and where they are most convenient for your crowd/audience to use. This gives the event organiser the opportunity to influence crowd movement and can also prevent overcrowding in certain areas of the site.

Audience profiles were discussed earlier in this book. It is very important to understand the audience. Crowds predominantly made up of teenagers will behave and react differently from those made up of older people or family groups. Music genre can also influence the crowd; there are big differences between crowds watching hip-hop, dance, heavy metal and classical concerts. Entertainers can incite the crowd but at the same time can also be useful to relay safety messages. Each type of crowd has its own particular elements for the event team to monitor: 'moshing' and 'crowd surfing' are examples. Some organisers even ban these activities from their events. Excessive alcohol and drug use will have an impact as well. Crowd behaviour in front of stages can vary from country to country and from genre to genre; 'it is clear that the British crowd is by far the most boisterous and that dealing with their behaviour needs a much more creative management strategy than most places in Europe' (Kemp et al., 2007, 169). There may be outside influences that can impact upon the event that may be much more difficult to plan for proactively. These might include political activities either nationally or internationally, acts of terrorism or even strikes by transport operators, all of which will require reactive management.

Finally, the weather will also have an impact on the crowd and how it will need to be managed. In extreme heat, consideration should be given to making sure that messages go out encouraging people to drink plenty of water, apply sunscreen and wear hats, especially to more vulnerable groups. Make sure that catering vendors do not increase bottled water prices; this should be pre-agreed as part of the contracting. Some organisers even provide free water and sunscreen. If the weather is cold and wet or windy, the risk of hypothermia increases. If the event is taking place outdoors, there may be a risk from thunder and lightning causing temporary loss of power as happened at Glastonbury Festival in 2014. The ground can become muddy due to crowd movement and it may be that operationally the site cannot function. For example, if toilets cannot be properly serviced, a health and safety issue can arise and the organiser may need to consider cancellation. In all cases it is important that as problems and challenges arise and decisions are required, full consultation between all agencies takes place, and the resulting actions are carefully logged together with the other options discussed and the rationale behind those chosen.

Tip box

It is important to ensure that contact details are available and contact methods work so that when problems and challenges arise the full consultation advised in this chapter can take place. The logging of resulting actions and their rationale provides a clear audit trail, if it is needed.

11.5 Phases four and five: Breakdown and debrief

The breakdown phase of the event (sometimes referred to as the load-out time) is as important as the build-up phase and comes with the same set of risks and potential problems. There is also one additional risk, however: the excitement is over, the staff are often tired and everyone is eager to leave. The breakdown phase is the period when all the equipment, temporary demountable structures and services at the event site are cleared and restored back to how they were before the event. There is also the additional problem of clearing the waste. Details of the breakdown phase will also be included in the event schedule and should be managed appropriately by the event safety officer together with the event team. This is often in the reverse order of the build-up schedule. Some larger event organisers use run sheets at their events. Run sheets are lists of the order of specific tasks and jobs that are required to be undertaken by contractors or key members of the event team, examples of which include stage builds, catering, artists or entertainment, and waste management considerations. All these run-sheet lists are usually located in one folder called the production schedule.

During debrief it is important that all the problems and decisions made during the previous four phases are properly recorded. All areas of the event should be included in the process along with the event team, emergency services and other agencies (if present at the event), and critical contractors/suppliers. This allows the event to evolve and can save both time and money for future projects. Some event organisers like to hold 'hot debriefs' where they get all the staff together at the end of their shifts to find out what went well, what did not go quite so well and identify ideas and lessons learnt for the future. This procedure is carried out at this time so that information is still fresh in the minds of those taking part.

Others like to hold a debrief at a date agreed some time after the event. The rationale behind this is that it gives time for people to take stock and evaluate their thoughts. It may also be that there is not enough time to hold a hot debrief when staff and resources may be moving to another venue or site. This method is also useful if supervisors have more than one shift of staff; it allows them time to collate the information before attending. Whichever method is used, all the information gained should come together in the form of a debrief document which is shared between all interested parties, and which, if the event is to take place again, should form the first item on the agenda at the first planning team or SAG meeting for the next event. If an emergency has taken place at the event, this process will be especially important as the document may be used as evidence in any resulting criminal or enquiry proceedings. With the growth of the 'no win no fee' solicitors that now advertise in handling personal injury claims, records of the treatment and actions taken by both the medical teams and the event management team should also be kept for some years afterwards.

11.6 Problem-solving strategies

In order to solve a problem it is important to understand a wide range of potential solutions to that problem. It is also important to have some method of understanding which solution may be the most appropriate.

> The complexity of the problem needs to be determined by taking the following steps in account: naming and analysing the problem; understanding the problem and developing the right problem attitude; defining the types of problems and problem-solving processes; and collecting the experiences of experts.
>
> (Ellert et al., 2015, 63)

It is much better to develop a range of options for solving problems rather than to rely on just one. The best way to learn is to study what other event organisers have done in the past. The event organiser needs to remember that they are not the first person to arrange an event. Most of the problems the organiser will face will have been faced before by others and it is possible to make use of others' experiences in relation to event management. Doing this will help to solve any problems that may be encountered by efficient and effective means that may also have financial benefits.

Figure 11.1 and the following discussion highlight some strategies and examples that can assist with problem solving at an event. This is not an exhaustive account but is designed to give some context when considering problem solving and decision making; the organiser may implement additional solutions along the way. The important thing is to always review ways of working and implement any new systems as they are identified or become available. This will ensure that the event takes place in as safe a manner as possible and that the organiser is able to provide a clear audit trail regarding safety and working practices if required.

- *Clarify the problem*: it is much easier to solve a specific problem than a vague one so the organiser should make sure they know what the problem is and have gathered all of the information before looking for a solution. If a member of the team reports that they are having difficulty with a piece of equipment, stating that it does not work, try to establish what does not work and what they were expecting that piece of equipment to do.

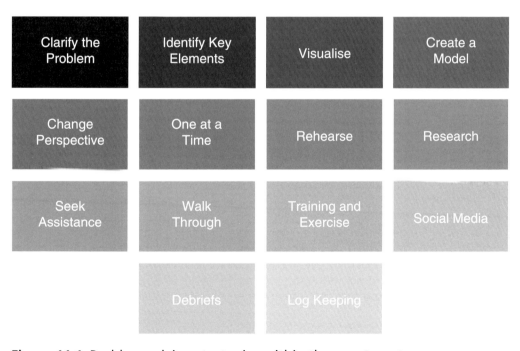

Figure 11.1 Problem-solving strategies within the events sector

- *Identify key elements of the problem*: when problems are presented they can some-times arrive with little information, lots of information and/or useless information. Valuable time can be wasted going through the useless information and it can distract from the really important pieces of detail. Try to establish the key elements of a problem before looking for the solution; there may be hidden agendas behind people presenting information, so try to establish the bigger picture, and keep an open mind where possible. For example, if there is a problem with a large piece of equipment try to establish the specific part that is causing the problem and what overall effect it may have on the event.

- *Visualise the problem*: sometimes the problem and all the important details are visible. This helps to understand the problem, but when this is not the case it is important to try to visualise it; it may be beneficial to draw pictures and diagrams, or use technology, such as mobile phone photographs or Apps. This is useful if the event organiser has been taken away on another job and needs to return at a later time, and it is also useful if the organiser is trying to explain the problem to others. If trying to explain the site plan of the event to other members of the team it is easier to do this with the aid of a site drawing.

- *Create a model of the problem*: this is a particularly useful tool when trying to estab-lish how crowds will behave and move through the event, knowing that the site capacity, the location of toilets and catering units and the audience profile can all influence the crowd. Creating a model and trying different methods will help to understand the customer experience before the event and identify any potential problems before they occur. It will also help in understanding how the crowds will move through the site, identifying any potential bottlenecks or any necessary site design amendments.

- *Change perspective*: when considering problems and making decisions, looking at the issues from somebody else's perspective can help change the way the organiser may view them. It can also help in understanding the impact of decisions made on others and the environment. It is always useful to empathise with the customer's position and to try and understand how the event site design and actions can affect their visitor experience. If their experience at the event is poor, they are less likely to return to future events and this could have both a financial and a reputational impact.

- *Solve one problem at a time*: there are times when multiple problems are presented simultaneously. It is important to make sure all are considered but that the most serious are given priority ranking. There can sometimes be problems that can remain problems which do not have a bearing on the safety of the event; these should be noted and considered at a later date.

- *Rehearse the problem*: there are some risks that will always remain risks to the event; it is important that the events team are aware of these types of risk and that they are continually monitored. It is good practice also to include these risks in the planning phase of the event and in any exercises used to validate plans. For example, crowds will always remain a risk to an event as they can sometimes become unpredictable due to their response to other influences such as the genre of music, an incident or even the weather. It is important that the organiser has contingencies in place to manage this.

- *Do the research*: as stated earlier in this chapter, there will be very few problems encountered at the event that others have not experienced before and found solutions to previously. As these problems come to light in the preparation of event plans and risk assessments, it is good practice to do some research and try to contact other event organisers to see if they can provide guidance and solutions. This can help to save time and money, and may make the organiser re-think activities at the event.

- *Get someone else involved*: it is always a valuable idea to get someone who has not been involved in the event at all to look at your plans with a fresh set of eyes; they have no preconceived ideas and could come up with a much better way of working. As the event organiser, sometimes it is possible to become so familiar with the risk assessments, event plans and other documents that the obvious may be missed.

- *Have a walk through*: it is good practice for event management teams, key contractors/suppliers, local authorities and emergency services to have a walk through the event site before it opens to customers. This ensures that everyone is familiar with the site and its operations and that they know the procedures that are in place should an emergency occur; it will also identify any last-minute problems. Some event organisers also have a walk through when the event is in operation, again to identify any unexpected problems. Any problems or last-minute decisions or changes to the risk assessment or event management plan should be documented along with the rationale behind them.

- *Training and exercise*: in the planning stages of the event the organiser will have completed a risk assessment and an event management plan; both of these documents should go through a validation process to ensure that systems and processes are appropriate for the event and that they will work should the need arise for them to be implemented. The best way of achieving this is to bring all interested parties together and run through some relevant scenarios using the plans to address them; this results in everyone understanding their roles and responsibilities and the response to incidents if necessary. It also ensures that the decision-making process is understood. This process is commonly referred to as a *table-top exercise*, a process which will be familiar to the emergency services and most other organisations within the event industry. It should be made clear at the start of these events that this process is designed to test and validate the event documents and not the individuals attending, as this can sometimes be a common misconception. It is also important that the event team and those teams belonging to critical contractors/ suppliers understand their roles and responsibilities both during the day-to-day operation of the event and in the case of an emergency. Training sessions should take place so that individuals are both competent and confident to undertake their duties; this is especially important for roles such as safety officers, stewards and security.

- *Monitor social media*: the use of the internet and in particular social media is becoming increasingly important in influencing the way that people both receive and share information about an event. It can be used to inform attendees of the latest line-up information, health and safety arrangements, travel updates, site layout and welfare arrangements. If the event takes place annually, it can give prospective customers an idea of what to expect by showing pictures and videos from the previous year. There are numerous other social media platforms available and customers may be using them all to communicate with each other before, during and after the event. It is very important that these platforms are monitored at all times to understand what customers are doing and planning to do. It also helps to gather intelligence in the run-up to the event, to understand what they are enjoying and also not enjoying as part of the event, and to gather feedback post-event. It can also assist in getting information out to both the local community stakeholders and those attending the event. If there is an incident, it helps to dispel any rumours that may become apparent and can help to inform and calm the crowd, giving them timely and accurate instruction regarding evacuation of the site, for example.

- *Debriefs*: a debrief should be conducted following the event; this helps to identify what went well, what did not go quite so well, any lessons learnt and better ways of working for future events. It helps to inform the event organiser about what people attending the event enjoyed and did not enjoy, making future events easier to plan for, and it will assist in bettering the customer experience for the following event.

- *Log keeping*: it is vitally important that problem solving and decision making are properly documented; the rationale behind decisions should also be included. This becomes especially important if there has been an incident and/or the event organisation is subject to any legal claim. Records should be kept for a number of years afterwards; for exact details it is important to seek advice from local stakeholders. These documents can also ensure that past mistakes are not repeated and that if problems reoccur they can be dealt with more efficiently. Refer to Malouff (2015) for some useful strategies, together with examples that can be used by event organisers to assist with problem solving during all stages of their event.

11.7 Decision making

In all five phases of the event, there will be a need to make decisions. Some will be relatively simple whilst others will be more complex. Some decisions will be routine and others may be difficult or challenging; some may even have to be made in the context of an emergency situation and whilst under pressure. Although problem solving and decision making are different processes, it is often necessary to combine them when making complex decisions. During the decision process, event organisers may be unaware of all the facts, there may be interrelated factors to consider, and the impact of the decision may be significant. There will almost certainly be several alternatives, each with its own set of uncertainties and consequences, which is why it is imperative that an event organiser not only records the decisions taken but the rationale behind them, especially in emergency situations if they occur. It is good practice to give someone this sole task and this role is usually referred to as a loggist. As specified by Van Knippenberg, Dahlander, Haas and George, (2015), even with technological advancements now available, knowing how to make an effective decision and what to do with the information present is still a concern for the human mind.

Decisions can often fail because the best alternatives are not clear at the outset, or key factors are not considered as part of the process: 'essential decisions for event processes are more difficult to make since obvious and less obvious side effects are hard to anticipate' (Ellert et al., 2015, 55). It is therefore important that problem-solving and decision-making strategies are combined to clarify understanding. A logical and ordered process will assist and ensure that all critical elements needed for a successful outcome have been considered. Often, when responsible for making a decision, support from others will still be required to implement it, so it pays to gain their trust. If possible make sure that those who will be affected or asked to implement a decision are involved in the process and asked their opinions. A single perspective can result in 'tunnel-vision' so a fresh view can be very useful.

People should be encouraged to contribute to the discussion without any fear of other participants rejecting their ideas. Make sure everyone recognises that the objective is to make the best decision possible in the circumstance. Team work should always be encouraged under normal circumstances. The exception to this would be emergency situations where it becomes necessary for a clear command and coordination hierarchy to exist. Before a decision can be made, the event organiser must be fully aware of the situation. It may be that the objective can be approached in isolation, but it is more likely that there will be a number of interrelated factors to consider. For example, organisers of the Lincoln Christmas Market regularly have to consider implementing crowd-thinning techniques during peak times in several areas of the event. Clear processes are in place but it is important that the organisers understand what the implications that a decision made in one area of the market can have for the rest of the market.

Different options may seem to make the decision more complicated at first, but coming up with alternatives enables a more in-depth look at the problem from different angles. When alternatives have been established, it is important to then evaluate the feasibility, risks and implications of each one, as almost every decision involves some degree of risk. It can be tempting to forge ahead at this stage. But now is the time to take stock and 'sense check' the decision. Hindsight is a luxurious thing and useful for identifying why things went wrong, but it is far better to prevent mistakes happening in the first place. The reliance on trust and effective networks is paramount in decision-making situations:

> They must be able to transfer that knowledge effectively, requiring robust network ties. And they must also decide how to react and respond to the information they receive, making concerns such as trust and trustworthiness central to the effective utilization of information.
>
> (Van Knippenberg et al., 2015, 651)

When making that final decision it is important to check that the organiser has based it on sound intelligence and research. It is important to double check to make sure that the information is still reliable and that there has been no change to the situation. It is also important for the organiser to trust their own instinct and judgement. The event organiser should use their previous training and experience to evaluate the decision made, especially if there are still elements that are uncertain. Once the decision has been reached, it must be communicated to everyone affected. Ensure that this done in a comprehensive way, that all interested parties understand the implications and can ask any questions they may have. You may even find that during this discussion other options come to light; if so, be sure to incorporate them into the solution and thank those who offered them. There are a wide variety of tools, techniques and software available to event organisers to assist them with their decision-making process. As with the risk assessment process, it is up to the individual to adopt or pick the most appropriate method for both themselves and the event.

Study activity

Look at the list of activities below and, together with your peers, put them into the correct phase of the event (planning, build-up, the event, and breakdown and debrief). Discuss your answers and provide the rationale behind your decisions.

- liaison with the Safety Advisory Group
- implementation of a site health and safety policy
- introduction of an event log
- validation of the event management plan
- completion of a site design and plans
- licence application
- validation of contractor's documentation
- completion of the event schedule document
- handover from the SAG to event control
- completion of a fire risk assessment
- emergency site evacuation procedures
- site communications systems
- traffic management plan
- cancellation policy
- monitoring of social media
- document any lesson learnt
- site security and stewarding
- implement decision-making roles and responsibilities
- engagement with local authority environmental health officers
- monitoring of noise

11.8 Conclusion

The focus on problem solving and decision making overlaps with many other areas of event project management as already discussed within this book. Risk management, feasibility, structures and teams, and also law and legislation all play a significant role in the event organiser's need to act in an effective and decisive manner in each phase of the event. It is sensible to think that problems and incidents will occur during an event, and it is the event organiser's duty to provide clear guidance and management in terms of planning for and managing these problems and risks. This chapter has provided some useful strategies to assist with problem solving and decision making within the events sector.

Case study 11: Walking conference in the Himalayan mountains of Nepal

The Tourism Education Futures Initiative (TEFI) walking conferences are designed to take participants completely outside of their normal daily environments and connect them with like-minded participants and colleagues from the same subject disciplines from around the world. The aim of the event is to facilitate cross-fertilisation of ideas with participants whilst trekking. This is to allow for communication and reflection without the constant time pressure that is common in traditional conference settings.

The first walking conference/workshops were organised in Nepal in 2014 by TEFI as an inspirational event for tourism and hospitality educators. The organisation had aspirations for a series of yearly events; however, the 2015 workshop was cancelled due to an earthquake in Nepal.

The first walking TEFI conference was designed and organised based on the following format:

- Walking Up: the Quest; the Query; Walking papers
- The Peak – Camp – Rest – Reflection; awareness-raising workshops on social entrepreneurship and tourism; observation in the villages
- Walking Down: Waking Up; Stepping Up, Commitment, Action. Reflections on how participants have changed and how they will make changes on returning.

Figure 11.2 Walking conference, Nepal

Source: © Georgiana Els

The main focus for this case study is the dynamic decision-making process that was required from the planning to the organisation and operation of the event organiser and their team. The case will be approached from two different perspectives: that of the organiser who is responsible for taking decisions and

(Continued)

Case study 11 (*continued*)

preventing all potential risks, and that of the attendee who wants to participate in a safe and enjoyable event. Roberto Daniele organised the first walking conference in 2014 for TEFI and will provide the organiser's perspective and Dr Georgiana Els attended the walking conference in 2014 and will make contributions from a participant perspective in relation to the decisions taken and the experience of the entire event.

The format of the walking workshop is innovative, refreshing and engaging. The conference provides the opportunity to share ideas and interact with peers that you would not typically approach in a traditional conference setting. In this way, historical preconceptions about conferences are dispersed, which allows for new ideas to emerge. The experience was enriching and life-changing from both a personal and professional point of view as new ways of thinking unfolded.

How did the initial idea of a 'walking workshop' emerge? How long did it take for it to materialise?

RD: The initial idea came to me out of frustration with traditional conferences which often take place in venues that are completely removed from the context of the topic being discussed, and are often too short, leaving very little time for thinking and reflection. Ten days working away from the desk or office meant that participants could use this time to escape their usual routines and ways of thinking and enter a more open and relaxed space for listening to others and letting new ideas, projects and links emerge from our interactions.

GC: Participants were asked to deliver one or several 'walking papers' whilst trekking. The task was more challenging than initially thought as it was quite difficult to trek and talk on steep hills. Usually, papers were delivered in small groups of two to three people due to the slenderness of the mountain paths. As a participant, however, this was a memorable, enjoyable experience as papers were sometimes delivered in extreme weather conditions – heavy rain, mud or amongst curious donkeys. From an organiser's perspective, there were several risks to be considered such as: weather conditions, slippery terrain, narrow and steep mountain paths or open fields.

What was the planning process behind it? Would you do anything different at the second workshop (to be organised in May 2016)?

RD: I think that an important aspect of the planning process was the clear demarcation between the roles and responsibilities of the organisers. So from day one I was clear that all the travel and trekking logistics were to be handled by our expedition operator Adventure Alternative, a tour operator that works on a social entrepreneurship business model and which therefore was very much in alignment with our thinking and fully understood the purpose of our workshop. On the other hand, a TEFI committee led by myself but including other members

Figure 11.3 The curious donkeys, Nepal

Source: © Georgiana Els

(Continued)

Case study 11 (*continued*)

of the executive, took care of the academic content and structure of the work-shops. This, however, was also done in close consultation with Adventure Alternative as we wanted to make sure that we had strong input from those who knew the region and its communities much better than we did.

GC: Due to the remote location of the walking workshop, facilities were quite basic, meaning no internet, limited electricity, no normal conference equipment and sometimes limited hot water supplies.

How did you decide what aspects of the conference were compulsory to have, would be desirable and/or not needed? Was it a decision taken in the planning process or along the way?

RD: As the focus of this workshop was really to do things differently and not replicate existing formulas we used some of the location shortcomings to actually play to our advantage: great *not* to have PowerPoints as this forced presenters to be more natural; great to have basic facilities and lots of walking to tackle and some mildly adverse weather. This created a spirit of camaraderie within the group and the big hierarchical distinctions which are often very visible at tradi-tional academic conferences pretty much disappeared so that 'big name' professors were suddenly on an equal footing with junior lecturers!

Taking into consideration the five phases of an event (planning, build-up, the event, break down and debrief) what was the most challenging stage of the first walking conference?

RD: I think that the most challenging aspect of this conference was that of 'selling the model' to academics. This was pretty much the first walking confer-ence ever organised in the tourism and hospitality sectors and it was obvious from many emails I was getting that academics were baffled by the format and could not quite make sense of it. Lesson learned from this is about being much clearer in future communication strategies, making sure that key differ-ences or novelty aspects are communicated well in advance. The second chal-lenge was actually during the event. Even though we were organisers of the workshop everything was a first for us too as due to time and budget constraints we were not able to do a pre-conference visit so we were seeing and experien-cing all aspects of the workshop for the first time, just like our participants! This often involved having to make quick decisions on the go, and again the strong partnership with Adventure Alternative was invaluable with regard to providing the right advice and local knowledge to make the right decisions in the end.

GC: From a participant perspective, there were no obvious problems or conflicts while in Kathmandu or while trekking in the Himalayas and that is why it would be interesting to know if you had any organisational problems or conflicts whilst in Nepal?

RD: Thankfully there were no major organisational problems whilst in Nepal with the exception of two participants who had dramatically overestimated their fitness levels and ability to take part in the workshop. Again, thanks to the expertise and local contacts of Adventure Alternative we were able to fly those participants back safely to Kathmandu, allowing the rest of the group to stick to the original plan of the workshop which went as anticipated.

Figure 11.4 Himalayan mountains of Nepal

Source: © Georgiana Els

(*Continued*)

Case study 11 (*continued*)

What would you say was the most difficult decision taken during the ten-day conference?

RD: I think that the most difficult decision taken during the conference was actually to stick to the conference plan. Towards the end of the conference we were getting reports that due to bad weather there was a bottleneck at Lukla (Tenzing-Hillary) airport with several trekkers missing their flights back to Kathmandu. My concern was that delays in Lukla could mean participants missing their flights back home from Kathmandu and the temptation here was to shorten the conference by one or two days to allow some buffer time in Lukla. Once again we turned to Adventure Alternative for advice and they were able to convince us to stick to the original plan as they were confident about their ability to get us all on board our originally planned flight, which they did!

What was the impact of the walking workshop on the local community, businesses and development of tourists in the Lower Solu Khumbu region of the Himalayas?

RD: Apart from the impact of local spending, of delegates staying in villager's guesthouses, using porters, etc., one of the unintended consequences of the conference was that the delegates were so impressed with what they saw in the villages and with the work that Adventure Alternative (and its sister charity organisation Moving Mountains Trust) carried out in the region, that they decided to commit to help Adventure Alternative and Moving Mountains in their quest to develop a local tourism training institution. We are now returning to Nepal in May 2016 to plan the first Tourism Summer School which will be the precursor of the first Himalayan Tourism Institute in the region, and TEFI has committed to giving academic support and input into this venture.

What advice would you give to students studying events management about event project planning?

RD: Two pieces of advice here:

1 Think outside the box and outside the norm if possible. The sector is increasingly competitive and clients are increasingly looking for event organisers that enable them to provide their stakeholders with events which stand out from the crowd.
2 More importantly, think about your sector (event management) as one that can play a big role in making this world a better place, and try to focus on events which make a real difference. There is a growing market and appetite for this and I would love to see students identifying with a cause and building a social enterprise events company around this!

Evaluative student questions

1 How did the concept, design and implementation of the walking workshops manifest?
2 If you were to organise the event yourself, how would you devise the planning of the event? What contingency plans would you put in place to assist with potential problems that may arise?
3 How important is it to maintain and develop relationships with colleagues and stakeholders? In what way do you think strong collaborations and community partnerships make problem solving and decision making easier?

Further reading

Ellert, G., Schafmeister, G., Wawrzinek, D. and Gassner, H. (2015) 'Expect the unexpected': new perspectives on uncertainty management and value logics in event management. *International Journal of Event and Festival Management*, 6(1) 54–72.

Malouff, J. (2015) *Over 50 problem solving strategies explained*. Available from: http://www.une.edu.au/about-une/academic-schools/school-of-behavioural-cognitive-and-social-sciences/news-and-events/psychology-community-activities/over-fifty-problem-solving-strategies-explained [Accessed 14 July 2015].

Van Knippenberg, D., Dahlander, L., Haas, M. and George, G. (2015) Information, attention and decision making. *Academy of Management Journal*, 58(3) 649–657.

Note

1 Sourced from a conversation with Nick Sentance, Divisional Resilience Manager for East Midlands Ambulance Service.

References

Bowdin, G., Allen, J., O'Toole, W., Harris, R. and McDonnell, I. (2011) *Events management*. 3rd edition. London: Butterworth-Heinemann.

Civil Contingencies Act 2004 (c.36). London: HMSO.

Ellert, G., Schafmeister, G., Wawrzinek, D. and Gassner, H. (2015) 'Expect the unexpected': new perspectives on uncertainty management and value logics in event management. *International Journal of Event and Festival Management*, 6(1) 54–72.

Griffiths, B., Woodham, R. and Stuart, E. (2015) *The UK good practice guide to working in Safety Advisory Groups*. York: Emergency Planning College.

Health and Safety Executive (2015) *Getting started*. Available from: http://www.hse.gov.uk/event-safety/getting-started.htm [Accessed 14 July 2015].

Kemp, C. Hill, I., Upton, M. and Hamilton, M. (2007) *Case studies in crowd management*. Cambridge: Entertainment Technology Press.

Kiaffas, Z. and Afthinos, I. (2013) Simulations for correct organizational decision making processes in sport events project production management. *Hellenic Journal of Sport and Recreation Management*, 10(1) 1–15.

Malouff, J. (2015) *Over 50 problem solving strategies explained*. Available from: http://www.une.edu.au/about-une/academic-schools/school-of-behavioural-cognitive-and-social-sciences/news-and-events/psychology-community-activities/over-fifty-problem-solving-strategies-explained [Accessed 14 July 2015].

Management of Health and Safety at Work Regulations 1999 (n.3242). Available http://www.legislation.gov.uk/uksi/1999/3242/contents/made [Accessed 4 March 2016].

National Fire Protection Association (2015) *The station nightclub fire*. Available from: http://www.nfpa.org/safety-information/for-consumers/occupancies/nightclubs-assembly-occupancies/the-station-nightclub-fire [Accessed 14 July 2015].

O'Toole, W. (2011) *Events feasibility and development: from strategy to operations*. London: Butterworth-Heinemann.

Still, G.K. (2013) *Introduction to crowd science*. Boca Raton, FL: CRC Press.

Van Knippenberg, D., Dahlander, L., Haas, M. and George, G. (2015) Information, attention and decision making. *Academy of Management Journal*, 58(3) 649–657.

Chapter 12

Project completion and review

12.1 Introduction

This final chapter will concentrate on an essential phase of the event project management process. The project completion and review stage is the final segment that completes the event planning cycle and ensures that all aspects of the project reach proper conclusions and that any lessons learnt are taken forward and included in future projects. This phase can all too easily be completed in haste or, worse, be overlooked in the rush to break down and move on to the next project. Bowdin et al. (2011, 212) state, 'it is only through evaluation that event managers can determine how successful their efforts have been in achieving whatever goals and/or objectives they have set'. The importance and significance of project review and completion should not be ignored.

Tip box

Planning for the project's completion should be part of the initial project plan. If no thought is given to this phase until it commences, it may be too late to assimilate the necessary resources and information and things will get missed.

It is particularly important that the event undergoes a proper evaluation as it is this procedure that will enable the event organiser to take stock and capture information on a range of subjects and procedures such as health and safety, contractor/supplier performance, stakeholder and customer feedback. This data can then be used to look at what went well, what did not go quite as planned and ideas for the future. Information gained can then be used for new projects to assist with event planning and delivery. It also provides a clear audit trail as to how both the event and the event organiser have evolved and taken into account their past experiences and how they have been used to plan and manage events. This process arguably enables the event organiser to save money as a result of better practices and systems, and also to identify and contract reliable contractors/suppliers and remove those that did not perform to the standards expected of them.

As soon as the event comes to a conclusion, there are many tasks and procedures that will need to be undertaken before the project can truly be labelled complete. It may be some weeks and even months before this is fully achieved. Tasks will include the breakdown, returning the site/venue to its original condition, artists/performers' payments, contractors/suppliers' payments, human resource issues, paperwork, including letters of thanks, and event management plan amendments that were identified during the actual event.

12.2 Shutdown

Once all audience members have left the venue the event shutdown can begin in earnest although at some larger events with multiple attractions or stages, such as festivals for example, this may have begun prior to audience departure. If some of the audience are still in attendance this will require careful management with these areas appropriately risk assessed, signed and cordoned off whilst any work is being undertaken. The conclusion of the event requires careful consideration. If the entertainment is a single performance, show or activity, the majority of the audience or attendees will all want to leave the venue or site at the same time. They will all have arrived at different times but this 'hard stop' will put additional pressure on both crowd and traffic management systems. Thought should therefore be given to the entertainment programme and if possible the addition of extra attractions to help stagger the departure phase.

The organisers of RAF Waddington International Air Show used this particular approach effectively to manage the departure of crowds from the event. Historically, research showed that many people started to make their way home immediately after the RAF Red Arrows aerobatic display team had performed; this had traditionally been the last display of the air show and resulted in large traffic tailbacks around the site inconveniencing the local community. To stagger the exit phase at future air shows, the Red Arrows performed in the middle of the afternoon and not at the end of the show. This meant that those wishing to depart following the display could do so, leaving others to enjoy the rest of the flying programme. Fairground rides, stalls and static displays remained open after the flying display had ended, which took the pressure off the traffic management system and lessened the impact on the local community.

The shutdown process can also sometimes be referred to as the breakdown, load-out or site phase-out. The event breakdown phase will include the removal of all equipment, final liaison with the entertainment including payment, cleaning and returning the site or venue to its pre-event condition, disposal of waste, removal of staging areas and event signage, and any other financial transactions. It is also important that time is taken to thank crews, contractors/suppliers, volunteers and sponsors for their support throughout the project. For any event, especially larger ones, the breakdown schedule should be carefully considered and properly risk assessed with appropriate systems put in place to manage it safely. There can be a danger that site health and safety procedures may not be fully adhered to in the rush to clear and dismantle equipment and the site. All staff and contractors/suppliers should be reminded that what was not considered safe practice during the build and at the event will not be considered safe practice during the breakdown, and the same rules still apply. Fatigue can sometimes play a part as crews may have been working long hours, especially at events such as music festivals which span a number of days, and there may be an element of complacency. Crews may face uncertainty over future employment and this may have an impact on morale and output. There may also be time constraints which play a part; for example, equipment may be required at another event site or the event may be part of a tour and the pressure is on to move to the next venue. The weather can also be a contributing factor and every effort must be made by the event management organising team to oversee and face these challenges efficiently:

> Disbanding event teams can be problematic if not planned well in advance. Many event personnel can experience concerns about future employment, so there can be a tapering of team morale. Some event organisations try to combat this by holding debriefing meetings and end-of-event parties, which may include recognition and rewards for performance achievement.
>
> (Bladen et al., 2012, 44)

During the breakdown phase, the security of the site should be maintained at all times. There may be many new contractors/suppliers and vehicles arriving on site to assist with this stage of the project. Some will have been used during the build or during the event but others may be unfamiliar to the event management team. It is prudent to keep security on site as it is at this time that the site and equipment may become vulnerable to theft or damage.

The site may appear to be clear but it is important that a final check is made to ensure that any smaller equipment such as hand-held radios and other small items are accounted for. Some events adopt a sign-in and sign-out policy for such items to avoid this issue and some get the event team together and jointly walk the complete event site as a final check before handing it back over to the site owner. As suggested by Bowdin et al. (2011, 550), 'a member of staff needs to walk the site to check whether anything has been left behind – called the "idiot check" in the music industry. At this point, the event manager realises the value of a torch!'

It is good practice to hold regular team meetings to capture any examples of good practice, lessons learnt, near misses and any areas for improvement not only during this phase but throughout the build and the actual event. It is also a good way of sharing the latest information and intelligence and helps to foster a good teamwork ethos. When referring to crowd management and learning from past experiences, Still (2013, 19) explains:

> Near misses are rarely documented, and neither are things that work *well*. The events industry has no requirement for formal qualifications – either for crowd risk analysis or crowd safety engineering; the risk assessment process is, at best, subjective and in general unstructured. There is a clear need for a more formalised approach to best practices, and for the continual development of information capture systems to improve our understanding of events and, specifically, to reduce accident potential.

Due to the lack of clarity about expectations and documentation in the events industry, it is crucial that the events organisation develop a best practice of its own that is thoughtful, safe and detailed.

Tip box

Use checklists to help manage the process, key staff and supervisors should be encouraged to use them to ensure that all necessary tasks are completed. They can also assist with task allocation, responsibilities and prioritisation.

The use of checklists combined with a methodical approach to the breakdown of the event can facilitate the redeployment of staff and equipment. This in turn can have financial benefits for the event organiser as, for example, money can be saved on daily hire costs, and this information can be especially useful when contracting for future events. It may be useful to prepare a checklist of everything that must be done before the project can be officially closed. Using a checklist as part of the project management process is very important:

> The simple checklist represents the combined experience and knowledge of the corporate event management team. It is the final document output of the work breakdown structure and could be thought of as a list of mini milestones . . . It is the fine mesh of the net that stops anything from slipping through and escaping attention before it is too late.
>
> (O'Toole and Mikolaitis, 2002, 54)

Table 12.1 lists items that may be included on such a checklist. It is not intended to be exhaustive but merely provides examples, and more may be required at individual and specific events dependent on a number of influencing factors such as location, time of day, site restrictions, activity and entertainment, audience profile, crowd numbers and weather, to name but a few. It is important to revisit the checklist at each event to ensure that it is still appropriate and meets the requirements of the individual event.

Tip box

All items in Table 12.1 should be allocated to a role which will be responsible for its reporting and completion along with timescales and any necessary resources.

Once the breakdown of the site has been completed, the event shutdown will continue but it will take on more of an administrative function and will include tasks such as acquitting all the contracts, final invoice payments, collation of event records and data and collation of customer, stakeholder and any media feedback. All of this information will be necessary in compiling event evaluation data and the final event report.

Table 12.1 A project completion checklist

Project Completion Checklist

Ensure event site is cleared and returned to original condition
Clean, sell or repair any equipment as necessary
Ensure all project activities have been completed
Complete all required project deliverables and objectives
Gather all necessary acceptances and approvals of project results
Check event logs have been completed
Ensure any incidents have been properly recorded (contacts, photos, logs)
Ensure thank you letters are disseminated to all relevant parties
Assess the extent to which project results met expectations
Perform all required administrative tasks
Terminate all related contracts for goods and services
Ensure all outstanding invoices are paid
Complete all human resources tasks
Ensure that all project documentation and deliverables are archived
Gather customer, stakeholder and any media feedback
Undertake proper event evaluation and debrief
Prepare event report
Include any good practice or lessons learnt in future event management plans

12.3 Evaluation

The importance of evaluating the event cannot be underestimated. The project should undergo proper evaluation and review during all stages of the planning cycle. It can help to avoid any unnecessary delays and may be used to manage any emerging challenges or risks which may in turn impact on costs or the effective delivery of the event:

> The events industry is still young, and is struggling in some areas to establish legitimacy and acceptance as a profession. One of the best means for the industry to gain credibility is for events to be evaluated honestly and critically, so their outcomes are known, their benefits acknowledged and their limitations accepted.
>
> (Bowdin et al., 2011, 629)

It is only through proper evaluation and review that event organisers can be certain that their events have achieved their aims and objectives, and that they are still relevant to and appropriate for their next event. Each of the different event areas such as operations, finance, logistics, marketing and human resources should have control measures in place so that accurate and detailed reports and documents are produced to ensure that planned procedures and activities are being adhered to and any necessary amendments and the rationale behind them are captured for future use.

Many events rely heavily on stakeholder engagement and involvement and their promised legacy, especially if there are to be benefits to the local economy or the event is to become an annual occurrence. Large-scale events with high-profile enter-tainment often attract intense media scrutiny. Discussion on social media sites can also impact upon its reputation and popularity. Taking this into account, it is important that an evaluation is undertaken to provide these stakeholders with financial data and that it is used to measure performance against agreed project objectives and deliver-ables. This should be a mixture of both quantitative and qualitative feedback to properly understand any impacts. It can also assist with protecting not only existing stakeholder investment but in attracting future sponsors and investors as well.

During the evaluation process it will be more straightforward to measure or assess certain impacts of the event as these will be tangible and clearly intelligible. Examples include financial costs and benefits, ticket sales and attendance. This type of data are quantitative in nature, and facts, figures and statistics from financial reports, media analysis and questionnaires can be utilised. It is also important that the process includes factors that are more elusive and imperceptible and cannot be easily measured or assessed, such as specific impacts on the local community. Qualitative methods are required to understand community wellbeing or sense of community (SOC) (Van Winkle and Woosnam, 2014) as a result of the event, as well as civic pride and the impact on the location from the perspective of tourism. Appropriate means of gathering this inform-ation, which is rich and people-focused, would be interviews, focus groups, observa-tions and, potentially, online forums. This type of feedback is especially useful in gaining sponsorship, support or acceptance by local communities for future events in the locality.

12.3.1 The process

The event evaluation process requires a mixture of observation, measurement and continuous assessment of the project to ensure that objectives and outcomes have been suitably met. It should be included in the initial project planning phase with a commitment for staff and resources to be made available to undertake and document the task. Procedures necessary may have significant budgetary implications and can often be a limiting factor in the application of any evaluation process; this may mean that it can be downgraded or, even worse, forgotten about as other areas of the event budget receive greater priority. The basic process of event project evaluation involves four main reflective stages, these stages formulate an event project evaluation cycle as shown in Figure 12.1 (Bladen et al., 2012).

It is important to review and reflect upon the event project cycle and Verhaar and Eshel (2013, 149) offer a number of questions that could be posed as part of the event evaluation process:

- Has the target group been reached and were they satisfied?
- Did the event run as expected and have the desired effect?
- Were the methods used during planning and execution adequate?
- Were the budgets and targets met?
- Were deadlines met?
- Were all tasks and responsibilities carried out satisfactorily?
- Was co-operation, liaison and teamwork achieved during the project?
- How was the event project managed?

These questions take into account stakeholder needs, project success, financial targets and communication benchmarks. To reiterate, the event evaluation process should

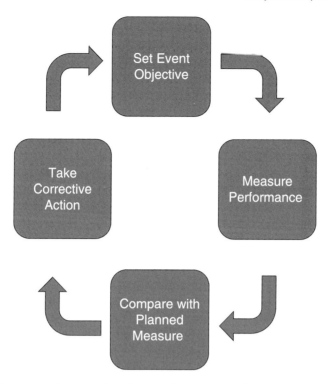

Figure 12.1 Event project evaluation cycle extracted

Source: Bladen et al., 2012, 39

take place during all stages of the event and be undertaken by competent staff and properly documented. The following sections will review the evaluation process under the three areas of data analysis and collection, impact and legacy, and finally reporting and dissemination.

Study activity

Write a list of all of the possible stakeholders involved in a one-day music event and next to each stakeholder write down what procedures would need to take place to ensure effective completion and review with that company or person (e.g. contractors/suppliers – contracts signed off, payment).

12.3.2 Data collection and analysis

After it has been established and agreed what to evaluate and what process is to be used, the next step is to collate and analyse the data. The event evaluation process is also a time when the event organiser and the management team can reflect upon the process used to manage all stages of the event. For example, some event organisers choose to write the risk assessment before the event management plan, whilst others may do this at a later stage. Whichever way is chosen, it is important that these documents, along with all other documents pertaining to the event, are suitably reviewed. This will enable the team to properly capture any learning, amendments and good practice established during the event project; this can then be disseminated to all relevant staff and contractors/suppliers, which helps to inform future projects. Experience and the information gathered can also identify any training and development gaps and opportunities both for the event management team and any other staff/volunteers that haves roles and responsibilities at the event.

There are several documents that will provide substantial amounts of data during the evaluation process, the most significant of which should include financial performance, ticket sales, attendance figures, demographic information, performance data and medical and safety event logs. Financial performance data should include information regarding the event budget and the balance sheet, and details of all income and expenditure together with profit and loss figures. This information will be of particular interest to the event organiser who will be able to use it to evidence success and attract future sponsorship and other investment in their future projects. More information about this can be found in Chapter 9 on cost and financial planning. After consideration of this data, the organiser may also decide the viability of future events of this type. Evaluation of ticket sales is particularly important, especially if the event organiser is planning future events of a similar nature with the same entertainment or performances in the same area. It is really useful to know how quickly the tickets sold and, if there were differing types, which sold first or were more popular. This information can also be used during future planning and is something that SAGs will be interested in as liaison and planning progresses.

Collation of accurate attendance figures will be able to demonstrate either the event's success or failure. For paid events data is gathered on the demographics and potentially socio-personality details in terms of age, gender and income. Postcode analysis is especially useful when trying to gauge how the intended audience will travel to the event and for putting together traffic management options and plans. This in turn can have significant financial benefits to the event organiser when contracting parking and traffic management companies at other events, and also helps to target areas for promotion of future projects.

For free events, attendance figures can be ascertained by calculating the area of the site and the area that will be used by the crowd. These areas can then be looked at in people per square metre and a safe capacity agreed; site design, crowd movement and flow should also be incorporated into this calculation. Public transport and parking companies will be able to provide data in relation to usage. Event staff may use observation and photographic evidence to estimate the crowd size.

Chapter 3 discusses stakeholder relationships and makes reference to different audience profiles at the event and it is useful to use this information to build a proper demographic profile of the event audience or crowd. This can be achieved through the use of surveys or questionnaires at the event and focus groups post-event. Information that could be sought may include gender, age range, spending patterns, levels of education and income, where they live, how they travelled to the event, and any features for inclusion in future events. It is also useful to find out both what people enjoyed and, more importantly, what they did not. All this information will ensure that the event organiser is better informed in relation to staging future events. The perceptions of both local residents and tourists were explored by Chan (2015) in relation to Hong Kong's Rugby Sevens event and it was discovered that local residents felt that the event was more tailored to younger people. This evaluative insight will have repercussions for the event marketing team and project planning for the following year. Chan (2015) interviewed 14 participants, 11 of whom were men and three of whom were women, and this may have skewed the results in terms of sample size and gender bias. Regardless of this limited sample, the findings of Chan's (2015) research remain useful and rich, but it is advisable that event evaluations consider an appropriate sample size and coverage to increase the reliability of data collection. Sometimes aspects of event evaluation can be overlooked, such as the participation legacy of the Sydney 2000 Olympic Games, which was not specifically or initially targeted (Veal, Toohey and Frawley, 2012). Instead, it was necessary to analyse national participation surveys that were conducted by telephone or face-to-face interviews in order to review sports participation figures. As Veal et al. (2012, 166) state, 13 out of the 17 national surveys only included participants aged 15 years or older, making it difficult to provide a full picture of children's sporting legacies.

On occasion the image or status of the event may need to be analysed, something that can be a reasonably subjective and open-ended process. Stakeholders may wish to understand the local or national perception of the event and how well it has been received by the attendees and those affected by it. Deng, Li and Shen, (2015) attempted to explore the event image of the 2010 Shanghai World Expo by conducting in-depth interviews and sending out questionnaires. The qualitative evaluative method used was 'free association', in which participants were asked what thoughts came to their mind when they thought of the World Expo. In conclusion, the research named five labels that contribute to event image; benefit, facility, service, theme and event content. Event managers may wish to evaluate the perception of their event using labels such as these, but the subjectivity of this particular research method might incur the need to combine it with other mixed method approaches.

The use of ICT and project management tools will be required to properly manage and evaluate the event and should include the use of Gantt charts, critical paths, milestones and budgetary indicators, for example, all of which are discussed in Chapters 5 and 9 of this book. These techniques will become particularly useful if deadlines and other milestones need to be amended or adjusted as the project progresses. Critical success factors (CSFs) refer to the direct and indirect inputs which lead to project success (Alias, Zawawi, Yusof and Aris, 2014) and can be referred back to and monitored during the event evaluation process. There are many different examples available to event organisers and their management teams and they can be used as part of the project management process. It is good practice to evaluate several before deciding upon which are most suitable to the particular event.

12.3.3 Media and social networking

Positive media coverage of all aspects of the event will be important to any event organiser as it can be used to negotiate the occurrence of future events in the locality, and to help attract sponsors and encourage ticket sales, but it is equally important to be aware of the negative connotations of media publicity as well. Social media is a tool people use to update and report on events happening around them: 'For instance, during recent social upheavals and crises, millions of people on the ground turned to Twitter to report and follow significant events' (Atefeh and Khreich (2015, 132).

> ## Tip box
>
> Try to build good working relationships with the media throughout all phases of the event. The local media can be especially useful in providing information, sponsorship and local area comment and feedback.

Media coverage of the event should be monitored and collated as part of the evaluation process. Large-scale organisations and events usually have people or teams that will look after this process but it is good practice at any event. Effective media monitoring and a proactive stance can help to eliminate any misinformation that may arise, but it can also assist with providing timely and accurate information from the event organiser in reply to specific issues or situations as they occur. Ultimately, the event organiser's reputation can be enhanced or destroyed in equal measure by the media if not managed correctly.

Monitoring social media sites and platforms, both during the actual event and during the days immediately following it, will also provide valuable information and data regarding visitor experiences:

> Download was one of the first festivals to embrace social networking, encouraging fans to have their say and to voice their thoughts and opinions. They really put the fans at the heart of the festival – encouraging their input and valuing their thoughts and ideas. Some fans are even invited to sit with Download organisers and discuss the festival face-to-face. Download's online interaction and forums are a key part of the success of the festival and something its organisers have won awards for.
>
> (Bowman, 2015, 39)

If event organisers encourage and promote interaction between stakeholders and organisers on virtual networks then an evaluation and monitoring of this process is necessary. The ease with which social media enables voices to be heard and opinions to be raised means that the event organisers have access to feedback at speed and in large volumes.

Study activity

Compile a SWOT analysis (strengths, weaknesses, opportunities and threats) in relation to the use and analysis of social media sites during and after the event. Is it useful? Could it be misleading?

12.4 Event observation

The best way to see how the event is operating at all stages is to take a moment to step back and actually look at it. For this process to be most effective, all elements should be covered including performance of contractors/suppliers, entertainment, audience responses and behaviour, crowd dynamics and flow around the site, general ambience and any security or safety issues. All staff and contractors/suppliers working on it should be consulted and their opinions, ideas and feedback listened to and taken on board. This is where checklists for staff may become particularly useful.

A spirit of cooperation and team working should have been established early in the planning stages of the event and this should have been driven through whilst plans were being developed, during their validation and as part of any exercises held, but most importantly during the event operation itself. If this has been the case, all staff and critical contractors/suppliers should be aware and knowledgeable of the event objectives and management plans, and have a good idea of how the event should operate so that they are able to comment on operations and procedures with a degree of authority. Data gathered should therefore be informed and accurate and will help identify the most popular attractions or aspects of the event, any lessons learnt, different ways of working, any unsafe practices and cost savings for the future.

As well as the event team, it is equally important to involve other agencies and stakeholders in the process. Each organisation will have its own roles or responsibilities within the event project and will be able to compare activities taking place at this event with those taking place at others either that they have been involved in or that have taken place in the vicinity. These agencies will be able to provide their own thoughts on planning and operations which will be useful to the event organiser. Examples of agencies that should be asked for their observations include the emergency services, local authorities, vendors, sponsors and other contractors/suppliers that are involved in the project. All documentation and feedback should be kept and included in the final event report.

Tip box

Remember, 'a picture is worth a thousand words'. Use photographs, video and audio to capture any information, incidents and occurrences that need to be taken to debriefs and form part of the evaluation report, as this can illustrate points raised and will be especially useful if future evidence is required or as part of any future training initiatives.

12.5 Debriefing

Debriefing is a crucial element of this final phase of the event cycle. It provides an opportunity to look in detail at all aspects of the project, the things that went well, others that did not go quite so well, any incidents, lessons learnt and ideas for future projects. As stated previously, it is important that everyone involved in the project is included, no matter what their role, and that their ideas and opinions are recorded. Attendees must be made to feel comfortable and have the confidence to share their views and opinions in order for the debrief meeting to be truly representative of the event. Those that are not truly representative often fail, and valuable information and experience may be lost. There are several ways that debriefs can be conducted and each has its own benefits and downfalls; the event organiser must choose the one most appropriate to their event.

For larger-scale events, it may be necessary to hold individual departmental or team debriefs ahead of the main event debrief meeting. This may be the case because there would simply be too many people to invite to one single debrief meeting. The event management team should allocate this task to a key member of staff to conduct. Once this meeting has been held, the information and feedback captured should be properly documented, and that member of staff invited to the main debrief meeting to represent the group. It must be noted that the time frames for conducting debriefs may vary from event to event, more of which is discussed in the previous chapter in relation to phases four and five of the event cycle.

Information and feedback can also be gathered by conducting surveys or focus groups. Surveys can be used to evaluate the whole event or different or particular aspects of it. They can be used to establish the opinions and responses of an agreed number of event attendees. Careful thought should be given to questions included in the surveys as it will be the replies to these that will influence the quality of the data and information captured. Surveys are a useful tool for providing accurate statistical data and can be undertaken either by face-to-face interaction at the event or by telephone or post after the event. A good incentive is to offer some sort of reward such as free tickets or event merchandise to increase the response; the more returns, the more accurate the data. It must be noted, however, by the answers they provide that incentivised responses may lead to bias as the participant may want to return their gratitude for the incentive. Face-to-face interviews, however, require a team of people to conduct them and this can be an additional expense for the event organiser unless volunteers can be sourced. Focus groups are typically directed discussions that are normally held with small groups of people and are qualitative in nature. They can be used to provide detailed and targeted information on attendee experiences and perception of the event, to discuss future proposals and activities, and to ascertain perceptions and attitudes towards the event.

There may also be some existing forms of data that have been gathered from different sources which may not be related to the event but could be used as part of the evaluation process. These data are sometimes referred to as secondary data and can be obtained from several different sources. Examples include publicly or privately funded research companies that can provide data either free of charge or under contract, use of the internet to research similar or previous event data, journal databases, research reports and other academic reports also available through university libraries or the internet.

Tip box

Network and take time out to speak with others in the event industry as there are very few things that, collectively, event organisers have never experienced. Other organisers' experiences can help you and save both time and money in future event planning and delivery projects.

12.6 Event impact and legacy

The impact that the event has on both the local community and the local economy will be of much interest to event stakeholders, the local authorities and other agencies such as the emergency services. It is therefore important that data and evidence is gathered to enable both positive and negative aspects of the event to be properly reported. Previous research into event impacts has focused on urban settings but many events take place in rural surroundings (Wood and Thomas, 2008). Regardless of the setting, the evaluation methods, in a practical sense, should be proportionate to the size and scope of the event (Davies, Coleman and Ramchandani, 2013). Methods and processes should be manageable and appropriate for the event team. It is beyond the scope of this book to provide detailed information regarding measurement of impact and legacy. This section, however, will highlight the key aspects of impact that the event project team will need to be aware of in the project completion stages. Event impact can generally be split into three main areas – economic, environmental and social, also known as the triple bottom line.

12.6.1 Economic impact

Data gathered around the economic impact of the event will be of particular interest to the stakeholders and sponsors as they will be keen to establish the benefits and return from their investments and it may be that future funding and investment can be secured on the basis of this. These organisations can also use this data to prioritise which events they will support going forward, and event organisers will be keen to harness any funding as soon as possible to enable planning to commence on any annual or future projects. One important aspect of economic impact analysis (EIA) is to take into account the expenditure of the stakeholders involved in the event (e.g. visitors, sponsors) (Dwyer and Jago, 2015).

There are many different methods of using economic impact toolkits, which will vary in approach and can be very complicated. Ultimately, event organisers must be able to evidence and document an evaluation of the event that is compliant with stakeholder needs and requests. With ever-decreasing budgets, staff and resources and the pressure on organisations to justify expenditure, it is little wonder that the evaluation process tends to focus on the economic impacts of events and that much of the academic literature and evaluation studies concern this particular area (Swart and Bob, 2013). Wood (2005) argues that the prevalence of economic measurement is an extension of traditional tourism impact research.

12.6.2 Environmental impact

The environmental impacts of the event are of great importance and if not properly addressed can lead to the event not being funded, supported or permitted to take place in the future. Most events, especially the larger ones, create a great deal of waste. This can be in the form of litter and personal belongings left behind by those attending, but also waste from temporary toilets and catering units, all of which will require responsible disposal. The case study of First Choice Conferences and Events featured at the close of this chapter illustrates the importance of sustainability, which is arguably now a key focus of event organisations. Recycling and sustainability should therefore be built into any event aspirations, objectives and planning. They can also be built into event contracting, as this can be an expensive operation and take up a large portion of the event budget. Chapter 7 looks in detail at using technology to assist in sustainable event practices.

If the event experiences bad weather, the site may become churned up and muddy and require substantial remediation measures before the site can be handed back to the owner. It may mean that larger equipment and machinery may be on site longer than expected, all of which may mean financial implications and penalties for the event organiser. There is also the impact of traffic, both traffic attending the event and traffic involved in the logistics surrounding it. Most events try to encourage greener options for travelling to and from the event site but events taking place on greenfield sites tend to attract more vehicles as the local transport systems may not be able to fully support adequate public transport or park-and-ride operations. In unfavourable weather conditions, these vehicles will also add to the problem and may even require additional resources and equipment to be brought in, such as towing vehicles and road sweepers if there is mud on public highways as a result of the event. It is worth remembering that traffic management around the event is the first and last impression that both those attending and the local community have of the event. If people attending are stuck in long traffic delays entering the event site, they arrive disgruntled and are likely to be less compliant. If it takes a long time to exit the event, they may decide not to return to future events at the same site or attend those staged by the same event organiser.

Tip box

A few simple calculations can be used during traffic management planning:

- an average of 2.5 people to a car
- 150–180 vehicles (depending on size) can be parked properly per acre
- a maximum of 1000 cars can leave a site per hour when exiting onto a single carriageway
- if vehicles are exiting into flowing traffic, the figure drops to a maximum of 600 per hour
- on semi rural sites, 60 per cent of visitors are likely to arrive by vehicle

Please note that these figures are only likely to be achieved if all management processes are working at optimum potential.

12.6.3 Social impact

The social, intangible aspects of events can be difficult to measure and economic measurement tools cannot be easily transferred. 'Social impacts generally refer to the effect the event has had on people's lives' (Swart and Bob, 2013, 259). It is very important to measure the effectiveness of the event on its local community, and community perception is quantifiable using multi-item attitude scales (Wood, 2006). Although the measurement and feedback of social impact can be something of a double-edged sword for the event organiser, if the event has gone well, there should be much positive media reporting and comment on social media sites, resulting in interest and support for future events. It is a good idea to collate data regarding numbers of the local community that were contracted to work, either paid or voluntary, at the event in any role or capacity, and those local businesses that benefited either directly through being contracted by the event organiser to provide goods or services, or indirectly through passing trade from those attending the event. Lastly, evaluate the number of local community members that bought tickets or attended the event. This information can be used to gauge local support and appetite for future events.

The flip side to this is negative impact, which may arise as a result of any traffic issues that may, for example, have prevented the local community from going about their daily business due to congestion or illegal parking. This may have had a negative impact on local businesses if they were not able to undertake normal work or receive deliveries because of traffic restrictions or congestion. This would also be reported through the local media and social networking sites. Disorder may have occurred at the event or an increase in crime and theft in the local community as a result. This could have had an impact on the local emergency services or hospitals, and they may have had to implement plans and provide additional resources to deal with incidents of this nature, resulting on a reluctance to give their support or backing to future events as a result of this unexpected additional expenditure and pressure. In their research reviewing the perceived social impacts of the F1 Korean GP, Kim et al. (2015) collected 1567 host community residents' views via questionnaire and measured responses on a six-factor model for perceived social impact. The six factors that were viewed as being most significant in relation to event social impact were economic benefits, community pride, community development, economic costs, traffic problems and security risks. It is possible to use quantitative methods in an attempt to research social and potentially intangible responses.

12.6.4 Event legacy

Preuss provides an all-encompassing definition of legacy (2007, 211): 'Irrespective of the time of production and space, legacy is all planned and unplanned, positive and negative, tangible and intangible structures created for and by a sport event that remain longer than the event itself.'

This presents legacy as complex and arguably highly interdependent on the relationships between social, political, environmental and economic indicators and perceptions. Every event organiser wants their event to be the best it can possibly be and for it to be enjoyed by all those attending. Most local authorities like to encourage event organisers to bring their events to their areas as they perceive them to bring potential benefits to both the local community and the local economy. Legacy therefore becomes very important, especially if the event is to become an annual occurrence or tour within the locality. To make sure that it leaves a positive impression, it is important that it is well planned, has minimum disruptive impact on the local community, with traffic management and waste properly addressed, and, most importantly, takes place in a safe and enjoyable manner both for those attending and those working there. In terms of global events, potential socio-economic benefits of mega-events are often used to justify significant government spending without evidence that long-term legacies exist (Swart and Bob, 2013).

The 2012 Olympic and Paralympic Games in London arguably left a positive infrastructure legacy. Sites used during the games are still being used as venues for other activities; the athlete's village has been turned into housing and many other venues continue to be redeveloped for alternative uses. A lasting legacy was factored into the initial bid for the games, which arguably had an influence on the final decision to award the games to London. Visitors may recall the importance of the 'Games Makers' and their friendly, helpful and positive interaction with the public during the games. The volunteers of the London 2012 Games were highly satisfied with their experience and felt their skills had developed, but how to harvest this potential social legacy needs further work (Dickson and Benson, 2013). Many other comparable sporting events have adopted similar practice at their own large-scale events, including the 2014 Commonwealth Games in Glasgow. According to Masterman (2009), consideration of the handover of legacies from Olympic Games must be fully planned for and monitored throughout the project management process. The example he gives is from the 2002 Manchester Commonwealth Games in which no construction of facilities started until the after-users of the facilities were in place and agreed. Furthermore, mega-events such as the London 2012 Games have a positive effect on the project management industry in terms of mobilisation and bringing together professionals (Grabher and Thiel, 2014).

Not taking into consideration safety risks during an event or the project review and shutdown can lead to devastating legacies. If there were to be an incident or any negative publicity at an event, there is a high chance that it may not be granted a licence or be allowed to take place in the future. An infamous example of this is the 2010 Duisburg Love Parade event which took place in Germany. This was a popular, free-to-enter electronic dance music festival and parade staged on the site of a former freight station. A mixture of overcrowding and poor management resulted in a crowd crush and stampede which claimed the lives of 21 people as well as resulting in injures to over 500 people (BBC, 2014). Dr Motte, the original founder of Love Parade, later stated in the wake of the disaster, 'it is the fault of the organizers . . . It is just about making money; the organizers did not show the slightest feeling of responsibility for the people' (*Local*, 2010, online). Event disasters such as this have significant consequences for the future planning and evaluation of events:

> At mass events, there is always the potential that panic or other catastrophes can occur. A disaster on the scale of Duisburg might lead one to expect major changes in event planning. After all, the trust of city and local authorities would be shaken, especially the assumption that events are the best option for promoting economic growth and cultural prestige.
>
> McKay (2015, 125)

Needless to say, the event never recovered and has not taken place since, nor have there been any similar events like it in Germany. Investors and sponsors are often reluctant to become involved with future projects of a similar nature. It should be remembered that more often than not events do run smoothly and provide benefits for both those who attend and the organisers. It is advised that event legacies should be measured for a minimum of 20 years after a mega-event to evaluate sustainable impact (Cornelissen, Bob and Swart, 2011).

12.7 Reporting and dissemination

Once all evaluative data is gathered and a detailed analysis of the results has been undertaken, the final step in the event project management process is to write up and disseminate the event report. It may be necessary to complete several smaller reports in order to satisfy the demands of the event investors and sponsors. Thought should therefore be given to the report layout and use of appendices. This could enable one document to be completed; all interested parties could navigate straight to sections of relevance and interest more easily. The report should be a definitive account of the whole event and it is important that it begins at the very beginning of the planning process and follows through to the very end of the project in a sequential manner. The use of statistics, comments and feedback from both those involved and those attending, repeated later, should form part of the report. The report should be the first document that is discussed at the first event planning meeting or SAG meeting held in preparation for the next event. This closes the planning cycle and ensures that any good practice and lessons learnt are incorporated into future events, also providing a clear audit trail. Table 12.2 presents suggested items which should be included in the formulation of the event report. It is important that the report accurately reflects the event project management process and includes all necessary data, evaluation and the methodology used as part of its compilation.

When the report has been compiled and deemed complete, it will require dissemination to all stakeholders and other interested parties. There are a number of ways in

Table 12.2 Developing the event report

Provide event synopsis and background information	List any injuries or incidents
State project aims and objectives	Include any photographic evidence to support issues raised
Include initial event budget details	Provide detailed financial analysis of the event
Summarise marketing and media plans	Provide community impact details
Summarise event management plans	Provide evaluation and methodology used
List investors and sponsors	Outcomes from any focus groups or surveys undertaken
List contractors and suppliers	Details of the data analysis undertaken
Include thank you/appreciation notes for relevant stakeholders	Detail customer, media and local community feedback
Outline project timescales and deliverables	Discuss supplier, contractor and entertainment performance
Summarise the planning process and consultation	Discuss what went well and what did not
Include summary of any event exercise reports	Compile list of lessons learnt
Summarise the build, delivery and breakdown phases of the event	Include ideas for future events
List number of attendees	List recommendations

which this task can be undertaken. Examples include posting the report out to all parties. Care should be taken if this method is adopted; it needs to sent out by some recorded method to ensure delivery and receipt, as there may be sensitive commercial information included within the detail of the report. The report may be presented at a meeting of all interested parties either by way of presentation of the most important points or as an agenda item at a wider planning meeting. There may even be a requirement for a launch style event with media involvement. The worst case of disseminating event information is if it is required as evidence as part of any prosecution or public enquiry following an incident. The most important thing to remember is that a well-written and comprehensive event report can positively affect the event organiser's reputation and help to gain funding and sponsorship for future projects. A badly written report that is inconclusive will not be useful to the event team or the stakeholders investing time, money and effort into the event.

12.8 Conclusion

The project completion and review stages of the event management process are crucial to assist the sustainability of the event. Project shutdown is a systematic process that involves careful planning to ensure that the needs of the event organisers and immediate public and locality are looked after. Crowd control and traffic management can be handled effectively if managed alongside the event schedule. It is crucial that the final event stages are not rushed but completed in a professional manner. The venue needs to be restored, equipment returned, contracts paid and staff congratulated. Debriefing of staff and other appropriate stakeholders is needed to collate evidence for the event report, and to gather opinions of, and perspectives on, the event and process. Events and festivals are essential to local strategic planning in terms of economic and community developments (Wood and Thomas, 2008). The economic, social and environmental impacts of events are highly significant to many event stakeholders. Project completion may lead to sustained event legacies, but this is a controversial and contested area of discussion. Finally, an event report must be written and disseminated to those involved in order to assist both in the review and in the planning stages of the next event. Remember, that when an event draws to a close, the planning stages for the following event will soon be under way.

Case study 12: First Choice Conferences and Events, South Africa

This case study is provided by Lethea Louw, Owner and Founder of First Choice Conferences and Events.

Please could you provide us with some background information about the organisation and your role?
First Choice Conferences and Events is an events company, now in its 13th year, which is situated in Pretoria, South Africa. After studying Hotel and Tourism, I

started my career in the hospitality industry. From there I worked in various hotels and departments and finally started my own events company in 2003.

What are the main types of events you organise?
First Choice organises mainly conferences, symposiums and association conferences, typically in South Africa. We also assist clients with gala dinners and end-of-year functions, when the need arises.

What are the benefits/challenges of working in your current location?
South Africa has a wealth of conference and exhibition facilities, including custom-built centres designed to top international specifications in all major cities. Settings for your conference in South Africa range from beach resorts to exclusive golfing estates or game reserves. From a geographical point of view, running an events company in South Africa is comfortable due to the great weather which is generally consistent throughout the year. Winter seasons may be cold, however, but never as uncomfortable as in the UK or other European countries.

First Choice is situated in Gauteng, which has a moderate climate and lovely summer temperatures. During the summer, we host a lot of events outside, especially dinner functions such as cocktail parties. During the winter season, we will make use of the indoor venues, but you will still get clients that prefer a barbeque (braai) outside during the winter time.

One challenge we have in South Africa is that of *load shedding*, which occurred in 2015. Load shedding is the control and management of the nation's power system to ensure usage remains balanced and supply can meet demand. However, most of the venues now have generators installed which are equipped for load-shedding time schedules that might come up. We do get notified in advance, so we can make preparations for this. When selecting a venue for an event, this is a very important check on our check list.

For how long have you worked in the corporate sector? Has the South African corporate events environment changed significantly over that time, and if so, in what way?
I have worked in the conference/hotel industry for 20 years. There have been a lot of changes in the industry, due to financial implications, such as rates increases and budget restraints. In terms of budgets, clients are cutting down on their costs and will sometimes make use of smaller or less expensive venues, or even make use of their own offices. The conference industry market is in a constant state of transition and no more so than in the present day. With the growth of hosted audio, web and video conferencing, the tightening of budgets across the board, and an increase in the demand for sustainable conferencing facilities, there are many influences on the industry. Clients have also cut down on hosting conferences, team-building activities and/or end-of-year events due to costs and budget. They are not allowed to spend as they used to in order to save money for the company. Even the government sector, which used to have an extensive amount of conferences during the year, has had to start cutting down on conferences and events.

(Continued)

Case study 12 (*continued*)

How do you measure success in the events you/your company organise?
Success for me as an events coordinator is really measured by the feedback I receive from my client after an event. Therefore the evaluation process that we implement in the final stages of the event is crucial to measuring impact and success. The venue that we select for a specific event also plays a big role in its success, in terms of service and standard of food, as well as location. At the end of an event, it is vitally important for me to know whether my client has received the best value for their money and the best service possible from the venue (we have recommended) and our company. I do this through clear and transparent client communication and consultation at every aspect of the event planning and hosting stage.

What are the event management phases and time frames that you use? Do you follow the same framework for all of your events (in terms of events management stages: concept, planning, implementation, actual event, project completion and review) or is each one differently structured?
Event management stages are very important, but we aren't always able to follow the stages in a structured fashion. Due to the fast-paced nature of the events industry, we may receive very short notice of event/conference bookings and therefore have to work quickly to finalise bookings and deals. With larger events, i.e. symposiums, I would most definitely recommend adhering to the event management stages to ensure that your event is successfully planned.

Are there any specific project management tools or computer software programmes you use to organise and evaluate your events?
Over the years we have used spreadsheets to help us keep to a schedule and enable us to review our tasks and objectives as we progress. We also make use of Smartsheet, a programme that we use for event registrations. It allows you to create/build your own registration page in line with the specific needs of the event and/or client. Each event/conference differs, and therefore you will never use the same information on a registration page. We also make use of checklists to assist us in organising events and to make sure that all aspects are covered. Timelines and to-do lists are also part of project management planning, and they allow us to view the event holistically and review it when it is completed. A management plan is another tool that we use for conferencing, which is especially useful in the completion and review phase. Furthermore, we assist our clients to draw up budgets for their event to make sure that they stay within the allocated costs and do not overspend. Our ability to manage these processes within the planning and execution stages of the event ensures we are able to measure our success during the completion stages.

Please would you describe the process you undertake once the event has come to an end?
At the end of the event we will make sure that all the suppliers involved have taken down or dismantled all of their decoration, draping, staging, sound

equipment, etc. and that the venue is cleared at the specific time as per the contract. Part of the venue service that is offered involves the clearing and cleaning away of equipment and supplies; it is our role to ensure this is communicated effectively between venue and supplier. We will, however, be on site to ensure that all is cleared and returned to its original condition. We usually inform all parties involved about the breakdown/clearing procedure before the event starts or during the pre-conference or event meeting.

After completion, how do you make sure that the event has achieved its aims and objectives, and that they are still relevant and appropriate for the next one to be organised?
We set up a post-event meeting with our client(s) after each event to ensure that the event has achieved its objectives. From there we can determine the outcome and also make notes on what to do and not to do for the next one.

Event impact is usually evaluated in terms of the triple bottom line (economic, environmental and social). Can you please provide an example of one of the events you have organised and the impact it generated in relation to the three pillars?
In South Africa we are currently focusing on going green with events/event greening. Our venues are all in the process of going down this sustainability route. Event greening should start at the conception stage of the project and involve all the key stakeholders. We use the following list to ensure the events we associate with accommodate green values:

- use water jugs rather than water bottles
- email invitations or use recycled paper
- caterers must use minimal, environmentally friendly packaging
- venues to have natural light and ventilation
- recycling stations through the venue.

Sustainability across each dimension – economic, environmental and social – is of continuing concern for meeting professionals, and an increasingly central issue for clients and meeting participants, who ultimately determine the industry's success. The meetings and events industry can be a powerful accelerator of sustainable development, and hosting sustainable events can drive economic growth and advance social and environmental awareness in cities.

Is there anything else you can share with us in relation to project completion and review stages in your place of work?
It is always important for me to conduct a post-conference meeting with my clients to ensure that they were satisfied with the standard of service received from us, that their needs were met for their specific event and that they have achieved their objectives. After an event, we will always ask the client to complete an evaluation form for both our events company and the venue. This helps us to

(Continued)

Case study 12 (*continued*)

determine the success of the event or conference. Event evaluation is an extremely important aspect of event management and helps to revise and improve events for future occasions.

Thank you to Lethea Louw for sharing your experiences with the authors to formulate this case study.

Student evaluative questions

1 In what way does effective event planning assist with effective event evaluation?
2 Provide five reasons why it is important to effectively complete and review an event.
3 Do the three pillars of sustainability have a significant role to play in event closure and evaluation? If so, in what way?

Further reading

Dwyer, L. and Jago, L. (2015) Economic evaluation of special events: challenges for the future. In: Yeoman, I., Robertson, M., McMahon-Beattie, U., Backer, E. and Smith, K.A. (eds), *The future of events and festivals*. London: Routledge, 99–114.

Grabher, G. and Thiel, J. (2014) Projects, people, professions: trajectories of learning through a mega-event (the London 2012 case). *Geoforum*, 65 328–337.

Health and Safety Executive (2014) *Managing crowds safely: a guide for organisers at events and venues*. Available from: http://www.hse.gov.uk/pubns/books/hsg154. htm [Accessed 2 December 2015].

References

Alias, Z., Zawawi, E.M.A., Yusof, K. and Aris, M.N. (2014) Determining critical success factors of project management practice: a conceptual framework. *Procedia: Social and Behavioral Sciences*, 153 61–69.

Atefeh, F. and Khreich, W. (2015) A survey of techniques for event detection in Twitter. *Computational Intelligence*, 31(1) 132–164.

BBC (2014) *Love Parade deaths: 10 charged over crush at festival*. Available from: http://www.bbc.co.uk/news/world-europe-26152045 [Accessed 29 March 2016].

Bladen, C., Kennell, J., Abson, E. and Wilde, N. (2012) *Events management: an introduction*. Abingdon: Routledge.

Bowdin, G., Allen, J., O'Toole, W., Harris, R. and McDonnell, I. (2011) *Events management*. 3rd edition. London: Butterworth-Heinemann.

Bowman, E. (2015) *Edith Bowman's great British music festivals*. London: Blink Publishing.

Chan, G.S.H. (2015) Perceived impact of hosting a sport event in a destination: a case study of the Hong Kong Rugby Sevens. *Journal of Management and Sustainability*, 5(3) 49–60.

Cornelissen, S., Bob, U. and Swart, C. (2011) Towards redefining the concept of legacy in relation to sport mega-events: insights from the 2010 FIFA World Cup. *Development Southern Africa*, 28(3) 307–318.

Davies, L., Coleman, R. and Ramchandani, G. (2013) Evaluating economic impact: rigour versus reality? *International Journal of Event and Festival Management*, 4(1) 31–42.

Deng, C.Q., Li, M. and Shen, H. (2015) Developing a measurement scale for event image. *Journal of Hospitality and Tourism Research*, 39(2) 245–270.

Dickson, T.J. and Benson, A.M. (2013) *Games Makers: towards redefining legacy*. Available from: http://www.researchgate.net/profile/Tracey_Dickson/publication/250310094_London_2012_Games_Makers_London_2012_Games_Makers_Towards_Redefining_Legacy/links/0046351eb2ac085831000000.pdf [Accessed 2 December 2015].

Dwyer, L. and Jago, L. (2015) Economic evaluation of special events: challenges for the future. In Yeoman, I., Robertson, M., McMahon-Beattie, U., Backer, E. and Smith, K.A. (eds), *The future of events and festivals*. London: Routledge, 99–114.

Grabher, G. and Thiel, J. (2014) Projects, people, professions: trajectories of learning through a mega-event (the London 2012 case). *Geoforum*, 65 328–337.

Kim, W., Jun, H.M., Walker, M. and Drane, D. (2015) Evaluating the perceived social impacts of hosting large-scale sport tourism events: scale development and validation. *Tourism Management*, 48 21–32.

Local, The (2010) *Love Parade founder Dr Motte blames new organisers for disaster*. Available from: http://www.thelocal.de/20100725/28727 [Accessed 2 December 2015].

McKay, G. (2015) *The pop festival: history, music, media, culture*. London: Bloomsbury.

Masterman, G. (2009) *Strategic sports event management: Olympic edition*. 2nd edition. London: Butterworth-Heinemann.

O'Toole, W. and Mikolaitis, P. (2002) *Corporate event project management*. New York: Wiley & Sons.

Preuss, H. (2007) The conceptualisation and measurement of mega sport event legacies. *Journal of Sport and Tourism*, 12(3–4) 207–227.

Still, G.K. (2013) *Introduction to crowd science*. Boca Raton, FL: CRC Press.

Swart, C. and Bob, U. (2013) The methodology of mega events: the culture of vanity and measuring real benefit. In: Hassan, D. and Lusted, J. (eds), *Managing sport: social and cultural perspectives*. London: Routledge.

Van Winkle, C.M. and Woosnam, K.M. (2014) Sense of community and perceptions of festival social impacts. *International Journal of Event and Festival Management*, 5(1) 22–38.

Veal, A.J., Toohey, K. and Frawley, S. (2012) The sport participation legacy of the Sydney 2000 Olympic Games and other international sporting events hosting in Australia. *Journal of Policy Research in Tourism, Leisure and Events*, 4(2) 155–184.

Verhaar, J. and Eshel, I. (2013) *Project management: a professional approach to events*. London: Eleven International Publishing.

Wood, E.H. (2005) Measuring the economic and social impacts of local authority events. *The International Journal of Public Sector Management*, 18(1) 37–53.

Wood, E.H. (2006) Measuring the social impacts of local authority events: a pilot study for a civic pride scale. *International Journal of Nonprofit and Voluntary Sector Marketing*, 11(3) 165–179.

Wood, E.H. and Thomas, R. (2008) Festivals and tourism in rural economies. In: Ali-Knight, J. (ed.), *International perspectives of events and festivals*. London: Elsevier, 149–158.

Glossary

This textbook refers to many different terms throughout the chapters and this glossary will assist in understanding what the phrases mean.

ABNT NBR ISO 20121 An international standard aimed at providing a sustainable event management system approach that is applicable, consistent and relevant to the entire event supply chain.

Breakdown The breakdown phase is the period when all the equipment, temporary demountable structures and services at the event site are cleared and restored back to how they were before the event.

BS8901 Guidelines which provide the framework to measure sustainable practices.

Build-up The build-up phase is the time when the necessary infrastructure is brought in, unloaded, built and set up.

Carbon calculator Calculates and determines the CO_2 emissions of a certain activity such as public transport or flights.

Carbon footprint The total amount of greenhouse gases, usually calculated in tons of CO_2 (carbon dioxide), that a certain activity (e.g. an event) produces.

Category 1 responder Category 1 responders are organisations at the core of the response to most emergencies (the emergency services, local authorities, NHS bodies). For more information see https://www.gov.uk/guidance/preparation-and-planning-for-emergencies-responsibilities-of-responderagencies-and-others [Accessed 1 April 2016].

Codes of Practice These are not legislation that must be complied with, however, they are documents which give standard guidance to assist users in achieving their desired result.

Context intelligence A leader who is able to 'read' a situation and respond to it with the most appropriate and relevant type of action for the specific event context.

Contract An agreement between parties to provide a product(s) or service(s).

Contributory negligence A situation whereby the defendant may have contributed to their own injury.

Critical path The critical path through any project network is the one which takes the longest time to complete.

Crowd management The management and facilitation of a crowd under normal event circumstances.

Crowd control The act of controlling a crowd once it has become unruly.

Debrief A means for event organisers and their stakeholders to review, discuss and record what went well at the event, what did not go so well, any lessons learnt and what could be improved at future events.

Deindividuation Loss of self-awareness in groups.

Due diligence Due diligence in the event world is the verifying of details relating to a contractor/supplier to ensure they are suitable and capable of carrying out the task they are contracted for.

Duty of care Event organisers have a duty of care to ensure all stakeholders involved in their event are safe and protected against all reasonable risks.

Event concept Event concept is concerned with the idea of the event which may connect to a target market or set theme.

Event management plan An event management plan is the document which contains all of the information about how the safety of the event will be managed, roles and responsibilities of key staff and safety procedures. It is shared between the event organiser and their contractors/suppliers as well as external agencies and emergency services with the aim of ensuring that the event takes place as safely as possible and that any incident is dealt with in the most timely and effective way.

Event objectives The objectives state the goals and aims of the organisation and/or event.

Event project(s) The utilisation of project management techniques and processes within an events management setting.

Events Events can be understood as social occasions which are limited in time, involve an audience and fulfil complex and varied objectives dependent on the stakeholders involved.

Events management Events management brings together the practical tools, resources and expertise needed to bring an event to fruition.

Feasibility At the event planning stage the viability or workability of the event needs to be analysed by researching the internal and external event environment.

Gamification The use and application of game design principles and theories in other fields of activity, including the one of events management.

Gantt chart A chart that allows project managers to collate the entire project tasks within one document in a manner which measures the tasks to time frames.

Geofence A virtual perimeter around any defined geographic area (e.g. convention centre, exhibition, hotel, etc.) which delivers relevant customised location information to mobile subscribers, when entering or exiting the geofence, by mobile notifications and alerts.

Glocal or glocally This term encompasses both local and global considerations

Governing Bodies Groups of officials who draw up the rules and formulate policy that govern the direction, actions and conduct of a body organisation.

Groupthink A collective taking an easier decision in order to maintain cohesion and keep all parties happy and on side.

Human resource management The management and grouping of people to work as a team to meet event objectives.

Initiation phase   This is the first stage of event planning which focuses on the objectives, concept and feasibility of the event.

Leadership   The ability to influence, persuade, encourage, enthuse and motivate others to meet common event goals.

Marketing mix   A strategy outlining the varying aspects of price, product, place, physical evidence, participants, process and promotion that needs to be considered when working towards event marketing objectives. (refer to Booms and Bitner, 1981, 50).

Multi-Agency control room   A multi-agency control room is the location in which all external agencies/emergency services work together with the event organiser during the event to monitor and respond to any incidents that may occur.

Negligence   Negligence is the failure to take the level of care that a reasonable person would expect, it falls below the standard of care expected by a reasonable person.

Network planning   Network planning provides event project managers with both a relational view of project tasks as well as a scheduling framework incorporating instances of delay and budgetary concerns.

Occupier   Anyone who has responsibility for a site or premise. In the event industry this can mean the land/venue owner, the person or organisation hiring the land/venue or the person or organisation that has been contracted to put on the event on behalf of the person or organisation hiring the land.

Outsourcing   Outsourcing is a means through which a company acquires the processes it lacks or is unwilling to perform.

Path networks   Path networks are the set of tasks that needed to be carried out in the right order for the overall project to be successful.

Plaintiff/claimant   The plaintiff is a person who brings a case to court; the claimant is someone who makes a claim, but not necessarily a court case (e.g. a claimant could be claiming tax relief, unemployment benefit).

Primary/critical supplier/contractor   Primary contractors/suppliers are fundamental to the implementation and delivery of a safe and successful event.

Project   In essence, a project is an idea which is implemented into action until completed.

Project management   Involves the careful monitoring and management of each project stage to ensure it is completed efficiently, professionally and to brief.

Public liability insurance   Covers the event organiser for the cost of claims for injury or damage made by members of the public at their event.

Pulsating Structure   The way in which the events team expands at the time of an event and contracts back to its core team at the event close (refer to Getz, 2012, 297).

Purple Guide   An event industry publication, written by the Event Industry Forum to advise event organisers about health, safety and welfare at events.

Rider   Term used in the event world for a clause in a contract, usually relating to the needs or wishes of the artist/band/group/performer.

Ringlemann effect   Individual input and effort for team tasks reduces exponentially with the increase in team size.

Risk   Any hazard or uncertainty that, if to occur, would impact on overall event safety and/or success.

Risk assessment   Documents which are created by the event organiser to record and assess the risks relatable to the event.

Risk impact   The outcome generated by a risk.

Risk probability   Risk probability indicates a chance of a risk even occurring.

Run sheets   Lists of the order of specific tasks and jobs that are required to be undertaken by contractors or key members of the event team.

Secondary supplier/contractor   Secondary contractors/suppliers can be said to be those that influence the quality levels of the event.

Shutdown   Shutdown is the period of time at the end of the public phase of the event, usually after the public have left, when the event is being deconstructed and contractors/suppliers are removing their equipment. This can also be referred to as the breakdown or load-out.

Slack   Slack time can be understood as the contingency or spare time available to use if a particular task overruns.

SMART technique   A method used to assess whether event objectives are valuable by assessing how specific, measurable, attainable, realistic and time limited they are.

Social media   Virtual networking sites accessed via computers and/or electronic devices to allow for information sharing, interaction and communication.

Supplier/contractor   A person or company who fulfils a role or provides a service relating to the management or planning of the event for the event organiser.

Supply chain   A supply chain can be viewed as the pathway in which a resource is supplied.

Supply chain management   The alignment between the event organisation's supply/demand processes with those of its suppliers/contractors.

Sustainability   Sustainability in relation to event projects will be defined as the successful management of event projects in a way which consciously values the current and future economic, social and environmental factors affecting the planning, promotion and hosting of events in relation to local, regional, national and international communities.

SWOT analysis   The analysis of the internal (strengths and weaknesses) and external (opportunities and threats) situation of the event undertaken as part of a feasibility study.

Table-Top exercise   An exercise involving the organisers and contractors/suppliers meeting together in a room (or round a table) to test and validate the event management plan through a series of scenarios.

Threat assessment   Threat assessment is the assessment of risk relating to terrorism, the security of VIPs or high-profile visitors such as members of a royal family, or the security of sensitive or secure venues such as military bases holding public events.

Triple bottom line   Building sustainable business opportunities by aiming for a balance between three main pillars: economic, social and environmental.

Volunteer   A person who provides their services, help and expertise free of charge to support and/or work at an event.

Work breakdown structure   A visual mapping of tasks and/or roles allocated to the workforce team.

References

Booms, B.H. and Bitner, M.J. (1981) Marketing strategies and organization structures for service firms. In: Donnelly, J.H. and George, W.R. (eds), *Marketing of services: conference on services marketing*. Chicago: American Marketing Association, 47–51.

Getz, D. (2012) *Event studies: theory, research and policy for planned events*. 2nd edition. Abingdon: Routledge.

Index

Locators in **bold** are for tables and those in *italics* for figures.